CHINA IN TRANSITION
VOLUME 1

China in Transition
Volume 1

K. S. Sim

Nova Science Publishers, Inc.
New York

Senior Editors: Susan Boriotti and Donna Dennis
Coordinating Editor: Tatiana Shohov
Office Manager: Annette Hellinger
Graphics: Wanda Serrano
Editorial Production: Vladimir Klestov, Matthew Kozlowski, Tom Moceri,
Anthony T. Sovak, Alexandra Columbus and Maya Columbus
Circulation: Ave Maria Gonzalez, Vera Popovic, Luis Aviles, Raymond Davis,
Melissa Diaz and Jeannie Pappas
Marketing: Cathy DeGregory

Library of Congress Cataloging-in-Publication Data
Available Upon Request

ISBN: 1-59033-627-5.

400 Oser Ave, Suite 1600
Hauppauge, New York 11788-3619
Tele. 631-231-7269 Fax 631-231-8175
e-mail: Novascience@earthlink.net
Web Site: http://www.novapublishers.com

Printed in the United States of America

CONTENTS

Preface **vii**

Chapter 1 Changes In The Source Of China's Regional Inequality **1**
Jongchul Lee

Chapter 2 China's Perceptions of the United States and Strategic Thinking **15**
Andrew K. Semmel, et al.

Chapter 3 Cross-Strait Security Issues **39**
Lori Esposito Murray, et al.

Chapter 4 China's Outward Foreign Direct Investment in Southeast Asia **51**
Hsiu-Ling Wu and Chien-Hsun Chen

Chapter 5 China and the World Trade Organization **69**
Kathleen J. Michels, et al.

Chapter 6 China's Growth as a Regional Economic Power **99**
Carmen Arleth, et al.

Chapter 7 The Defense Budget and the Military Economy **117**
Quentin G. Koffey, et al.

Chapter 8 Integration of China and Asia: Economic Reform and Policy Shifts **129**
Eddie Chi-Man Hui

Chapter 9 Dimensions of Doing Business in China **153**
Heidi Dahles and Harry Wels

Index **163**

PREFACE

China is a country in the midst of a transition which is inscrutable to almost all observers. The leadership has changed from the 'old guard' to the 'new guard' with hardly a slip. Capitalism is roaring but somehow at the same time doesn't exist. The economy is booming in virtually all areas. The military is growing more powerful each year, many industries are at world level, and China is taking more and more steps to join the international community at the same time as she doesn't snuggle up too closely. Still, with a population of 1.3 billion and staggering poverty in the rural areas making up the vast part of the country, the face of China remains centuries old. Where she will go, nobody knows. This series examines the issues, policies and progress of China's transition.

Chapter 1

CHANGES IN THE SOURCE OF CHINA'S REGIONAL INEQUALITY

Jongchul Lee*
Chung-Ang University

ABSTRACT

This paper examines whether the dominant sources of China's regional inequality have changed since the early 1980's. We adopt the decomposition method introduced by Tsui (1993) to facilitate comparisons with his results for 1982. The decomposition analysis shows that the dominant sources of the overall regional inequality in output have shifted from the intra-provincial to inter-provincial inequality, from the rural-urban to intra-rural inequality, and also from the disparity within the coast to between the coast and the interior. In the case of consumption, however, the intra-provincial inequality, the rural-urban inequality and the disparity within the coast are the major factors of the overall regional inequality. *JEL: O18, O53*

I. INTRODUCTION

The question of whether China's regional inequality has increased in the post-reform period is one of the major issues of empirical Chinese studies. A literature survey reveals that inter-provincial inequality has been the focal point of study (e.g., Chen and Fleisher, 1996; Denny, 1991; Du, 1996; Jian, Sachs, and Warner, 1996; Lee, 1995; Lyons, 1991; Raiser, 1997; Tsui, 1991, 996; Xiaobin, 1996). However, since the impact of economic reforms are regionally dissimilar in such a vast country as China, intra-provincial, intra-rural, intra-urban, and rural-urban inequality may also be crucial in analyzing China's regional inequality. A difficulty facing previous studies was the fragmentary nature of data (Tsui, 1993). The paucity of statistical data

* Corresponding Author: Jongchul Lee Mailing Address: Department of Economics, College of Social Science, Chung-Ang University, Ansung, Kyung-gi-Do, 456-756, Korea. E-mail Address: jc3253@cau.ac.kr Telephone: 82-031-670-3253 Fax: 82-031-675-1384

has often restricted the studies to a limited number of provinces (e.g., Chen and Ravallion, 1996; Cheng, 1996; Hare, 1994; Rozelle, 1994; Tsui, 1998a, 1998b). Rozelle (1994), for example, analyzed the intra-rural income inequality using per capita *gross value of industrial and agricultural outputs* (GVIAO) of a limited number of counties, townships, and villages of Jiangsu province.

In his pioneering work, Tsui (1993) developed a rigorous technique to decompose China's regional inequality into its inter-provincial, intra-provincial, intra-rural, intra-urban, and rural-urban components. He utilized the per capita GVIAO of the counties and cities of China (excluding Tibet) for 1982 to sort out the relative importance of the five facets of regional inequality.[1] The major findings of Tsui (1993) included the followings:

(a) The intra-provincial inequality is relatively an important source of China's overall regional inequality. The inter-provincial inequality, on the other hand, is by no means a major source of regional inequality.
(b) The disparity among the coastal, central, and western regions is insignificant while the variance within the coast is substantial.
(c) The rural-urban inequality accounts for a large share of intra-provincial inequality and in fact, is the most important source of the overall inequality. Neither of intra-rural and intra-urban inequality is a crucial factor.

As Tsui's results are based on the data for 1982, it would be interesting to reinvestigate his findings using more recent data. In 1997, China's Statistical Bureau and Development Center for the State Department released a compendium of the data for all the cities and counties in China. The primary purpose of this paper is to investigate the sources of China's regional inequality by adopting the decomposition method proposed by Tsui (1993). It will facilitate the comparison of new results to the previous ones of Tsui's. This paper also supplements Tsui (1993) by using per capita consumption as well as per capita GVAIO.[2] Per capita GVIAO and per capita consumption may have different implications with respect to the five dimensions of regional disparities, i.e., inter-provincial, intra-provincial, intra-rural, intra-urban, and rural-urban.

The next section describes the data and method used in this paper. Section 3 presents the new results on the relative contributions of the intra-provincial and inter-provincial inequality to the overall regional inequality. As the regional inequality with respect to the coastal, central, and western provinces has been a major issue of recent studies, we also decompose the overall regional inequality into the intra-regional and inter-regional components. Section 4 reports the major observations on the relative contributions of intra-rural, intra-urban, and rural-urban inequality to the overall regional inequality. The final section summarizes the results and discusses their policy implications.

---

[1] Tsui (1993) also used infant mortality rate, illiteracy and semi-illiteracy rates. In this paper, we limit our comparisons to the results with respect to per capita GVIAO due to the lack of availability of the data.

[2] GVIAO is used as a proxy for income because GDP for each city or county was not available. The concept of gross value of output is different from GDP in that it excludes services. GVIAO is just a part of gross value of output because it excludes gross outputs of construction, transportation, and commerce. There is also a double counting problem in the GVIAO measure to the extent that intermediate inputs from one sector are used in the production of another. Since double counting is more serious in the industrial sector, the use of GVIAO may exaggerate the output of a county or city whose share of gross industrial output is above average, thus overstating the degree of rural-urban inequality. For the definition and caveats with respect to GVIAO, see Rozelle (1994) and Tsui (1993). Despite the

II. DATA AND METHOD

Source and Profiles of the Data Set

The source of the data used in this paper is the State Statistical Bureau and Development Center for the State Department of China (1997). Excluding Tibet due to data limitations, we have used data on per capita GVIAO and consumption for China's 2,165 cities and counties for the year 1994.[3]

Table 1 and 2 report the summary statistics at the level of the provinces. The entries in column A and B, respectively, are the average per capita GVIAO of each province in 1982 and 1994. Each entry in column C is the average per capita consumption of each province in 1994. Columns D and E correspond to the ratios of average urban to average rural per capita GVIAO in 1982 and 1994. Column F is the ratios of average urban to average rural per capita consumption in 1994. In the last three lows, the same data are given for the coastal, central, and western regions.[4]

Even our data set at the provincial level demonstrates the differences in per capita GVIAO from the early 1980s. First, the rural-urban disparity has been reduced. One then would expect a reduction in the intra-provincial inequality as the rural-urban inequality accounted for a large share of intra-provincial inequality in 1982. Second, the disparity among the coastal, central and western regions has increased while the rural-urban gap within each region has narrowed. Thus the disparity among the three regions is possibly a dominant source of the current regional inequality with respect to per capita GVIAO.

In contrast, in 18 out of 26 provinces the rural-urban ratio of per capita consumption is higher than that of per capita GVIAO. Furthermore, the rural-urban disparity in per capita consumption within the three regions is higher than in per capita GVIAO. Table 2 also shows that the intra-provincial inequality in terms of the per capita consumption remains substantial. There are nine provinces in which the maximum per capita consumption is more than 30 times larger than the minimum while there are only four such provinces in the case of per capita GVIAO. Therefore, in the case of consumption, one would expect that the intra-provincial inequality, rural-urban inequality and the disparity within the coastal region are still crucial factors of the overall regional inequality.

shortcomings, per capita GVIAO is adopted by some other previous studies due to the lack of availability of the data (e.g., Knight and Song, 1993; Lardy, 1980; Paine, 1981; Riskin, 1987; Rozelle, 1994).

[3] Since the data were collected in 1996, Hainan is treated as a province. Tsui (1993) treated the three centrally administered municipalities as separate provinces. In our analysis, however, we combine the three centrally administered municipalities with their adjacent provinces, i.e., Beijing and Tianjin with Hebei, and Shanghai with Jiangsu, due to the data availability of the three municipalities.

[4] The coastal region includes Liaoning, Hebei, Beijing, Shandong, Tianjin, Shanghai, Jiangsu, Zhejiang, Fujian, Guangdong, Guangxi, and Hainan. The central region encompasses Heilongjiang, Jilin, Neimenggu, Shanxi, Henan, Anhui, Hubei, Hunan, and Jiangxi. The remaining provinces belong to the western region. For the partition of the provinces into coastal, central, and western, see Yang (1990) and Tsui (1993).

Table 1: Per Capita GVIAO and Consumption by Provinces

	A(1982)	B(1994)	C(1994)	D(1982)	E(1994)	F(1994)
Hebei	546.65	7,693.58	867.77	4.86	1.23	1.22
Liaoning	1,259.07	7,309.94	1,065.16	4.43	1.17	1.12
Jiangsu	1,350.80	17,876.16	2,010.98	5.49	2.26	2.42
Zhejiang	859.00	13,879.98	2,047.99	2.79	1.29	1.39
Fujian	609.60	8,752.26	1,560.12	3.52	2.07	2.99
Shandong	795.40	11,852.91	1,150.53	4.69	2.11	2.34
Guandong	685.53	7,992.91	1,705.49	4.26	2.37	2.09
Guangxi	441.70	4,194.71	869.66	4.72	2.77	3.65
Hainan		3,624.64	1,061.71		1.45	3.01
Shanxi	570.94	4.022.17	697.14	4.05	1.86	1.85
Neimenggu	544.79	3,051.89	1,129.33	2.30	1.40	3.80
Jilin	827.76	4,106.35	1,228.25	2.76	1.06	1.50
Heilongjiang	874.64	3,798.76	1,017.37	3.12	1.21	1.32
Anhui	627.98	5,150.51	768.39	5.25	1.57	2.25
Jiangxi	550.15	5,310.40	820.17	2.81	1.72	2.24
Henan	570.38	4.957.16	679.60	5.98	1.73	2.66
Hubei	882.27	5,440.84	977.88	7.18	1.03	1.02
Hunan	708.33	3,618.85	848.49	5.08	1.80	2.24
Sichuan	449.59	3,397.71	640.83	4.01	1.79	1.66
Guizhou	341.49	1,645.96	331.14	4.24	1.92	1.05
Yunnan	406.08	2,453.03	659.19	3.58	4.28	2.87
Shaanxi	433.87	2,131.53	492.00	4.66	1.03	1.78
Gansu	490.53	2,587.13	494.07	7.19	2.17	3.13
Qinghai	610.07	2,357.69	706.25	1.29	0.67	3.14
Ningxia	543.17	2,372.39	566.78	2.99	1.38	2.19
Xinjiang	584.15	3,008.32	812.22	2.73	1.14	2.18
Beijing	3,654.58			9.19		
Tianjin	1,952.50			7.33		
Shanghai	3,382.18			2.32		
Coastal	863.83	9,679.00	1,334.00	5.06	2.13	2.41
Interior	665.17	4,414.00	866.00	4.26	1.68	2.20
Western	459.66	2,627.00	594.00	3.92	1.95	2.21

Sources: For 1994, State Statistical Bureau and Development Center for the State Department (1997) and author's calculations. For 1982, Tsui (1993).

Note. Columns A and B, simple averages of per capita GVIAO (yuan) of counties and cities in 1982 and 1994; column C, simple average of per capita consumption (yuan) of counties and cities in 1994; columns D and E, the ratios of average urban to average rural per capita GVIAO in 1982 and 1994; column F, the ratio of average urban to average rural per capita consumption in 1994. The last three lows are the figures for the coastal, central, and western regions.

Table 2: Ratios of Maximum and Minimum Values of Per Capita GVIAO and Consumption

Province	A(1982)	B(1994)	C(1994)
Hebei	20.45	78.65	54.87
Liaoning	17.57	10.14	8.35
Jiangsu	21.30	22.23	16.60
Zhejiang	20.55	26.04	16.84
Fujian	15.48	12.55	23.45
Shandong	24.92	15.42	36.19
Guandong	23.54	29.35	65.40
Guangxi	20.87	27.55	21.36
Hainan		4.53	20.48
Shanxi	17.50	15.32	34.74
Neimenggu	9.53	13.76	85.55
Jilin	7.35	3.90	13.31
Heilongjiang	30.18	12.28	65.11
Anhui	20.69	12.35	12.85
Jiangxi	8.10	7.38	32.24
Henan	23.79	17.66	53.36
Hubei	29.07	27.91	23.12
Hunan	18.88	12.36	30.56
Sichuan	12.75	54.54	8.62
Guizhou	10.53	17.79	26.51
Yunnan	21.69	93.44	20.47
Shaanxi	17.86	6.47	13.23
Gansu	46.70	28.24	23.80
Qinghai	23.07	10.16	9.61
Ningxia	20.83	9.76	9.48
Xinjiang	39.17	12.78	26.09
Beijing	44.28		
Tianjin	10.10		
Shanghai	3.91		

Sources: See Table 1.
Note: Column A and B = maximum per capita GVIAO / minimum per capita GVIAO; column C = maximum per capita consumption / minimum per capita consumption.

Method

This paper follows the method suggested by Tsui (1993) in decomposing the overall regional inequality into the inter-provincial, intra-provincial, intra-rural, intra-urban, and rural-urban components. The inequality index, Theil's entropy measurement, is defined as follows.

$$I(y) = \sum_{i=1}^{n} f_i \log(\frac{\mu}{y_i})$$

where y denotes the vector of per capita GVIAO or per capita consumption; $f_i = P_i/P$, P_i is the population of the ith counties and/or cities and P is the total population; y_i is the value of the ith observation of y; $\mu = \Sigma_i f_i y_i$ is the mean of y_i, $i = 1, 2, \ldots, n$. Then the Theil's entropy index may be decomposed in the following way[5]:

$$I(y) = \sum_{g=1}^{G} w_g I(y_g) + I(\mu_1 e_1, \ldots, \mu_G e_G), w_g = \frac{n_g}{n}$$

where G is the number of the sample subgroups; y_g is the subvector of y consisting of the per capita GVIAO or consumption of the gth subgroup; μ_g is the population-weighted mean of the observations of the gth subgroup; n_g is the number of observations in the gth subgroup; e_g is an n_g vector of ones; $I(y_g)$ is the inequality index of the gth subgroup. The first term on the right-hand side of the equation is the weighted sum of the group-specific inequality indexes, i.e., the intra-group inequality. The second term is the inter-group inequality when all the elements in each group are set equal to the group mean. We use the difference between $I(y)$ and the first term to derive the value of the second term.

The counties and cities are grouped by: (1) provinces, (2) regions, i.e., coastal, central, and western, (3) rural and urban areas ignoring provincial boundaries, (4) rural and urban areas of each province and region. For instance, in the case of (2), each group g may include the observations of a given region which is either the coastal ($g = 1$), central ($g = 2$), or western ($g = 3$). Then $I(y_1)$, $I(y_2)$, $I(y_3)$ are the inequality within the coastal, central, and western region, respectively. The weighted sum, $w_1 I(y_1) + w_2 I(y_2) + w_3 I(y_3)$ is the intra-regional inequality while $I(\mu_1 e_1, \mu_2 e_2, \mu_3 e_3)$ is the inter-regional inequality.

III. Intra-Provincial and Inter-Provincial Inequalities

Table 3 shows the inequality indices with respect to both per capita GVIAO and consumption of each province. It also provides the relative contributions of the intra-provincial and inter-provincial inequality to the total inequality. Of the total GVIAO inequality, 0.39, 49% is due to the intra-provincial inequality while the remaining 51% is from the inter-provincial inequality.[6] Thus the inter-provincial inequality turns out to be the dominant source of the current overall regional output inequality.

In contrast, in the case of per capita consumption the intra-provincial inequality accounts for 63 percent of the overall inequality and hence is the major source of the overall regional inequality. It is consistent with the result of Cheng (1996), who analyzed the rural households income data of five provinces for 1994. According to his analysis the intra-provincial income inequality contributed 61% of the overall inequality. Our decomposition analysis suggests that income is more closely associated with consumption rather than output.

---

[5] Shorrocks (1980, 1984), Morduch and Sicular (1998) show that the only additively decomposable inequality measure simultaneously satisfying a set of desirable axioms is the class of generalized entropy measures.

[6] According to Tsui (1993), the overall per capita GVIAO inequality was 0.32 in 1982 and only 24% of overall regional inequality were explained by dispersions within provinces. It should be noted that the figures in our results are not strictly comparable to Tusi (1993) because of the different data sources and the different treatment of the three municipalities.

Table 3: Intra-Provincial and Inter-Provincial Inequality

Province	GVIAO	Consumption
Hebei	0.29	0.23
Liaoning	0.16	0.07
Jiangsu	0.33	0.32
Zhejiang	0.18	0.18
Fujian	0.19	0.31
Shandong	0.20	0.25
Guandong	0.28	0.24
Guangxi	0.20	0.30
Hainan	0.10	0.44
Shanxi	0.13	0.17
Neimenggu	0.11	0.21
Jilin	0.03	0.15
Heilongjiang	0.05	0.23
Anhui	0.11	0.18
Jiangxi	0.14	0.22
Henan	0.18	0.29
Hubei	0.17	0.16
Hunan	0.12	0.14
Sichuan	0.22	0.12
Guizhou	0.15	0.21
Yunnan	0.39	0.21
Shaanxi	0.09	0.09
Gansu	0.22	0.24
Qinghai	0.16	0.12
Ningxia	0.30	0.22
Xinjiang	0.12	0.29
Intraprovincial Inequality[a]	0.19 (48.5%)	0.21 (63.2%)
Interprovincial Inequality[b]	0.20 (51.5%)	0.12 (36.8%)
Total inequality	0.39	0.33

Source: See Table 1.

Note. [a] The number in brackets is the percentage contribution of intra-provincial inequality to overall inequality, i.e., $[\Sigma_g w_g I(y_g)/I(y)] \times 100$; w_g and $I(y_g)$ is the weight and inequality of the gth province.

[b] The number in brackets is the percentage contribution of inter-provincial inequality to overall inequality, i.e., $[I(\mu_1 e_1, \ldots, \mu_G e_G)/I(y)] \times 100$; μ_g, $g = 1, 2, 3, \ldots, G$, is the mean value of the gth province and e_g is a vector of ones.

The regional inequality in the coastal, central, and western provinces has been a major issue of recent studies (e.g., Chen and Fleisher, 1996; Fleisher and Chen, 1997; Jian, Sachs and Waner, 1996). Our analysis in Table 4 shows that inter-regional inequality, namely, the inequality among the coastal, central, and western regions accounts for 39% of the overall inequality with respect to per capita GVIAO.[7] Thus the output disproportion among the three regions is a significant source of the current regional inequality. Note that the importance of inequality in terms of per capita GVIAO within the coastal and interior provinces has dimished.[8] This is consistent with the previous observations of Chen and Fleisher (1996), Jian Sachs and Warner (1996), Raiser (1997), and Yang and Wei (1996). Jian, Sachs and Warner argued that the widening income gap between the coast and interior after 1990 more than offset the continued convergence within the coast so that overall regional income variance increased.

Raiser (1997) pointed out that the still existing system of inter-provincial fiscal transfers, which concentrated transfers to richer western provinces, had prevented convergence among the interior provinces, in particular, among western provinces. For instance, the western provinces of Xinjiang, Qinghai, and Ningxia, all with relatively higher incomes, have received much larger subsides. The result in Table 4 fortifies the arguments: the percentage contribution to the total per capita GVIAO inequality is higher within the western regions than the central region. In the case of per capita consumption, however, the inequality among the three regions constitutes 28% of the overall inequality. The consumption dispersion among the coastal provinces is the dominant source of the overall regional inequality.

Table 4: Regional Inequality among the Coastal, Central, and Western Regions (Percentage)

Region	GVIAO	Consumption
A. Coastal	27.6	31.2
B. Central	13.1	22.8
C. Western	20.3	18.0
D. Between Group	39.0	28.0

Source: See Table 1.

Note. The decomposition is based on the formula $I(y) = w_1I(y_1) + w_2I(y_2) + w_3I(y_3) + I(\mu_1e_1, \mu_2e_2, \mu_3e_3)$, where the subscripts 1, 2, and 3 refer to the coastal, central, and western regions. Row A: Percentage contribution to overall regional inequality attributable to the coastal region, i.e., $[w_1I(y_1)/I(y)] \times 100$. Row B: Percentage contribution to overall regional inequality attributable to the central region, i.e., $[w_2I(y_1)/I(y)] \times 100$. Row C: Percentage contribution to overall regional inequality attributable to the western region, i.e., $[w_3I(y_3)/I(y)] \times 100$. Row D: Percentage contribution of between-group inequality among the coastal, central, and western regions, i.e., $[I(\mu_1e_1, \mu_2e_2, \mu_3e_3)/I(y)] \times 100$.

The sources of the overall regional inequality based on per capita GVIAO and consumption are different with each other. The inter-provincial inequality and inter-regional inequality are the dominant sources of the overall regional inequality in terms of per capita GVIAO. In contrast, however, in the case of per capita consumption the intra-provincial inequality and the dispersion among the coastal provinces are the major sources of the overall regional inequality. These differences would be resulted from the use of GVIAO as a proxy for income. As noted in footnote 2, GVIAO excludes outputs from service industries and is subject to a double counting

[7] The contribution of per capita GVIAO inequality among the three regions was only 10% in 1982 (Tsui, 1993). Tsui thus pointed out that the reduction of inequality among the three regions may not necessarily result in a substantial decrease in overall regional disparity. Jian, Sachs, and Warner (1996) also found that per capita GDP dispersion between the coastal and interior regions accounted for 36% of the overall regional inequality in 1993, in contrast to 17% for 1982.

[8] The percentage contributions of per capita GVIAO inequality within the coastal, central, and western regions were 38%, 29%, and 23% in 1982 (Tsui, 1993).

problem. As a result, the observed change in the source of regional inequality in GVIAO could have resulted from shifts in the regional structure of industrial activities. Thus the long-term changes in the source of the output inequality should be understood with more reservations.

IV. Rural-Urban Inequality

Rural-Urban Inequality for the Nation as a Whole

In Table 5 the overall regional inequality in terms of both per capita GVIAO and consumption is decomposed into the intra-rural, intra-urban, and rural-urban components. It shows that the dominant source of per capita GVIAO inequality is the intra-rural inequality which contributes to more than half of the total inequality.[9] The dominance of intra-rural inequality confirms the major finding of Rozelle (1994) that the distribution of income among counties became notably inequitable between 1984 and 1989. He argued that the policies favoring the industrial development of rural area would create a more unequal income distribution on the observation that the large regional differences among the counties of Jiangsu Province were almost totally attributable to the differences in the development of the rural industrial sector. Hare (1994) also observed that in Guangdong Province a significant part of the increase in intra-county inequality was due to the growth of rural nonagricultural sector.

Table 5: Percentage Contribution of Intra-Rural, Intra-Urban and Rural-Urban Inequality

	GVIAO	Consumption
A. Intra-rural	52.8	39.6
B. Intra-urban	21.4	22.7
C. Rural-urban	25.8	37.7

Source: See Table 1.

Note. The decomposition is based on the equation $I(y) = w_R I(y_R) + w_U I(y_U) + I(\mu_R e_R, \mu_U e_U)$, where $I(y_R)$ and $I(y_U)$ are the overall intra-rural and intra-urban inequality; w_R and w_U are their respective weights; $I(\mu_R e_R, \mu_U e_U)$ is the overall rural-urban inequality; μ_R is the mean value of the counties and μ_U is that of the cities; e_U and e_R are vectors of ones. All the counties, regardless of province, are grouped under the rural sector. All the cities are grouped under the urban sector. Row A: Percentage contribution of intra-rural inequality to overall inequality, i.e., $[w_R I(y_R)/I(y))] \times 100$. Row B: Percentage contribution of intra-urban inequality to overall inequality, i.e., $[w_U I(y_U)/I(y)] \times 100$. Row C: Percentage contribution of rural-urban inequality to overall inequality, i.e., $[I(\mu_R e_R, \mu_U e_U)/I(y)] \times 100$.

In contrast, the rural-urban inequality, the previous dominant sources, now accounts for only 26% of the overall inequality. As observed by some authors (Jian, Sachs and Warner, 1996; Tsui, 1993; Xue and Liu, 1996), the effects of the rapid growth in rural enterprises and the relaxed rural-to-urban migration regulation have mitigated rural-urban output inequality. The relaxed regulation enabled poorer agricultural households to move into rural industrial sector with rising wages and employment opportunities to result in a more equitable rural-urban income distribution.

[9] The contributions of intra-rural, intra-urban, and rural-urban inequality to overall per capita GVIAO inequality were 40%, 8%, and 52% in 1982 (Tsui, 1993).

Table 5 also shows that intra-rural inequality with respect to per capita consumption stands out as the biggest component of overall regional inequality. Compared to the case of GVIAO, however, in per capita consumption, the contribution of intra-rural inequality is relatively low: 52.8% versus 39.6%. In contrast, the contribution of rural-urban inequality is higher in consumption than in GVIAO.

Following Tsui (1996), the *relative factor inequality weights* denoting the percentage contributions of the rural industrial sector to overall inter-county inequality are presented in Table 6.[10] It shows that the rural industrial sector exerts a predominant influence on the inter-county inequality in every province except Heilongjiang, Neimenggu, and Ningxia, where rural industry is responsible for less than half of inter-county inequality. For example, in Jiangsu province, one of China's most industrialized provinces and a leader in the township and village enterprises (TVE) movement, the contribution of rural industry to inter-county inequality is as high as 91%.

It is also worth noting that in per capita GVIAO the relative contribution of intra-urban inequality is similar to that of rural-urban inequality. As pointed out by Tsui (1993), intra-urban inequality was insignificant in 1982 because urban residents were mostly employed by the state sector which provided the same package of benefits to workers throughout the country. A consequence of the government's central control over wages was largely to eliminate the intra-provincial and inter-provincial wage differences (Knight and Song, 1991). This was reflected in the relatively low degree of intra-urban income inequality in the early 1980s. The remarkable development of the non-state sector, however, has changed the urban wage structure. The diversification of ownership structure due to the dynamic growth in the non-state sector implies that workers are paid different wages by the ownership category. This wage segmentation may be reflected in the higher intra-urban inequality in the 1990s.

Rural-Urban Inequality by Province and Region

The relative contributions of rural-urban and intra-rural inequality to the overall regional inequality for each province are provided in Table 6. The intra-rural inequality accounts for a large share of the intra-provincial per capita GVIAO inequality for many provinces. Although not so prominent as in GVIAO, the importance of intra-rural inequality is also somewhat greater than that of rural-urban inequality on average in terms of per capita consumption.

Separating the data of the counties from those of the cities makes it possible to decompose the overall inequality of each region along the rural-urban dimension. Table 7 summarizes the relative contributions of intra-rural and rural-urban inequality of the three regions. It shows the intra-rural inequality is the dominant source of the overall inequality in every region. It is interesting that the intra-rural disparity is greater in the poorer inland region than in the richer coastal region. Chen and Ravallion (1996), who analyzed the rural households data for four southern provinces over 1985-1990, found that low growth and adverse distribution effects slowed progress in the poorer inland provinces.

[10] It can be shown that if per capita income, y, is broken into the sum of its k sectors, the kth sector being y_k, the relative factor inequality weight measuring the percentage contribution of the kth sector to overall inter-county inequality can be expressed as $s_k = \text{cov}(y_k, y)/\text{var}(y)$, where $\text{cov}(y_k, y)$ is the covariance between y_k and y, and $\text{var}(y)$ is the variance of y. See Tsui (1996) for a detailed explanation. In this application, the per capita income of a county is rewritten as the sum of the per capita income from agricIture, forestry, livestock, and fishery as well as rural industry.

Table 6: Percentage Contribution of Rural-Urban and Intra-Rural Inequality by Province

Province	GVIAO		Consumption		
	Rural-urban	Intra-rural	Rural-urban	Intra-rural	Inequality weight[a]
Hebei	1.7	92.2	10.4	80.1	96.6
Liaoning	6.5	67.9	9.5	57.0	76.0
Jiangsu	23.0	38.4	35.0	25.4	91.3
Zhejiang	1.7	78.7	38.7	25.8	92.2
Fujian	50.2	25.9	58.5	11.3	82.4
Shandong	36.5	35.8	18.5	61.8	65.7
Guandong	26.9	17.3	27.6	20.7	69.0
Guangxi	38.9	43.9	59.6	22.1	82.0
Hainan	38.7	33.9	45.3	7.0	64.8
Shanxi	10.9	83.7	23.4	64.8	96.1
Neimenggu	19.0	64.1	58.3	30.3	48.6
Jilin	17.2	44.0	9.6	21.4	63.9
Heilongjiang	14.7	67.8	0.3	92.2	35.7
Anhui	17.3	47.5	42.5	31.1	88.2
Jiangxi	34.9	46.9	48.5	19.4	85.3
Henan	23.3	52.1	35.3	19.1	92.5
Hubei	20.3	39.0	24.0	19.8	83.1
Hunan	14.0	43.9	21.6	25.6	75.3
Sichuan	6.4	85.5	17.4	71.9	93.9
Guizhou	30.3	47.3	30.3	48.0	91.6
Yunnan	48.4	30.0	27.8	61.7	79.1
Shaanxi	2.5	86.2	27.5	57.9	90.4
Gansu	18.8	71.8	46.6	49.9	84.5
Qinghai	11.7	88.1	40.2	54.4	58.9
Ningxia	3.2	94.8	54.1	27.7	35.2
Xinjiang	15.8	53.3	26.6	69.9	68.3

Source: See Table 1.

Note. The contribution of rural-urban, intra-rural, and intra-urban inequality of the gth province is derived from $I(y_g) = w_{gR}I(y_{gR}) + w_{gU}I(y_{gU}) + I(\mu_{gR}e_{gR}, \mu_{gU}e_{gU})$, where $I(y_{gR})$ and $I(y_{gU})$ are the intra-rural and intra-urban inequality of the gth province, w_{gR} and w_{gU} are their respective weights; $I(\mu_{gR}e_{gR}, \mu_{gU}e_{gU})$ is rural-urban inequality of gth province, and μ_{gR} and μ_{gU} are the rural and urban means. The percentage contribution of intra-rural inequality to overall inequality is $[w_{gR}I(y_{gR})/I(y_g)] \times 100$; The percentage contribution of intra-urban inequality to overall inequality is $[w_{gU}I(y_{gU})/I(y_g)] \times 100$; The percentage contribution of rural-urban inequality to overall inequality is $[I(\mu_{gR}e_{gR}, \mu_{gU}e_{gU})/I(y_g)] \times 100$.

[a] The relative factor inequality weight measuring the percentage contribution of the rural industrial sector to overall inter-county inequality is based on the formula $s_k = \text{cov}(y_k, y)/\text{var}(y)$, where y is per capita GVIAO of a county, y_k is output of rural industry, $\text{cov}(y_k, y)$ is the covariance between y_k and y, and $\text{var}(y)$ is the variance of y.

Table 7: Percentage Contribution of Rural-Urban and Intra-Rural Inequality by Region

	GVIAO		Consumption	
Region	Rural-urban	Intra-rural	Rural-urban	Intra-rural
A. Coastal	21.3	51.8	36.1	36.5
B. Central	20.3	52.0	28.4	38.1
C. Western	14.1	71.0	21.1	67.5

Source: See Table 1.

Note. The percentage contribution of intra-rural and rural-urban inequality by region is calculated from the equations: for the coastal region, $I(y_1) = w_{1R}I(y_{1R}) + w_{1U}I(y_{1U}) + I(\mu_{1R}e_{1R}, \mu_{1U}e_{1U})$; for the central region, $I(y_2) = w_{2R}I(y_{2R}) + w_{2U}I(y_{2U}) + I(\mu_{2R}e_{2R}, \mu_{2U}e_{2U})$; for the western region, $I(y_3) = w_{3R}I(y_{3R}) + w_{3U}I(y_{3U}) + I(\mu_{3R}e_{3R}, \mu_{3U}e_{3U})$, where the subscripts 1, 2, and 3 refer to the coastal, central, and western regions, and the subscripts R and U refer to the rural sector and urban sector respectively. Row A: Percentage contribution of rural-urban and intra-rural inequality to overall inequality within the coastal region. Row B: Percentage contribution of rural-urban and intra-rural inequality to overall inequality within the central region. Row C: Percentage contribution of rural-urban and intra-rural inequality to overall inequality within the western region.

V. CONCLUSION

We have analyzed the source of China's regional inequality with respect to both per capita GVIAO and per capita consumption. This paper shows that since the early 1980s the dominant sources of overall regional inequality in output have shifted from the intra-provincial to inter-provincial inequality, from the rural-urban to intra-rural inequality, and also from the disparity within the coastal region to the gap between the coastal and interior regions. In the case of consumption, however, the intra-provincial inequality, the rural-urban inequality and the disparity within the coast are still playing important roles in the overall regional inequality. This paper also shows that the intra-rural disparity is greater in the poorer inland region than in the richer coastal region.

These results have important implications to the China's industrialization drive and regional development policies in the post-reform era. An outcome of rural-industry-led growth seems to the aggravation of the intra-rural output inequality. As a consequence, the intra-rural inequality has become the biggest source of the intra-provincial and overall regional inequality. Thus, as pointed out by Rozelle (1994, p.385), while rural industrialization has had and will continue to have a major impact on income levels in many areas, it is also critical to understand the role of rural industries in changing inequality patterns.

The impact of the contract responsibility system in the rural sector and the relaxed rural-to-urban migration policies may have mitigated rural-urban income inequality. In the case of consumption, however, intra-rural differences are not so conspicuous as in GVIAO. The rural-urban gap is still an important factor of both intra-provincial and overall consumption inequalities. Our Study also confirms that China's coastal-led development strategy has aggravated the output gap between the coastal provinces and interior provinces. In contrast, in the case of per capita consumption, the decomposition analysis revealed that a large share of the overall regional inequality is still accounted for by the inequality within the coast.

The findings of the paper reconfirm the viewpoint of Tsui (1993, p.620): in assessing the differences in well-being across regions, it may not be sufficient to concentrate on one single indicator. It should be pointed out that the regional polices may have different effects on different attributes of well-being. Different types of regional polices may also have different impacts on the intra-provincial, inter-provincial, intra-rural, intra-urban, and rural-urban inequality.

REFERENCES

Chen, J. and Fleisher, B.M., 1996, Regional Income Inequality and Economic Growth in China, *Journal of Comparative Economics,* 22, 141-164.

Chen, S. and Ravallion, M., 1996, Data in Transition: Assessing Rural Living Standards in Southern China, *China Economic Review*, 7, 23-56.

Cheng, Y., 1996, A Decomposition Analysis of Income Inequality of Chinese Rural Households, *China Economic Review*, 7, 155-167.

Denny, D.L., 1991, Provincial Income Differences Diminished in the Decade of Reform in *China's Economic Dilemmas in the 1990s: The Problems of Reforms, Modernization and Interdependence,* vol. 1 (Washington, D.C.: Congress of the United States, Joint Economic Committee, U.S. Government Printing Office), 186-208.

Du, J., 1996, Regional Inequality Variations in Post-reform China: Sources of Instability and Future Prospects, Paper for International Workshop on Income Distribution and Social Political Stability, Hitotsubashi University.

Fleisher, B. M. and Chen, J., 1997, The Coast-noncoast Income Gap, Productivity, and Regional Economic Policy in China, *Journal of Comparative Economics*, 25, 220-236.

Hare, D., 1994, Rural Nonagricultural Activities and Their Impact on the Distribution of Income: Evidence from Farm Households in Southern China, *China Economic Review*, 4, 59-82.

Jian, T., Sachs, J.D. and Warner, A.M., 1996, Trends in Regional Inequality in China, *China Economic Review*, 7, 11-21.

Knight, J. and Song, L., 1991, The Determinants of Urban Income Inequality in China, *Oxford Bulletins of Economics and Statistics,* 53, 123-154.

Knight, J. and Song, L., 1993, The Spatial Contribution to Income Inequality in Rural China, *Cambridge Journal of Economics*, 17, 195-213.

Lardy, N., 1980, Regional Growth and Income Distribution in China in R. F. Dernberg, ed., *China's Development Experience in Comparative Perspective*, (Cambridge, Harvard University Press, 153-190.

Lee, J., 1995, Regional Income Inequality in China, *Journal of Economic Development,* 20, 99-117.

Lyons, T.P., 1991, Inter-provincial Disparities in China: Output and Consumption, 1952-1987, *Economic Development and Cultural Changes*, 39, 471-506.

Morduch, J. and Sicular, T., 1998, Rethinking Inequality Decomposition, with Evidence from Rural China, Development Discussion Paper no. 636, Harvard Institute for International Development, Harvard University.

Paine, S., 1981, Spatial Aspects of Chinese Development Issues, Outcomes and Policies 1949-1979," *Journal of Development Studies*, 17, 133-195.

Raiser, M., 1997, Subsidizing Inequality: Economic Reforms, Fiscal Transfers and Convergence Across Chinese Provinces, Unpublished Discussion Paper, European Bank for Reconstruction and Development.

Riskin, C., 1987, *China's Political Economy: The Quest for Development Since 1949* (Oxford, Oxford University Press).

Rozelle, S., 1994, Rural Industrialization and Increasing Inequality: Emerging Pattern in China's Reforming Economy, *Journal of Comparative Economics*, 19, 362-391.

Shorrocks, A. F., 1980, The Class of Additively Decomposable Inequality Measures, *Econometrica*, 48, 613-625.

Shorrocks, A. F., 1984, Inequality Decomposition by Population Subgroups, *Econometrica*, 52, 1369-1385.

State Statistical Bureau and Development Center for the State Department, 1997, *Zhongguo Xianyu Jinggi*: *Huabei, Dongbei Quan* [China's County-level Economy: Huabei, Dongbei Volume] (Beijing, State Statistical Bureau Press).

State Statistical Bureau and Development Center for the State Department, 1997, *Zhongguo Xianyu Jinggi*: *Huadong Quan* [China's County-level Economy: Huadong Volume] (Beijing, State Statistical Bureau Press).

State Statistical Bureau and Development Center for the State Department, 1997, *Zhongguo Xianyu Jinggi*: *Xinan, Xibei Quan* [China's County-level Economy: Xian, Xibei Volume] (Beijing, State Statistical Bureau Press).

State Statistical Bureau and Development Center for the State Department, 1997, *Zhongguo Xianyu Jinggi*: *Zhongnan Quan* [China's County-level Economy: Zhongnan Volume] (Beijing, State Statistical Bureau Press).

Tsui, K., 1991, China's Regional Inequality, 1952-85, *Journal of Comparative Economics*, 15, 1-21.

Tsui, K., 1993, Decomposition of China's Regional Inequalities, *Journal of Comparative Economics*, 17, 600-627.

Tsui, K., 1996, Economic Reform and Interprovincial Inequalities in China, *Journal of Development Economics*, 50, 353-368.

Tsui, K., 1998a, Factor Decomposition of Chinese Rural Income Inequality: New Methodology, Empirical Findings, and Policy Implications, *Journal of Comparative Economics*, 26, 502-528.

Tsui, K., 1998b, Trends and Inequalities of Rural Welfare in China: Evidence from Rural Households in Guangdong and Sichuan, *Journal of Comparative Economics*, 26, 783-804.

Xiaobin, S. Z., 1996, Spatial Disparities and Economic Development in China, 1953-92: A Comparative Study, *Economic Development and Cultural Changes*, 27, 131-163.

Xue, J. and Liu, D., 1996, Urban-rural Income Disparity and its Significance in China, Paper for International Workshop on Income Distribution and Social Political Stability, Hitotsubashi University.

Yang, D., 1990, Patterns of China's Regional Development Strategy, *China Quarterly*, 122, 231-257.

Yang, D. and Wei,H., 1994, Rural Enterprise Development and Regional Policy in China, *Asian Perspective*, 20, 71-94.

Chapter 2

CHINA'S PERCEPTIONS OF THE UNITED STATES AND STRATEGIC THINKING*

Andrew K. Semmel, et al.

KEY FINDINGS

- The U.S. Government has dedicated insufficient resources to collect, translate, and analyze Chinese writings and statements. Consequently, it has a limited understanding of the perceptions of the United States held by Chinese leaders and the Chinese people. This undermines our government's ability to respond appropriately to the challenges and opportunities of the relationship, as well as to prepare for potential crises.

- China's leaders consistently characterize the United States as a "hegemon", connoting a powerful protagonist and overbearing bully that is China's major competitor, but they also believe that the United States is a declining power with important military vulnerabilities that can be exploited. China views itself as an emerging power.

- Chinese leaders say that they pursued World Trade Organization (WTO) membership as a means to continue China's rapid economic growth, which they consider essential to become a major power. Such rapid economic growth would also help the Chinese Communist Party maintain its monopoly on power. This objective is quite different from one of the main U.S. goals for China's accession, which is to promote the development of economic, legal and democratic reforms in China, as well as regional stability in Asia.

- China's leaders seek to deter the United States from effectively intervening in any Chinese use of force against Taiwan, by denying the United States the unfettered freedom under international law to operate in the seas and airspace near China.

---

* In: July 2002 - Report to Congress of the U.S. - China Security Review Commission - *The National Security Implications of the Economic Relationship between the United States and China.*

- The U.S.-China bilateral relationship is uncoordinated within the U.S. Government and does not include the necessary permanent institutions for managing and resolving conflicts. At worst, current U.S. practices have the effect of supporting Chinese efforts to enhance science, economic, financial and technology bases without adequate oversight within our government.
- Chinese strategic thinking and military planning differ markedly from our own, underscoring the need to study such differences more carefully. Such Chinese thinking draws heavily on ancient Chinese military lore and history, as well as Chinese Communist revolutionary history, and emphasizes nontraditional and asymmetrical techniques designed to enable an inferior power to defeat a superior one. Such techniques include deception, preemption, use of '"assassin's mace" or trump card weaponry, as well as information and cyber warfare. The possibilities of miscalculation, miscommunications, and misunderstandings are high, given the substantial differences in each country's thinking and planning, and require far more attention from U.S. policymakers and the Congress.
- Attempts to build crises-management and confidence-building measures (CBMs) between the United States and China have failed. This is due in part to Chinese strategic thinking which does not value openness, which the Chinese fear could result in revealing weaknesses, and also be construed as negotiation with a "superior" power. This has resulted in a dangerous lack of "circuit breakers" in the U.S.-China military relationship. This contrasts starkly with CBMs China has executed with India, Russia and the ASEAN and the Shanghai Cooperation Organization.

INTRODUCTION

The U.S.-China relationship is one of the most important and most difficult bilateral relationships for this nation. Yet U.S. Government officials know woefully little about prevailing Chinese perceptions and strategic thinking.

American policymakers know less than they should about how Chinese leaders assess U.S. foreign policy and the exercise of U.S. power, how China views its role in Asia and beyond, how Chinese leaders have incorporated their thinking and perceptions into economic, political and military planning, and how the Chinese Government has portrayed the United States to its own populace. Over the past year, the Commission has held a series of hearings and briefings with leading U.S. scholars, policymakers, and analysts and translated and analyzed official, semi-official and other Chinese publications, both unclassified and classified, to identify Chinese leadership perceptions and attitudes of the United States and how they might affect U.S. national security interests.

In addition, the Commission contracted independent research, including a major study conducted by the University of Maryland to provide empirical evidence on the messages and tone of Chinese reporting on the U.S. over time, and how it is affected by various events. Given the control of the Chinese leadership over the media, such messages give us insight into how the leadership attempts to portray the United States and thus develop attitudes toward the U.S. among the Chinese people.

The U.S. Government must dedicate far greater resources to collecting and analyzing both open and classified Chinese sources in order to better understand the views of Chinese leaders. U.S. Government efforts in this area are far less extensive than similar efforts our country made to understand the Soviet Union during the Cold War. As the Defense Department noted in its December 2000 Net Assessment Report to Congress, in order to judge whether China is deterred by U.S. military capabilities, we need to understand how the Chinese authorities assess the situation.

The Commission has found that while there are ongoing debates among China's leaders on various aspects and timelines of their security environment, China's strategic assessments and public portrayals of U.S. power are shaped by the view that U.S.-style democratic liberalism and the U.S. presence and position of power in the Asian periphery threaten the Communist Party's monopoly on political power. Specifically,

a) China sees the United States as a hegemonic power that is a major obstacle and competitor for influence in Asia;
b) China believes the United States is a superpower in decline, losing economic, political, and military influence around the world;
c) China aspires to be a major international power and the dominant power in Asia. To that end, China is actively pursuing a multipolar world where it could align with other rising powers such as Russia, Japan, and Europe in order to check or challenge U.S. power;
d) China's leaders want to maintain stable and good relations with the United States because the United States is an important market for Chinese goods and an important source of science and technology, financial capital, and foreign direct investment--all central components of China's rising status and strength.
e) China's leaders believe that the United States, although technologically superior in almost every area of military power, can be defeated, most particularly, in a fight over Taiwan in which China controls the timing. Along with logistical and operational weaknesses, Chinese analysts also believe that the United States will not and cannot sustain casualties in pursuit of its vital interests. China is dedicating considerable resources toward preparing for potential conflict with the United States, especially over Taiwan;[1] and
f) September 11 changed the context of China's approach to the United States but did not change the fundamentals.[2]

The beliefs of the Chinese leaders shape and direct China's relations with the United States and China's economic and military programs. They also influence China's relations with our major allies, its neighbors, terrorist sponsoring states, and its military doctrine and weapons acquisition programs.

[1] George Tenet, "DCI Worldwide Threat Briefing 2002: Converging Dangers in a Post 9/11 World," Central Intelligence Agency, 6 February 2002.
[2] Ibid.

THE UNITED STATES AS A "HEGEMON"

The term "hegemon," according to Chinese thinking, has a negative connotation, and depicts a power that desires imperialistic control over other powers, and is overbearing and controlling. China has traditionally characterized as hegemons only foreign powers with which it has highly antagonistic relationships. When China split with the Soviet Union during the Cold War, it began characterizing the Soviet Union as a Socialist hegemon. When Vietnam invaded Cambodia, and just prior to the Chinese invasion of Vietnam, Beijing characterized Hanoi as a "regional hegemon."

The word "hegemon," usually used alongside other terms such as "imperialist," "unilateralist," and "self-appointed world policeman," is precisely how official Chinese media characterize the United States. Such characterization communicates to the Chinese people that the United States, from the point of view of its foreign policies toward China, is a power with which China has a competitive, if not antagonistic, relationship.

Since the collapse of the Soviet Union, China has viewed the U.S. global position with deep suspicion, if not hostility. Chinese leaders believe that the fundamental drive of the United States is to maintain global hegemony by engaging in the shameless pursuit of "power politics," often disguised as a quest for democratization.[3]

China's Defense White Paper of 2000 reflects deep concern about an international order predominantly shaped by the United States. It states that "certain big powers" (i.e., the United States) are contributing to instability and "threatening world peace" by pursuing neo-interventionism, new gunboat policy, and neo-economic colonialism. The [4]document links such new problems to "hegemonism" and the hegemon's proclivities for playing "power politics."[5]

China has viewed high-profile U.S. military actions of 1999-2001–including the NATO campaign against Yugoslavia, the bombing of the Chinese embassy in Belgrade, the EP-3 incident over the South China coast–as glaring examples of "hegemonism" at work, and believes that they have produced an "extremely negative impact" on the international situation.[6] Beijing has compared the United States to Nazi Germany for the bombing of the Chinese embassy in Belgrade; it has labeled U.S. involvement in Bosnia and Kosovo as an attempt to maintain U.S. dominance in Europe; it has characterized the enlargement of NATO as an effort to contain and encircle China; and it has criticized U.S. development of ballistic missile defenses as contributing to the proliferation of weapons of mass destruction.[7]

Furthermore, Beijing has perceived Washington's "anti-China" streak — from what some American China policy analysts call the "China Threat" theory to others' regular condemnation of China's human rights record — as a U.S. attempt to preempt China's impending challenge to American influence in Asia. Persistent efforts by some members of the U.S. Congress to deny China most-favored nation (MFN) status for much of the 1990s, and to block Chinese accession to the WTO based on labor, human rights and economic grounds, were viewed by the Chinese

---

[3] U.S.-China Security Review Commission, Hearing on Security Issues: Strategic Perceptions, Written Testimony of Bates Gill, 3 August 2001, 10; Yong Deng, "Hegemon on the Offensive: Chinese Perspectives on U.S. Global Strategy," Political Science Quarterly 116 (2001): 350.

[4] Gill, Written Testimony, 8. ; "Text of PRC White Paper on National Defense in 2000," 2-3; translated in FBIS.

[5] Ibid.

[6] Ibid.

[7] Observer, "We Urge Hegemonism Today to Take a Look at the Mirror of History," People's Daily, 22 June 1999; translated in FBIS.

as a blatant intervention in China's internal affairs and a convenient excuse to prolong and protect U.S. hegemony.

To Beijing, the U.S. Government practices deception and repeatedly lies about its intentions to maintain hegemony. Therefore, U.S. actions, including those taken in the name of some global public good (such as humanitarian intervention in the Balkans), are seen as part of a conspiracy to impose the U.S. vision of the world on others.[8] By this logic, even the U.S. policy of engagement with China itself is a new form of "containment" and U.S. support for peaceful evolution toward democracy is no more than a sinister ploy to destroy the Chinese Communist Party.

For instance, even though the top Chinese leadership aggressively pursued China's entry into the WTO, many Chinese officials still view American support for China's WTO entry as part of a larger effort to promote democracy in China through economic integration and "peaceful evolution," or to maintain power by disseminating "Americanization."[9]

Paradoxically, Chinese suspicions of U.S. intentions and hostility toward American unipolarity exist alongside the recognition that U.S. trade and investment, technology, and know-how are crucial to China's search for modernization. The investigative research done by the University of Maryland indicates a contradiction in the leadership's characterization of the United States to the Chinese people. The contradiction is between their portrayal of U.S. foreign policy and that of the economic relationship, as well as general U.S. relations with China. The former is uniformly negative across the entire survey period by the researchers, and the latter is very positive across the same period. The characterization of the Sino-American relationship is generally positive. As pointed out by the research report to the Commission:

> A major theme emerging from the extensive reporting done on U.S. foreign policy is of the United States as a hegemonic power that acts unilaterally and in opposition to general international principles. Aside from the embassy bombing and reconnaissance plane issues, other major themes that emerged included the U.S. war on terrorism, in which the U.S. is taking increasingly strident steps away from international norms.[10]

Similarly, Chinese leaders can aggressively seek U.S. trade, investment and financial assistance while simultaneously denouncing U.S. intentions and power.

Post-September 11

Chinese suspicions of the United States did not subside even after a notable upswing in official Sino-American relations after September 11. Rather, official Chinese media has continued to portray the United States as a hegemon, albeit a wounded one. The state media blamed the September 11 terrorist attacks on a misguided and aggressive U.S. foreign policy. The University of Maryland study looked at Chinese media coverage in the time period after September 11 and found that the media, "although supportive at first of the U.S. anti-terrorist

[8] Deng, "Hegemon on the Offensive," 351; Su Ge, "Climbing High to See Afar," Xiandai Guoji Guangxi (Contemporary International Relations) (September 2001), trans., U.S.-China Security Review Commission.

[9] Zhang Minqian, "Globalization and U.S. Strategy," Xiandai Guoji Guanxi (Contemporary International Relations) 128 (20 May 2000): 28-31; translated in FBIS.

[10] University of Maryland's Institute for Global Chinese Affairs and the Department of Communication, "Perspectives toward the United States in Selected Newspapers of the People's Republic of China," prepared for the U.S. China Security Review Commission, 30 May 2002, 9.

position, soon after introduced a more wary tone" and characterized the U.S. war on terrorism as "taking increasingly strident steps away from international norms."[11]

In the month immediately following September 11, Chinese open sources reiterated three constant decades-old themes: a relative decline in U.S. power is underway, the U.S. Government practices deception and continually lies about its intentions, and China must be vigilant about U.S. actions against China, because the U.S. is making China its enemy. Two days following the attack, the Chinese owned Hong Kong newspaper *Ta Kung Pao* featured an interview in Beijing with two active duty colonels, who said, "The United States has been too self-willed and conceited, likes to dominate others, and has made so many enemies that it has been unable to determine who the enemies were since the attacks occurred."[12]

In a more lengthy analysis of the impact of September 11 on U.S.-Sino relations, the Deputy Director of the influential Chinese Institute of Contemporary International Relations (CICIR), Yuan Peng, challenged the analysis of some American scholars that counter terrorism cooperation between the United States and China would be the new strategic foundation of U.S.-China relations. Peng argued that cooperation over counter-terrorism "would hardly change [the United States'] deep prejudice towards certain countries. Fundamental contradictions will re-emerge at the end of the counter-terrorist war...And, second, differences between China and the US over a number of related important issues like the definition of terrorism, the goal of the current war, etc. have come to the surface despite good bilateral cooperation over counter-terrorism so far. Such divergences over concrete issues, plus existing problems between the two, might cast shadows over their future ties."[13]

Within days of September 11, videos and DVDs produced by the government appeared in China explaining the attacks.[14] Most notably, a video entitled *The Pentagon in Action* painstakingly portrays the U.S. Government as a wounded bully whose hegemonic power and ego have been challenged and which is obsessed with irresponsible military retaliations. Despite its occasional sympathetic tone, the video repeatedly cites "the world's opinions" to criticize America's "immature and revengeful" counter-terrorist measures. The French prime minister and foreign minister, the German defense minister, the Russian President and China's President, all "earnestly" urge the U.S. to be cautious, and "don't behave just like the terrorists." Saddam Hussein appears in this program as a rational statesman urging the U.S. to utilize wisdom rather than force. And Jiang Zemin advises the Americans to use "wisdom, rationality and courage," not just blunt force, in dealing with the world's real problems.

America's geopolitical position after September 11 continues to feed Chinese anxiety.[15] Russia, which China has actively courted to balance U.S. hegemony, has drawn even closer to the United States since September 11. This has been underscored by the U.S.-Russia agreement in St. Petersburg and the formation of the NATO-Russian Council. In Central Asia, the United States gained access to bases and facilities in Tajikistan, Kyrgyzstan and Uzbekistan and was

---

[11] Ibid.

[12] Michael Pillsbury, "China's Perceptions of the USA: The View from Open Sources," Report prepared for the U.S.-China Security Review Commission, 4-5; The two PRC colonels quoted were also authors of Unrestricted Warfare, a 1999 book that advocated asymmetric warfare with Chinese characteristics and called on the Chinese Government to explore all possible means—including political, economic, financial, and military—in warfare against a superior power

[13] Yuan Peng, "September 11 Event vs. Sino-US Relations," Xiandai Guoji Guanxi (Contemporary International Relations) (November 2001): 8.

[14] Peter Hessler, "Letter From China," The New Yorker, 15 October 2001, 83.

[15] Aaron Friedberg, "11 September and the Future of Sino-American Relations," Survival 44 (Spring 2002): 41.

granted permission to overfly the territories of Kazakhstan, Azerbaijan, and Georgia.[16] In South Asia, the United States cemented a crucial alliance with Pakistan through President Pervez Musharraf. In sum, America's heightened military presence in China's "backyard" and improved relations with its neighbors have created anxiety in Beijing about U.S. designs to encircle or contain it.[17] Furthermore, not only has the United States not condoned China's crackdown on Muslims in Xinjiang Province, it has stepped up pressure on issues ranging from religious freedom to controlling the proliferation of weapons of mass destruction (WMD).[18]

America's Relative Decline and Perceived Weaknesses

Relative Decline

China's leaders have been predicting the relative decline of American economic, political and military influence relative to other powers, for decades. Without the decline of the "capitalist" United States, Chinese Marxism would be proven wrong. The debate in China is how long it will take. In the 1990's, Chinese analysts were predicting that the decline would take five years. Today, revisionists admit that the rate of decline is going to be slower.[19]

U.S. unipolarity, they argue, will in time be balanced by rising poles such as the European Union (EU), Russia, Japan, and China. In a multipolar world, U.S. influence would be weakened to accommodate the interests and desires of other powers, especially China.[20]

Chinese strategists measure national standing by evaluating both quantitatively and qualitatively the politics, economics, military, science and technology, and foreign affairs of a country to determine relative "comprehensive national power (CNP)."[21] The analysts predictably see U.S. decline in virtually all arenas, and symbols of that decline can be seen everywhere in macro and micro trends, including, for example, the building of newer and higher skyscrapers in Asia.

Among Chinese strategic thinkers, the economic growth of the rising powers, particularly China, is a central component of (relative) U.S. economic decline and the inevitable trend toward multipolarity. An article from CICIR states: "As a result of their economic growth, more and more countries now dare to say 'no' to the United States."[22] U.S. hegemonic impulses and, consequently its "mistaken foreign policy", will, over time, alienate key European and Asian allies, who after the collapse of the Soviet Union, will be unwilling to remain subordinate to a grand U.S. strategy but instead will assert their own "polarity."[23] China believes that the enhancement of its economic and political power and international influence will lead the new poles, such as the EU and Japan, to seek better relations with Beijing as American hegemony

[16] . Ibid.

[17] Ibid., 42.

[18] Aaron Friedberg, Informal Presentation to the U.S.-China Security Review Commission, 24 April 2002.

[19] U.S.-China Security Review Commission, Hearing on Security Issues: Strategic Perceptions, Oral Testimony of Michael Pillsbury, 3 August 2001, 22.

[20] U.S.-China Security Review Commission, Hearing on Security Issues: Strategic Perceptions, Written Testimony of Larry Wortzel, 3 August 2001, 5.

[21] "U.S. Defense Secretary's Report on the Pattern of Military Modernization in China," Annual Report to Congress on the Military Power of the People's Republic of China, June 2000, 6.

[22] Yan Xiangjun, Yang Bojiang, Chu Shulong and Dao Shulin, "A Survey of Current Asian Pacific Security," Contemporary International Relations 8 (July 1994): 1-2.

[23] Pillsbury, "China's Perceptions of the USA," 8.

declines.[24] The results of the struggles among the Untied States, Europe and Japan will lead all three to "attach more importance to the China factor in their foreign strategies" because of the "enhancement of China's Comprehensive National Power and the extension of China's international influence."[25]

Perceived Military Weaknesses

Chinese strategists also view the United States as relatively weak militarily. Foremost in their strategic considerations are:

- The United States will not and cannot sustain casualties in pursuit of vital interests.[26] If China could kill or wound enough American service personnel, as occurred in Somalia, it could effectively deter U.S. forces or force their defeat in the event of a military conflict in East Asia, including in the defense of Taiwan.[27]
- Despite overwhelming U.S. military and technological superiority, China can still defeat the United States by transforming its weakness into strength and exploiting U.S. vulnerabilities through asymmetric warfare, assassin's mace weapons, deception, surprise, and preemptive strikes.

In general, Chinese authors assert: the United States barely won the Gulf War (Saddam Hussein could have won with a better strategy); the United States today cannot contain Chinese power; the United States cannot execute its past military strategy of two major regional contingencies; and that U.S. munitions cannot damage deep underground bunkers like those in China.[28]

Lieutenant General Li Jijun, Vice President of the Academy of Military Science, wrote about the weaknesses of the U.S. military during the Gulf War:

> U.S. Armed Forces revealed many weak points. For example, the combat consumption was too great, and it could not last long. There was great reliance on the allied countries. The high-tech equipment was intensive and its key links were rather weak; once they were damaged, combat effectiveness was greatly reduced. Also, if the adversary of the United States was not Iraq, if the battle was not fought on the flat desert, if the Iraqi Armed Forces struck first during the phase when U.S. Armed Forces were still assembling, or if Iraqi Armed forces withdrew suddenly before the U.S. Armed Forces struck, then the outcome of the war might have been quite different.[29]

---

24 Ibid., 6,9.

25 Xu Zhixian, Zhang Minqian, and Hong Jianjun, "On the Foreign Strategy and Trends of China Policy of the U.S., Western Europe and Japan at the Turn of the Century," Contemporary International Relations 8 (March 1998): 12-14.

26 Wortzel, Written Testimony, 5.

27 Thomas Christensen, "Posing Problems without Catching Up: China's Rise and Challenges for U.S. Security Policy," International Security 25 (Spring 2001): 14.

28 Pillsbury, "China's Perceptions of the USA," 20.

29 Li Jijun, "Notes on Military Theory and Strategy," Military Theory and Conflict, (Beijing: Academy of Military Science Press, 1994) cited in Michael Pillsbury, Chinese Views of Future Warfare (Washington, D.C., Nation Defense University Press, 1997), 227.

Chinese assessments of American military weaknesses have led to a broad conclusion by many Chinese strategists and military authors that the U.S. forces will one day be vulnerable to a Chinese strategy of deception, special silver-bullet "trump card" weapons, and classic defeat of the "superior" by the "inferior."

Finally, a recurring Chinese theme is that the "decay" of American global predominance stems from rampant social problems in the United States, including drugs, crime, social inequality, homelessness, racial tensions, and spiritual and moral crises.[30]

CHINESE STRATEGIC PRIORITIES

It is clear that China anticipates America's decline and is working to shape a world with a weaker United States and stronger competing poles of power where it can play a central role. China's strategy to help achieve this objective appears to include biding its time by avoiding confrontation with the United States, and meanwhile gaining access to American investment, technology and know-how. At the same time, Beijing is working to counter U.S. influence and competition by preparing if needed to subdue American forces via military modernization, including asymmetrical means of warfare.[31]

Economic Growth

Economic growth is a central pillar of Chinese power. The Chinese Government and its industries share an overwhelming common and driving goal to increase the power and international standing of China as a nation state. While China's leaders remain wary of U.S. support for WTO entry, they view accession as essential to continue rapid growth by accelerating economic reform, attracting higher levels of foreign investment, maintaining and expanding export markets and playing a more influential role in shaping the rules of the world trading system.

Over the past two decades, China has undertaken a prodigious economic reform and has seen a dramatic growth in its economy. This growth has been largely propelled by exports from China and foreign direct investment in China, in both of which the United States plays a lead role. China's growth strategy has also included a stringent commitment to improving its science and technology base by importing both civilian and military technologies from advanced industrial nations, again most importantly, from the United States.

Chinese policy has been guided since the 1970's by the maxim enunciated by Deng Xiaoping that science and technology from abroad is the prime force of production and central to China's rise from poverty and weakness. The United States is seen as a major source for this technology. The Chinese have used a variety of overt and covert methods to acquire this technology, including sending large numbers of students abroad to study relevant disciplines, forming joint

[30] Michael Pillsbury, China Debates the Future Security Environment (Washington: National Defense University Press), 2000), 86-87.

[31] Wortzel, Written Testimony, 1-2.

ventures, partnerships, and using the attraction of its potential consumer market to induce firms to sign investment agreements that require some form of technology transfer.[32]

Chinese leaders have repeatedly insisted that peace is fundamental for economic growth. As China's White paper on National Defense states, "A peaceful international environment and a favorable surrounding environment serves China's fundamental interests."[33]

In the short-to-mid term, China needs the United States to achieve its objective of developing its economy, its science and technology base and its military force.[34] While debate periodically erupts among its strategists on how to deal with the United States, patience has been the guiding dictum since Deng Xiaoping launched the modernization drive. Deng's often quoted advice was, keep cool-headed to observe, be composed to make reactions, stand firmly, hide our capabilities and bide our time, never try to take the lead and be able to accomplish something.

Deng's advice is followed today. The only real debate in China on U.S. decline is when. The leaders counsel patience, and tolerating whatever the United States does to China, in order to allow China to grow for the next 20 years. The leaders believe that at that time, China will, at best, be equal to the United States or, at least, be able to combine with other powers to check American power. There is a basic sense of confidence at the highest levels that the U.S.-PRC relationship is achieving China's immediate objectives of growth in exports and foreign direct investment, which will lead to economic growth.[35]

Strengthening the Party

Chinese leaders believe that American-style democratic capitalism threatens the Chinese Communist Party's political monopoly, but they believe they can grow economically and still maintain their power. This matter was recently addressed in Jiang Zemin's announcement of the "Three Represents" in which he called on the Chinese Communist Party (CCP) to represent the forces of production, the progressive course of China's culture, and the broad interests of the majority of the Chinese people. According to Jiang, the Three Represents would make the CCP more relevant to the Chinese people amidst the rapid social and economic developments now taking place within China.

Viewed as the centerpiece of Jiang's effort to modernize the CCP, the strategy was announced together with Jiang's invitation to intellectuals and entrepreneurs–traditionally viewed as "red capitalists" or the "exploiting class"--to join the CCP. These new members, Jiang argued, would strengthen the CCP with their technological know-how, education, and skills and therefore help strengthen "socialism with Chinese characteristics."

This theory was developed at the Party School, headed by Hu Jintao, Jiang's anticipated successor.[36] At the time that the theory was announced, approximately 100,000 CCP members were business owners.[37] If fully implemented, the strategy would fundamentally change the CCP

[32] "U.S Commercial Technology Transfers to the People's Republic of China," Bureau of Export Administration, January 1999, <http://www.fas.org/nuke/guide/china/doctrine/dmrr_chinatech.htm>(16 May 2002).

[33] "PRC White Paper on National Defense in 2000," Beijing Xinhua Domestic Service, 16 October 2000, 2. FBIS: CPP20000101600006O.

[34] Mark A. Stokes, China's Strategic Modernization: Implications for the United States (Carlisle, PA: Strategic Studies Institute, 1999), 140.

[35] Pillsbury, Oral Testimony, 22, 69.

[36] Party School of the Communist Party of China (CPC) Central Committee, Informal Meeting with the U.S.-China Security Review Commission, July 2001, Washington, D.C.

[37] Michael Dorgan, "China's Jiang Angers Ideologues by Embracing 'Red Capitalists,'" Knight Ridder, 18 August 2001.

and dilute its traditional membership of workers and peasants. For that reason, Jiang has been accused by ideological hard-liners of betraying the core principles. Some even argue that Jiang is using the Three Represents to build a cult of personality around himself before retiring as President at the upcoming Party Congress in October 2002.

Despite some internal dissent, the CCP has pressed on with a nation-wide propaganda campaign to spread Jiang's theory. Cadres, academic institutions and ordinary citizens have all been instructed to study and practice it much like they studied Mao Zedong Thought and Deng Xiaoping Theory.

Expanding China's International Role

In response to a world in which the United States has not declined as quickly as the Chinese hoped, Beijing put forth a "New Security Concept" in 1996-97, which calls for the abandonment of "Cold War mentality" and a new security order based on "mutual trust, mutual benefit, equality, and cooperation." Having failed to achieve parity or dominance through their own efforts and our failures, the Chinese are now attempting to gain equal footing through diplomacy. The emphasis on equality and cooperation reflects China's preference for a multi-polar world that conforms less to U.S. influence and more to their own desires.[38]

Beijing has described traditional U.S. alliances as vestiges of "Cold War Thinking" while at the same time it has sought to establish its own "partnerships" in Asia and around the world. In the past decade, Beijing has established multiple "cooperative" or "constructive partnerships" with countries from Japan to India, from the European Union to the United Kingdom, from Mexico to South Africa.[39]

Asserting greater influence in the Asia Pacific region is central to China's strategic policy. And Chinese analysts also see the region as an important source of technology, investment and modern management techniques.[40]

Since 1989, China has sought to create an environment conducive to domestic economic development and regional stability by engaging in confidence building measures (CBMs) with other Asian countries. Such measures have contributed to a reduction of tensions between China and border states such as India, Russia, and three Central Asia republics (Kazakhstan, Kyrgyzstan, and Tajikistan).[41] In addition, Beijing has agreed to CBMs with other key players in the Asia region, such as the Association of Southeast Asian Nations (ASEAN). As a result, China has successfully eliminated any dramatic or compelling military threat to its borders, at least for the short term. Most notably, Beijing aggressively sought and reached a friendship and cooperation treaty with Russia, which was intended, in part, to counter-balance U.S. and European global influence.

---

[38] Gill, Written Testimony, 10-11.

[39] Ibid., 13-15.

[40] Wang Yizhou, Multi-Polarity Does Not Equal an Anti-US Position, The Globe Times, (Summer 1999), 4, trans., U.S.-China Security Review Commission, Wang Yizhou argues: "To maintain good relations with our neighboring countries, especially with countries in the Asia-Pacific region, is and has always been our most important diplomatic task. In a new and multi-polar environment, our guidelines of 'maintaining friendly relations with our neighbors and stabilizing relationships with other surrounding countries' should not only be continued, they should even push for China to 'exert greater influence and become a leading force.' We should strive to make our voice heard more in regional affairs."

[41] Kenneth W. Allen, "China's Approach to Confidence-Building Measures," in Ranjeet K. Singh, ed., Investigating Confidence-Building Measures in the Asia-Pacific Region, May 1999, 23.

The record stands in stark contrast to the resistance by China to U.S. Government attempts to develop CBM's between itself and China. Authoritative U.S. Government sources involved in years of such futile efforts concluded the Chinese simply did not want such CBMs to have a central place in U.S.-China relations. The results were a nearly complete failure in the face of no interest by Chinese. Perhaps even more worrisome is the same lack of interest and success in reducing misunderstandings or miscalculations between Beijing and Taiwan, resulting in no CBMs between them.

Similarly, China's economic relations with Europe and Japan reflect both an interest in building relations with America's traditional allies and also decreasing China's own dependency on the United States. To this end, China has courted Europe and Japan for technology, investments, and markets. China has also thrown a broad net in its efforts to acquire advanced science and technology from abroad. China has cooperative arrangements in both civilian industrial and military areas with countries such as Germany, France, the United Kingdom, Russia, Israel, Brazil, Japan, Korea, and Australia. Its membership in WTO helps broaden China's outreach to all the players in the world trading system, lessens its dependency on the United States for investment and trade, and makes it even more attractive to foreign investors.

In addition, Beijing is attempting to broadly counter American influence by increasing its involvement in multilateral organizations. On the international level, Beijing has increasingly supported the United Nations, where it has a permanent seat or the Security Council, as a legitimate arbiter of conflicts around the world. Regionally, Beijing has actively sought to strengthen ties with neighbors by signing a statement of friendship and cooperation with the Shanghai Cooperation Organization, increasing involvement with the ASEAN Regional Forum (ARF), participating in ASEAN +3 discussions and hosting the all-Asia Boao Economic Forum.[42]

Military Modernization

On the military front, China is dedicating considerable resources to a military modernization effort, the focus of which is preparing for conflict involving the United States over Taiwan.[43] China is upgrading its missile force structure, shortening its response time, and enhancing its reliability and survivability.

Over the past year, China has emphasized a "real world focus" in its military training exercises, emphasizing "rigorous practice in operational capabilities and improving the military's actual ability to use force."[44] Among other measures, China is preparing to respond to U.S. forces, if necessary, by developing the capacity to control sea lines of communication and project force there. These objectives entail a substantial build-up of air, marine, airborne, and naval forces. China is not only adding longer range cruise missiles to its inventory, it is also developing through military purchases from traditional U.S. allies an over-the-horizon capability for its cruise missiles to extend the range at which they can strike U.S. naval forces.[45] China has also publicly stated its intention to be able to neutralize an American aircraft carrier. This objective may, in part, be based on its belief that the United States does not have the will to sustain casualties.

---

[42] Gill, Written Testimony, 14.
[43] Tenet, "DCI Worldwide Threat Briefing 2002: Converging Dangers in a Post 9/11 World".
[44] Ibid.
[45] Wortzel, Written Testimony, 10.

While reaffirming their commitment to economic growth and development, senior Chinese leaders have agreed to a significant increase in funding for military modernization, announcing in March 2002, a 17.6 percent increase in military spending.

The bulk of Chinese defense investment is still commanded by the PLA ground forces and the Chinese military school of thought that endorses the concept of People's War or Active Defense. This concept supports a large standing army, a suitable defense mobilization base, and opposes dependence on foreign weapons. Nevertheless, beginning in 1985, competition for resources has come from the Local War advocates who were embraced by Deng Xiaoping and have characterized China's most likely future conflicts as intense but limited local wars."[46] Since the Gulf War, competition for resources has also come from reformists who are "Revolution in Military Affairs (RMA)" advocates, who call for investment in the most exotic and advanced form of weaponry, including what they term "assassin's mace weapons," which can deliver decisive blows in carefully calculated surprise moves and change the balance of power. There is evidence that the Chinese leadership is allocating resources among these three distinct paths.[47]

Since the Gulf War, PLA analysts seem convinced that their traditional approach to warfare, which focuses on mass and the annihilation of their enemies, would not be successful against an enemy with advanced technologies. In facing a high-tech enemy that relies on the RMA concepts, the PLA's revised doctrine seeks to exploit perceived weaknesses in such concepts.[48]

Chinese thinking on military planning and action differs markedly from our own, underscoring the need to understand their thinking better than we do now. Drawing on analyses of ancient and modern warfare in China as well as their own extensive revolutionary experience, the Chinese conclude it is not necessary to match U.S. capabilities to achieve victory and believe that the "inferior can defeat the superior." According to such thinking, China can transform weakness into strength by employing deception, surprise and preemptive strikes, creating or leveraging discord amongst the enemy's internal units, capitalizing on the opponent's complacency, and using "trump cards" or "assassin's mace weapons." In fact, assassin's mace weapons have been given the highest level of attention since August 1999 when Jiang Zemin called for their priority development in a speech.[49] Such weapons fall in line with a host of other asymmetrical strategies–such as cyber warfare–that the Chinese believe would help to counter U.S. military superiority.[50]

Information warfare--focusing on gaining and exploiting information, attacking the enemy's information systems and defending one's own information--is an important component of this asymmetric warfare strategy. Asserted Major General Wang Pufeng, former director of the strategy department of China's Academy of Military Science: "In the future, information warfare will control the form and future of war. We recognize this developmental trend...and see it has a driving force in the modernization of China's military and combat readiness. This trend will be highly critical to achieving victory in future wars.[51]" One of the consequences of this analysis

[46] U.S.-China Security Review Commission, Hearing on Export Controls and China, Written Testimony of Bernard D. Cole and Paul H.B. Goodwin, 17 January 2002, 3.

[47] Michael Pillsbury, "China's Military Strategy Toward the U.S.: A View From Open Sources," Report prepared for U.S.-China Security Review Commission, November 2001, 4.

[48] Department of Defense, Annual Report on the Military Power of the People's Republic of China, 2002, 12.

[49] Pillsbury, "China's Military Strategy Toward the U.S.," 5.

[50] Richard Betts and Thomas Christensen, "China: Getting the Questions Right," National Interest, no. 62 (Winter 2000).

[51] Kathryn L. Gauthier, China as Peer Competitor? Trends in Nuclear Weapons, Space, and Information Warfare," Air War College Maxwell Paper, no.18 (July 1999) 19.

is that China is increasing its investment in space warfare.[52] China's efforts include the pursuit of a viable indigenous space force. Particular attention is being paid to the development of small boosters able to launch satellites at a moment's notice in a contingency.[53]

The PLA's strategy of defeating a "high-tech" opponent through surprise and preemptive attacks "calls for operations aimed at destroying the enemy command system, crippling the enemy information system, destroying the enemy's most advanced weapons systems, crippling the enemy support (logistics) systems, and disrupting the critical links in the enemy's campaign systems."[54]

To deal with the gap between mission requirements and capabilities, China's weapons acquisition policy continues to require weapons purchases and technology acquisition from a host of advanced industrial nations including, along with the United States, Russia, Israel, Great Britain, Italy, France, and Germany. It has also been relying very heavily on its ability to develop and produce missiles to bridge the gap,[55] while it seeks to build and improve its defense, science and technology and industry and develop its indigenous capacity to build weapons.[56]

Given the PLA assessment methods from the model of "weak defeating the strong," normal western strategies and communications may not operate effectively. The use of "direct" communications cannot be trusted to establish the credibility of Chinese intentions, and may not be interpreted correctly. Thus, so-called confidence building measures might be used to deceive or may be interpreted as a means of Western deception. Once in a crisis, the Chinese may not escalate at the same pace or by the same means as the West, which may lead to misperceptions of the Chinese level of commitment. Indeed, thinking on asymmetric warfare appears to be so pervasive in China today that the Commission believes the troubling possibility of Chinese self-deception could be worrisome in that it could lead to major miscalculations on their part. It is worthy of more attention by American policymakers.

Promoting Nationalism

On the domestic front, China has carefully fanned the flames of nationalism and anti-Americanism through state-controlled media. To counter persistent U.S. objections to China's behavior in areas from trade to human rights, from weapons proliferation to Taiwan, the Chinese state media has portrayed Washington as the self-appointed policeman of the world, whose foreign policy is inherently aggressive and bent on undermining others countries' national sovereignty.[57] The Chinese leadership has projected these negative images while also deliberately embracing those American achievements they would like China to emulate for its own development, such as American advances in high technology.

Years of anti-American propaganda greatly contributed to the popular reaction to September 11, as Chinese Internet users gloated online over America's national tragedy. The degree of anti-

52 U.S. – China Security Commission, Hearing on Security Issues: Strategic Perceptions, Oral Testimony of Richard Fisher, 3 August 2001, 183.

53 U.S. -China Security Review Commission, Hearing on U.S. Export Control Policy Toward China, Written Testimony of Lisa Bronson, 17 January 2002, 1.

54 Annual Report on the Military Power of the People's Republic of China, 15.

55 Gill, Written Testimony, 13.

56 PRC White Paper on National Defense in 2000, 5.

57 Ying Ma, "China's America Problem," Policy Review no. 111 (February/March 2002),44-45.

Americanism so embarrassed Beijing that Internet censors were instructed to delete such online content.[58]

China's promotion of nationalism and anti-Americanism reflects a larger strategy on the part of the CCP to maintain stability and control as the economy rapidly opens up to the outside world and American values and culture.

OFFICIAL SINO-AMERICAN RELATIONS

The U.S.-PRC bilateral relationship is at best, deficient for conflict resolution, uncoordinated within the U.S. bureaucracy and, at worst, has the effect of supporting Chinese efforts to enhance their science and technology base without adequate oversight within the U.S. Government.

Science & Technology Exchanges

The main elements of the existing bilateral relationship were established by President Carter in 1979, shortly after the normalization of relations with the PRC. At that time, President Carter and Premier Deng Xiaoping signed the U.S.-China Agreement on Cooperation in Science and Technology, which set up a series of joint commissions and committees to facilitate and promote bilateral dialogue and cooperation. Eleven U.S. Federal Agencies and numerous branches currently participate in cooperative exchanges under the Science and Technology agreement and its nearly 60 protocols, memoranda of understanding, and annexes. These agreements cover cooperative research in diverse fields, including energy, mathematics and chemistry, fisheries, the earth and atmospheric sciences, high-energy physics and other energy related areas, agriculture, cooperation in civil industrial technology, mine safety and miners' health and disaster research.

According to the Congressional Research Service, which was asked to examine the structure of these agreements, there is no centralized mechanism for coordinating, funding or reporting to Congress on the various cooperative programs occurring within these agencies or commissions.[59] However, the Department of State in its first comprehensive assessment to Congress of the history and implications of these arrangements reported that the bilateral S&T relationship is coordinated through two mechanisms: the Joint Commission on S&T Cooperation and the S&T Executive Secretaries.[60] But the Department of State acknowledged that these coordination meetings are infrequent and clearly insufficient to monitor, much less direct, set guidelines, or evaluate the detailed technology transfers being made. The Joint Commission Meeting originally scheduled to meet once a year to coordinate the overall effort meets customarily every two years with the personnel on both sides varying greatly from meeting to meeting. Similarly, according to State, the Executive Secretariat Meeting should annually occur, but in reality the meetings are less frequent.

---

[58] John Pomfret, "China Censors Anti-U.S. Reaction," Washington Post, 15 September 2001, sec. A.

[59] Kerry Dumbaugh, "The early infrastructure of U.S. relations with the People's Republic of China (PRC) during the Carter Administration," Congressional Research Service Memorandum, 23 April 2002. (This memorandum was requested on behalf of the U.S.-China Security Review Commission by Senator Robert C. Byrd).

[60] Washington, D.C.: Department of State, Report on U.S. – China Science and Technology Cooperation, 2002, 5.

During President George W. Bush's visit to China, he and President Jiang Zemin agreed to set up further exchanges and cooperation in the fields of trade, energy, science and technology, environmental protection, AIDS prevention and cure, and law enforcement. Given the history of these activities, the Commission finds that the Executive Branch needs to undertake a major effort to coordinate these exchanges and to inform Congress of the activities and progress on a regular basis.

The Chinese value the economic relationship with the United States very highly and have made strenuous efforts to insulate it from the vagaries of episodic military incidents, tensions, and even confrontations. For example, during the U.S. reconnaissance plane crisis, they "quietly" renewed, according to the Department of State, the agreement on scientific and technology exchanges with the United States. Furthermore, in the early morning after the plane incident, the mayor and other Shanghai officials fanned out across the U.S. firms located in the area to assure these executives that they and their firms would be protected, to encourage them to remain in a business-as-usual mode, despite the rhetoric and tensions associated with the military incident.[61]

Confidence Building Measures

The U.S. China relationship is event driven with very few structured mechanisms for conflict resolution or threat reduction. The Four Party Talks addressing the Korean Peninsula and the US-China coalition addressing the South Asian Nuclear Tests in 1998 are two examples of temporary mechanisms that terminated once the issue was resolved or was no longer of central importance. This lack of durable architecture is particularly important, and even dangerous, given the Chinese perceptions of the United States. The United States worked diligently for years with the Soviet Union to establish threat reduction mechanisms to avoid unnecessary or potentially cataclysmic conflict. Despite extensive efforts by the United States to do the same thing, the result has been near total failure.

Over the past decade, the United States has sought to establish a more stable architecture of military CBMs with China, in part, because of growing concern over China's negative perceptions of U.S. activities in the Asia-Pacific region, specific worrisome military incidents, and the general need to manage crisis. PLA reluctance to acknowledge any legitimacy to U.S. national security concerns has been mainly responsible for the general failure of these initiatives. An underlying factor complicating these efforts has been the Chinese Government's apprehension about revealing any weakness to the United States. On this latter point the Commission has noted that, whether in the area of threat reduction, budget discussions, or military to military exchanges, the Chinese pattern has been to absorb as much information as possible and share as little as possible.

The implementation of CBMs between China and the United States since 1989 has largely reflected these attitudes and the vicissitudes of a very contentious Sino-American relationship. Following the Tiananmen Massacre of 1989, the United States suspended all military cooperation with China. Regular contact did not resume until September 1993, when the Clinton

[61] U.S.–China Security Review Commission, Shanghai Meeting with U.S. Corporate Executives, November 2001, Shanghai.

Administration began its policy of "Comprehensive Engagement." Between 1993 to 1995, the following measures were established:[62]

- Restoration of high-level military exchanges, such as visits to China by Defense Secretary William Perry and two former commanders-in-chief of the U.S. Pacific Command;
- Enhanced military transparency, including consultations and briefings regarding defense budgets and military strategies;
- Restoration of exchanges of military academic units, such as visits between the American National Defense University (NDU) with the Chinese NDU;
- Establishing joint agreements on preventing nuclear proliferation and the proliferation of weapons of mass destruction
- Cooperation on defense conversion; and
- Reciprocal visits of naval warships.

The sum total of these efforts is meager, given the increasing level of military operations and interfaces between the Chinese and U.S. military and subsequent events. The CBMs were put aside after China became incensed by Washington's willingness to permit Taiwanese President Lee Teng-hui to attend his alumni reunion at Cornell University, on a private visit to the United States in 1995. Momentum was regained after the 1995-1996 Taiwan Strait crisis when the U.S. began a discussion with the Chinese about creating a crisis-management mechanism similar to the U.S.-Russian Incidents at Sea Agreement. Helped by the momentum of the 1998 Sino-American presidential summit, a direct presidential communications link (hotline) was established between Presidents Clinton and Jiang, several decades after one was established with the Soviet Union. Subsequently, the two militaries exchanged port visits and reciprocal senior defense and military visits were conducted through the respective National Defense Universities.[63]

After much effort, the Military Maritime Consultation Agreement was also established to foster a process for dialogue. Unfortunately, it is essentially a hollow shell and only calls for periodic discussions between U.S. and PRC military officials on navigation in international waters to enhance understanding when maritime and air forces operate in close proximity.[64] This arrangement fell far short of the more robust structure the United States wanted.

The shortcomings of our CBM efforts were dramatically evident in April 2001 during the EP3 incident. At that time the Chinese refused to use the Military Maritime Consultation Agreement to help resolve the crisis. The Chinese refusal was due, in part, to their reluctance to give legitimacy to U.S. activities in the region and also Chinese perceptions of the U.S. as a hegemon with aggressive intent. These elements help to block the development of crisis reduction mechanisms and, consequently, raise the possibility of conflict between the two countries. Similarly, the Chinese are very reluctant to engage in confidence building measures

[62] Xia Liping, "The Evolution of Chinese Views toward CBMs," Michael Krepon, ed., Chinese Perspectives on Confidence-building Measures, Report No. 23, May 1997, 31-33.

[63] Kenneth W. Allen, "China's Approach to Confidence-Building Measures," in Ranjeet K. Singh, ed., Investigating Confidence-Building Measures in the Asia-Pacific Region, May 1999, 14.

[64] Ibid.

with the Taiwanese. The overriding reason appears to be China's fears that they will convey legitimacy on the Taiwan regime and reveal their own weaknesses.

By stark contrast, the Chinese are far more forthcoming on establishing CBMs when they clearly perceive them as enhancing China's rising power. Beijing has successfully used a variety of CBMs to establish better relations with neighboring countries (See appendix for further discussion). The CBMs also have opened up doors to acquiring much-needed weapons systems and technology from Russia and have facilitated force reductions along shared borders with India and Central Asian states.[65] At the same time, the CBMs have allowed China to reassure its neighbors of the benign nature of its rapid military growth.

In sum, China is keen to encourage any organization or structure that could speed the formation of a multi-polar world. Beijing's participation in the Shanghai Cooperation Organization, which consists of China, Russia and four Central Asian Republics, could potentially serve as a counter to U.S. foreign policy, while its participation in the ASEAN Regional Forum (ARF), because of ARF's emphasis on consensus, prevents any major power (like the United States) from dominating the agenda. Beijing uses CBMs to achieve regional stability and create options that would undermine U.S. influence and power in Asia.

Library of Congress[66]

Understanding Chinese perceptions and strategic thinking is crucial to the formulation of a sound U.S.-China policy. The Library of Congress China collection is the national repository of published and other material on contemporary China, and plays a critical role in informing the Congress, the Executive Branch, and the public for the national policy debate on China. Unfortunately, in recent years, the Library's China collection has been poorly maintained and sorely neglected. Insufficient attention has been paid to collecting and organizing open source Chinese materials in key areas relevant to the policy debate, such as military affairs and national security, Chinese foreign policy, and Sino-American relations. Materials that do exist in the Library are not available for easy and free access to the public. Recent studies conducted by reputable China scholars have also called attention to this problem.[67] The Library's China collection needs to be greatly improved to serve the nation's policy debate on China.

NATIONAL SECURITY IMPLICATIONS

Chinese perceptions of the United States as a hegemonic power and China's principal rival and competitor have serious implications for U.S. national security.

China is seeking to enhance its national power relative to U.S. power. Potential conflict with the United States over Taiwan is the primary focus for that effort and the reason underlying China's growing interest in asymmetric warfare. We must not ignore China's dedicated effort to develop its science and technology base, to acquire advanced technology, and to intimidate and

---

[65] Ibid., 23.

[66] Joseph Cheng, "China's ASEAN Policy in the 1990s: Pushing for Regional Multipolarity, Association of South East Asian Nations," Contemporary Southeast Asia (1 August 1999): 5,6.

[67] Professors June Teufel Dreyer and David Shambaugh have conducted separate studies on the Library of Congress China collection and come to similar conclusions about its glaring deficiencies.

threaten Taiwan. In addition, U.S. security interests are put at risk by China's proliferation of WMD to terrorist sponsoring states.

Chinese perceptions of the United States as an aggressive power become highly destabilizing when combined with a deliberately weak architecture of crisis management. The efforts to resolve the EP-3 incident last year is an example of this deficiency.

Understanding Chinese perceptions of the United States is central to a successful deterrence and crisis management policy, military and diplomatic strategies and our economic relationship. We do not know as much as we should about Chinese perceptions; we do know that the Chinese have a world view very different from ours and that they devise their policies and strategies from such a view. Given, for example, the PLA's use of ancient models of the weak defeating the strong, western notions of deterrence may not operate effectively. In a crisis the Chinese may not escalate at the same pace or by the same means as the West, causing the West to miss the level of commitment the Chinese are applying. Unless we understand Chinese perceptions, we run the risk of implementing policies that are ineffective. All of this increases the potential for misunderstanding and miscalculations.

China's perceptions of the United States and its related strategic objective of multi-polarity impose limits on the extent of genuine cooperation with shared goals and a common agenda. China's reliance on deception casts further doubt on the credibility of its cooperation. Nonetheless, China's recognition that the United States is vital in its modernization, and its recognition that a peaceful international environment is essential for its growth, provides the Untied States important opportunities and leverage.

The combination of Chinese leaders' perceptions of America as an adversarial hegemon, and the lack of solid bilateral institutions for crisis-management response, is potentially explosive. Chinese leaders may well believe the worst of American intentions, and there is no regular mechanism for resolving misunderstandings. In the worst case, this could lead to military conflict. It is urgent for American leaders to work to correct mistaken Chinese perceptions of us, so that that future Chinese leaders will come to share more of our values–particularly in the areas of democracy and human and labor rights–and view us as reliable partners in the search for peace. There is no short-term solution, and we will most likely have to navigate some highly choppy waters before reaching mutual understanding. But there is no more important mission for our policymakers than this one.

RECOMMENDATIONS

- The Library of Congress China collection today is nearly unusable and is a disgrace, despite two major studies advocating a more robust and sophisticated collection. The Commission recommends, therefore, on an urgent basis that the Congress fund the appropriate implementation of the detailed recommendations already submitted by these two previous investigations.

- The Commission recommends that Congress expand the U.S. Government's capacities for collection, translation and analysis of open source Chinese language materials, including expanding the scope of Chinese materials translated by the Foreign Broadcast Information Service (FBIS) and enhancing the Library of Congress's collection. The Central Intelligence Agency, the Defense Intelligence Agency, and other appropriate

Executive Branch agencies should report annually to the Congress on their resources and progress in this area.

- The Commission recommends that Congress request that the Foreign Broadcast Information Service restore and maintain a national research data bank which identifies Chinese authors and publications and determines their relative authority. Such a data bank would help policy makers and scholars determine the significance of the publications and their relative influence on Chinese policymaking.

- The Commission recommends that Congress provide federal funding and other incentives to strengthen Chinese language and area studies programs in U.S. universities, similar to the program that was developed with regard to the Soviet Union and Eastern Europe in the National Defense Education Act of 1958. In conjunction, there should also be incentives given to post-secondary graduates in this field to provide government service.

- The Commission recommends that Congress request that the President designate an Executive Branch agency to develop a database of all government-to-government and government-funded cooperative programs between the U.S. and China. The database should include a full description of each program, including its history, origin, activities, and statutory basis (if any), and a status report on its achievements to date, and should be in both unclassified and classified form, as appropriate. Congress should receive an annual report on official U.S.-China bilateral programs, based on the database, and the agreements should be submitted to Congress pursuant to the Case Act (PL 92-403).

- The Commission recommends that Congress encourage the Department of Defense to make renewed attempts to develop military-to-military confidence building measures, within the context of a strategic dialogue with China and strictly based on the principles of reciprocity, transparency, consistency and mutual benefit.

Appendix: China's Confidence Building Measures with Neighboring Countries

India

The Sino-Indian relationship has experienced extreme animosity and repeated attempts to reduce bilateral tensions. China's invasion of India in 1962 has resulted in unsettled border areas and mutual distrust. In addition, India deeply resents China's effort to balance Indian power in South Asia through the persistent proliferation of nuclear technology and components to Pakistan. Hostilities between the China and India reached a new height in 1998 when India cited the rise of China and its close ties with Pakistan as key threats that led India to detonate a nuclear bomb. Despite these and other chronic disagreements, China and India have attempted to forge a more stable relationship. Most notably, they agreed to CBMs in 1993 and in 1996 to reduce tension in disputed areas along their common border.

In September 1993, India and China entered into an agreement to maintain peace and tranquility along the Line of Actual Control (LAC), declaring that the boundary question should be resolved through peaceful and friendly consultations.[68] Pending a settlement, the two countries will respect the LAC and rely on experts to check and determine the line where there are differences of alignment. Beijing and Delhi also agreed to a reduction of military forces along the border, to be maintained at levels in conformity with the principle of "mutual and equal security."[69]

As part of this agreement, the two sides agreed to a series of CBMs, including the prohibition of specified levels of military exercises in mutually identified zones and prior notification of exercises at specified levels near the LAC.[70]

In November 1996, during the visit of Chinese President Jiang Zemin to India, the two countries signed the Agreement on Confidence Building Measures in the Military Field along the Line of Actual Control in the India-China Border Areas. The agreement reaffirmed the 1993 commitment to seek a peaceful solution to the boundary dispute and to observe the LAC.[71] The two sides agreed to refrain from deploying armed forces along the LAC to attack the other side; to reduce the strength of armed forces to a minimum along the common border; and provide for bringing down the number of field army, border defense and the paramilitary forces to mutually agreed ceilings and the geographical zones.[72] In addition, both promised to avoid holding large-scale military exercises and to give prior information of any such exercise involving more than one hazardous chemicals within the 10 km area.[73]

CBM agreements between China and India have contributed to the reduction of military tensions on the two countries' shared borders. While mutual distrust and deep-seeded animosity linger, China and India today are no longer facing imminent war.

Shanghai Cooperation Organization (SCO)

Since the collapse of the former Soviet Union, China has pursued improved military relations and strategic partnerships with Russia and the central Asian republics, bilaterally and multilaterally, despite its continuing struggle in broader relationships with these counties.[74] Most significant is the creation of the "Shanghai Five" (later renamed as the Shanghai Cooperation Organization), which consists of Russia, Kazakhstan, Kyrgyzstan, Tajikistan and China and first convened in Shanghai in April 1996. The group signed the "Agreement on Confidence-Building in the Military Field in the Border Area," which called for mutual non-use of force and renunciation of military superiority through confidence building measures along their common

---

[68] Agreement on the Maintenance of Peace and Tranquility along the Line of Actual Control in the India-China Border Areas, 7 September 1993.

[69] "India's Prime Minister Signs "Landmark" Border Agreement with China," Press Trust of India News Agency, 7 September 1993.

[70] Agreement on the Maintenance of Peace and Tranquility along the Line of Actual Control in the India-China Border Areas, 7 September 1993.

[71] Agreement between the government of the republic of India and the government of the people's republic of china on confidence-building measures in the military field and line of actual control in the India-china border areas, 29 November 1996.

[72] "Accords Signed with China," All-India Radio, 2 December 1996, 16.

[73] Ibid.

[74] Sino-Russia Joint Declaration on the Basis of Mutual Relations, (1992); Agreement on the Western Section of the Boundary between the People's Republic of China and the Russian Federation",(1994).

border. Under the agreement, the armed forces deployed in the 100-km zone on either side of the border shall not be used in attacks against the other side and shall not be engaged in any activities that would endanger the other side or threaten peace and stability in the region.[75]

According to the CBMs, the parties shall:

- Exchange information on the number of personnel and amounts of essential armaments and equipment of land forces, paratroopers, border guards and air defense forces deployed in the 100-km zone;
- Refrain from carrying out military games aimed against the other parties; inform each otherof the military activities in the 100-km zone; invite observers to watch large-scale exercises along the border;
- Allow warships to enter the 100-km zone only on strictly specified occasions, with notable exceptions for Russian warships;
- Prevent dangerous military activities in the zone: redeployment should not acquire a dangerous form and the parties should take measures to prevent stray bullets, shells and rockets from hitting the territory of the other side during military games;
- Promote military cooperation in adjacent districts, such as official visits by military commanders, trips by teams of experts at various levels and observers to watch military exercises;
- Stipulate that border guard units establish contact and exchange information to promote cooperation.

Since 1996, the Shanghai Cooperation Organization has held annual summits and has deepened their cooperation in military, cultural and trade and security areas. Recently, statements by the group indicate an inclination to seek an expanded role in international affairs. For example, in July 2000, the group even voiced a thinly veiled criticism of U.S. policy when it declared opposition to "intervention in other countries' internal affairs on the pretexts of 'humanitarianism' and 'protecting human rights.'"[76]

Southeast Asia

China has pursued CBMs with individual Southeast Asian states to reduce tensions resulting from territorial or border disputes and with Southeast Asia in general through the Association of Southeast Asian Nations (ASEAN).

In the 1990s, China signed border agreements with Laos and Vietnam and set up CBMs to promote border cooperation. In 1999, China agreed to CBMs with Thailand, which included: enhanced cooperation between the two countries' strategic and security research institutes, strengthened consultations between military personnel and diplomatic officials in security issues,

[75] "Yeltsin Visits China: Details of Confidence-building Measures between Four CIS States and China," ITAR-TASS News Agency (World Service), 26 April 1996.

[76] Bates Gill, "Shanghai Five: An Attempt to Counter U.S. Influence in Asia?" Newsweek Korea, 24 May 2001.

exchange between the two militaries on humanitarian assistance and rescue, and general exchange of information on military science and technology.[77] China has also established CBMs with the Philippines to address their territorial dispute over the Spratly Islands in the South China Sea, especially after the Philippines accused China of taking over one of the islands, the Mischief Reef, in 1995.The CBMs undertaken have included vice-ministerial talks, promotion of high-level visits, agreement to establish a "bilateral consultative mechanism" to cooperate in the South China Sea, and the establishment of the China-Philippines Working Group on Confidence Building Measures.[78]

In addition to establishing CBMs with individual Southeast Asian countries, China has shown great interest in working with ASEAN and the ASEAN Regional Forum (ARF) to maintain good relations with Southeast Asia.[79] China proposed a free-trade area with ASEAN as a form of "political confidence-building." The Chinese initiative, endorsed by both sides in November 2001, offers to ASEAN trade liberalization measures and tariff reductions even greater than those that China agreed to under the WTO.[80]

China has viewed ARF as a useful venue for China to diffuse tensions with Southeast Asian countries over the disputed ownership of the Spratly Islands in the South China Sea. ARF have focused heavily on CBMs, which include: multilateral dialogues on security perceptions, a voluntary annual submission of a defense policy statement, high-level defense contacts and exchanges and participation and observation of other members' military exercises.[81]

China has actively pursued involvement in and CBMs with multilateral organizations such as the SCO and ARF for better relations with its neighbors and to seek arrangements that could serve as an alternative to U.S.-style bilateral alliances in Asia.

[77] "China-Thailand Joint Statement on Bilateral Cooperation," Xinhua English Newswire, February 5, 1999.

[78] Cheng, "China's ASEAN Policy in the 1990s"; "China, Philippines Sign Joint Statement," Xinhua News Agency, May 17, 2000.

[79] The ASEAN members are: Brunei, Burma, Cambodia, Indonesia, Laos, Malaysia, Philippines, Singapore, Thailand and Vietnam. The ASEAN Regional Forum is a 23-nation security forum, proposed in 1993, that groups the ten ASEAN members with Australia, Canada, China, Democratic People's Republic of Korea, European Union, Japan, Republic of Korea, Myanmar, Mongolia, New Zealand, Papua New Guinea, Russia and the United States.

[80] Susan Lawrence, "China –Asean Trade – Enough for Everyone," Far Eastern Economic Review, (13 June 2002).

[81] "Chairman Issues Statement," ASEAN Secretariat, 23 July 1996.

Chapter 3

CROSS-STRAIT SECURITY ISSUES[*]

Lori Esposito Murray, et al.

KEY FINDINGS

- The stated policy of the United States Government is to support Taiwan's security and democracy.
- Taiwan recently has undergone a remarkable political transition, rejecting authoritarian government in favor of free elections and a multi-party parliamentary democracy.
- China is increasing at the rate of roughly 50 per year the number of ballistic missiles it has deployed opposite Taiwan and could have 600 missiles within five years.
- China is enhancing its capability to carry out attacks across the Taiwan Strait with its special operations forces, air forces, and navy and missile forces with little notice.
- It appears the Chinese buildup is designed to forestall pro-independence political movements in Taiwan and help bring about an eventual end to the Island's continued separate status.
- Executive-Congressional consultations regarding Taiwan's security up until the most recent period have not been in conformity with the clear expectation of the Taiwan Relations Act (TRA). The Commission feels strongly that such consensus building is crucial given the clear security risks of this situation. In the last two years the Executive-Congressional consultations in this area have improved.

---

[*] In: July 2002 - Report to Congress of the U.S. - China Security Review Commission - *The National Security Implications of the Economic Relationship between the United States and China.*

Introduction

The Taiwan issue is the most dangerous flashpoint in U.S.-China relations. Prospects for maintaining peace and security in the region and in the Taiwan Strait depend on how Beijing and Taipei manage their significant political differences. While cross-strait economic interactions have flourished since the 1990's, the two sides remain locked in an uneasy standoff. The United States, with significant interests at stake in its relations with both parties and in the region, cannot stand aside. China's political and military strategy is designed to remind U.S. leaders of the significantly increased direct costs to America and its regional relationships should our military forces intervene to challenge Chinese interests. Even though China retains substantial incentives to collaborate with the United States in future years, the situation remains volatile over the medium and long terms. The real possibility that tensions could erupt into major crisis must be factored into U.S. policy and planning.

A military defense for an island of 23 million people, facing a nation of 1.3 billion people, is complicated and difficult. While recognizing that Taiwan's security depends on more than just military means, this chapter concentrates on the military dimension of the impasse between the two sides. Taiwan has made significant progress in its transition to democracy, a multi-party parliamentary system of government, and to a successful open-market economy. This chapter will examine China's position on the use of force to resolve Taiwan's status and its capabilities for exercising that option and will briefly look at the issues that Taiwan's defense planners are facing and conclude with a discussion of U.S. strategy.

China's Intentions and the Threat of Force

Chinese officials have long maintained that they cannot and will not rule out the use of force against Taiwan under certain conditions. These conditions include a formal declaration of independence by Taipei, internal unrest there, or even indefinite delays in the resumption of cross-strait dialogue.[1] The government has published two white papers concerning the "One-China Principle and Taiwan". These papers plus supporting reports and official statements set forth what Chinese officials perceive to be a viable foundation on which unification talks can proceed. The first white paper was released in 1993, which was then followed by President Jiang's Eight-Point Offer to Taiwan on January 30, 1995. The second white paper followed on February 21, 2000. The basic premise of the One-China Principle and the key points are:[2]

- China will do its best to achieve peaceful reunification, but will not commit itself to rule out the use of force;
- Will actively promote people-to-people and economic and cultural exchanges between the two sides;

---

[1] U.S. Department of Defense, Annual Report to Congress on The Military Power of the People's Republic of China (Washington, D.C.: U.S. Department of Defense, 1 May 2002), 47.

[2] The Taiwan Affairs Office and The Information Office of the State Council, White Paper: The One-China Principle and the Taiwan Issue, (Washington, D.C.: Embassy of the People's Republic of China in the United States of America, 21 February 2000).

- Start direct trade, postal, air and shipping services as soon as possible;
- Achieve reunification through peaceful negotiations; and
- Any matter can be negotiated on the premise of One-China.

Recent statements by China's leaders indicate that the use of force remains an option in dealing with Taiwan:

> The Hong Kong Paper Tai Yang Pao, reported last year that President Jiang expressed concern over the then deterioration in Sino-US relations. He is reported to have said that if the United States puts pressure on the Mainland through arms sales to Taiwan and blocks cross-strait reunification, China would be forced into a war between powers.[3]
>
> Chi Haotian, vice-chairman of the CPC Central Military Commission and the Minister of National Defense has stated that the Taiwan problem is the most serious and urgent problem for China's security. He added that the PLA must continue promoting the peaceful unification of the motherland, and must never allow any force to sever Taiwan from China by any means.[4]

Recent evidence also suggests that China's leadership is serious in its efforts to pursue unification. In the late 1990's, China made a critical decision to make its force deployment credible in order for the leadership to enhance its options in dealing with pro-independence forces in Taiwan. It is believed that the PRC military has been directed to have viable options ready by 2005-07. Late last year, there was a leak to the Hong Kong newspaper *Insight*, of what purports to be an August 1999, Central Military Commission (CMC) document discussing the plans for military action against Taiwan. On orders from Beijing, *Insight's* offices were subsequently closed for two weeks and the publication withdrawn from circulation. Analysis of the 2001 PLA Dongshan Island exercises of last year indicates the exercises focused on joint operations with the goal of taking Taiwan. The PLA exercised all elements of a potential war plan from the use of its Second Artillery Corps ballistic missiles, from information warfare to joint landings and potential anti-carrier naval operations at sea.

ASSESSING CHINA'S CAPABILITIES

Chinese authorities are apparently considering several broad classes of military contingencies available to impose their will on Taiwan:

- An invasion of Taiwan (or an offshore island), using amphibious or other sea or air-transported forces
- Air or missile strikes on its industrial infrastructure or commercial assets
- A blockade

---

[3] Wen Jen, "Jiang Reportedly Threatens War with US over Taiwan," Hong Kong Tai Yang Pao, 26 March 2001; translated in FBIS.

[4] "PLA NPC Delegates Stress Need for Expeditious Resolution of Taiwan Problem," Beijing Zhongguo Xinwen She, 9 March 2001; Meng Yan, "PRC's Chi Haotain: Any Attempt to Sever Reunification of Motherland 'Will Be Futile,'" Beijing China Daily, 1 August 2001; translated in FBIS.

Associated with each of these contingencies is some strategy for avoiding, discouraging, or defending against possible third-party intervention, that is, against a determined U.S. response. China's most formidable challenge would be to withstand international condemnation and the imposition of global economic sanctions.

Launching an Invasion

Beijing has increasingly focused on advanced training methods to demonstrate joint-service war-fighting skills that are steadily altering the balance of power with Taiwan. Over the past several years PLA exercises have shifted from intimidating Taiwan to a more serious effort to prepare its military forces to invade. Last year's Dongshan Island exercises illustrated an increasing level of sophistication in war-fighting tactics and interoperability. The PLA is radically overhauling its training regime and introducing more realistic exercises including night maneuvers, combined operations training, long-distance deployments and live-fire exercises.

In keeping with its recent efforts to implement a strategy based on "high-tech limited wars," the PLA's tactical goal would be to strike fast and hard in the event of a cross-strait attack. Planning for U.S. involvement compels the PLA's war-fighting plan towards a quick, decisive neutralization of Taiwan and the degradation of its ability to defend itself. The strategy is to present the United States with a significant political decision. Assuming the strategy was successful, rather than assisting in Taiwan's defense the United States would then be required to expel a Chinese occupational force.

The PLA is making wide-ranging advances in the size and sophistication of its forces arrayed along the strait. The combination of advanced surveillance, large numbers of ballistic and cruise missiles, and the element of surprise is a serious threat to the region's stability.

China has stationed some 75 Russian SU-27 fighters with advanced air-to-air missiles opposite Taiwan, and it will assemble another 125 fighters with Russian help. China also has purchased 40 SU-30 fighters, each of which can provide radar targeting through a data link to four SU-27s. The PLAAF's SU-27s and SU-30s are highly capable planes. Of particular concern is the massive numbers of less capable fighters possessed by the PLAAF. These aircraft can overcome by attrition the technologically superior planes of Taiwan's air force.

China poses an increasing threat to the region with its acquisition of Russian Kilo-class submarines and the indigenously produced Song-class submarines. The Song-class is the first Chinese submarine equipped with a submerged-launch anti-ship cruise missile. The Kilos are among the quietest conventional submarines in the world, and coupled with the Song-class submarines, provide a generational leap in China's conventional submarine technology.

China's has also purchased Russian Sovremenny-class destroyers. The SS-N-22/Sunburn/Moskit anti-ship missile on these destroyers is designed specifically to attack U.S. aircraft carrier battle groups and to defeat the U.S. Navy's Aegis air-defense system. The SU-30 fighter can also carry the air-launched version of the "Moskit" anti-ship missile as well as advanced air-to-air missiles that can travel farther than the 100 miles across the strait.

These actions are seriously affecting the region's balance of power. Within ten or fifteen years China will have the ability to project its forces and will probably possess sufficient air and sea capabilities to enforce her expanding perimeters. Even now at considerable cost and with substantial losses, the PLA Air Force could establish the air and sea superiority needed for a successful invasion.

Mounting a Missile Attack

An extensive increase in the number of operationally deployed short-and intermediate-range missiles is clearly in progress with many of the missiles positioned at bases near the strait.[5] The significance that PLA strategists attach to ballistic missiles was evident in the 1996 Taiwan Strait crisis, when the effectiveness of China's forces was fundamentally challenged by the deployment of two U.S. aircraft carriers. There are significant political costs associated with this buildup; the deployments radically increase the potential for miscalculation and decrease the time to make those decisions by both governments. Missile strikes are incalculably risky; once launched, the Chinese leadership cannot afford to fail. The initiative will have to be prosecuted until Taiwan surrenders.

Chinese leaders understand the inherent political risks to its survival should an attack fail. Failure would strip the regime of its domestic legitimacy and threaten its continuation in power. Failure would likely also mean de facto independence on Taiwan. This must give the leadership pause.

Admiral Dennis Blair, Commander-in-Chief, U.S. Pacific Command, stated that China had recently increased its deployment of short-range ballistic missiles against Taiwan. Another assessment of these missiles concludes that:

> They cannot make a decisive military difference yet, but if they continue to increase in number and accuracy there will come a time when they threaten the sufficient defense of Taiwan.[6]

Of concern, however, is the limited information we actually have on missile deployments, given their growing importance to PLA war strategy. The PLA could be increasing its current production well beyond current assumptions. Taiwan's national defense report published in August of 2000 indicated the PLA had approximately 400 ballistic missiles of different kinds covering Taiwan and estimated that this could increase to 600 in five years.[7] Ballistic missile batteries could easily be hidden in the rough terrain along the mainland's coastline. It is not just the numbers that are increasing; China is increasing the accuracy of its short-range ballistic missiles and Taiwan lacks an effective response to this threat.

Taiwan forces, however, would not be the only ones facing the missiles. The PLA, in anticipation of U.S. intervention, has indicated a willingness to use accurate short-range and medium-range ballistic and cruise missies against U.S. forces, including bases in Japan and aircraft carriers operating in the Western Pacific. All PLA missiles capable of hitting bases in Japan from China's territory are nuclear-tipped.

PLA strategists understand that modern battlefields will be nonlinear requiring a modern integrated force to be successful. Thus, the operational strategy of using air strikes or missiles to carry out accurate attacks on rear targets has been given particular emphasis. In terms of an emerging strategy, ballistic missile attacks will probably announce a PLA offensive operation against Taiwan. To be successful the PLA will need to disrupt, degrade, or destroy Taiwan's

---

[5] U.S. Department of Defense, Office of the Secretary of Defense, Proliferation: Threat and Response, Section 1, NBC Proliferation Challenges (Washington, D.C.: U.S. Department of Defense, January 2001), 8.

[6] Dickie Mure, Joe Leahy, Richard McGregor, and Andrew Ward, "US Warns it may aid Taiwan on missile defence," Financial Times, 19 April 2002, sec. Asia Pacific, p.11.

[7] 2000 National Defense Report, 8 August 2000, <http://www.mnd.gov.tw/report> (27 June 2002). Bill Gertz, "Admiral Calls for Pacific missile defense system", The Washington Times, 12 November 1999 <http://www.taiwandc.org/washti9903> (26 June 2002).

overall combat capability. PLA strategists have written on the need for missile attacks in the opening phase of combat in order to splinter Taiwan's fully integrated and developed air defense network. These strategists insist that the key parts of Taiwan's air defense system, such as airfields, ground-based radar stations, and command, control, communications, and intelligence centers become the first targets. Taiwan is virtually defenseless against a ballistic missile attack. Taiwan's missile defense forces are vulnerable and China's ever-strengthening ballistic missile capability can cause severe destruction.[8] Although expressing doubt that the PLA could coordinate simultaneous missile and military operations, the Defense Department's annual military report on China says that these weapons would be most effective when used in high-volume, precision strikes. Taiwan's resources and population centers are concentrated, and missiles pose a very serious problem for electric power production, oil storage and processing facilities, communications, ports, airports, railroads, and factories. A few ballistic missiles would be enough to destroy most of Taiwan's civilian oil reserves stored in the event of war.[9]

As long ago as October 1998, a Defense Intelligence Agency report outlined a major buildup of short-range ballistic missiles opposite Taiwan. Up until 1998 the missile deployment had been modest and was limited to a garrison of CSS-6 weapons. The Chinese plan to have in place a total of 600 missiles by 2005, by deploying about 50 new missiles a year.

Missile strikes have the advantage of speed: targets would be destroyed with little or no warning. If attack plans were implemented covertly over a period of time, a quick-strike missile attack would minimize the possibility of third-party intervention. Because of the speed of the missiles and the short distance across the strait, Taiwan would have very little time to prepare its defenses. A barrage even of hundreds of Chinese ballistic and cruise missiles fired against Taiwan, however, would actually do limited (or at least not permanently devastating) damage, unless China resorted to chemical, biological or nuclear warheads or the missile strike is coordinated with other concurrent military operations such as air and maritime engagements.

Threatening a Blockade

Because Taiwan will continue to maintain significant qualitative and technological advantages against Chinese forces over the near term, the issue of a Chinese blockade will be the most important defense issue in the coming decade. The primary objective of a blockade would be to cripple Taiwan economically and isolate it internationally. A review of available Chinese military literature indicates that China's leaders apparently believe a blockade would be less likely to provoke outside intervention than other actions. Beijing would probably initiate a blockade in steadily increasing steps. Escalating at will, Beijing could deploy successively more severe responses, beginning with stopping Taiwan-flagged merchant vessels operating in the strait and ending with mining harbors and ports and deploying submarines and surface ships.[10]

---

[8] U.S. Department of Defense, Report to Congress on The Security Situation in the Taiwan Strait Washington, D.C. 26 February 1999. <http://www.defenselink.mil/pubs/twstrait> (27 June 2002). See also Lin Tsung-ta "Taiwan Vulnerable to Ballistic Missile Attacks, Landing by China", Chien-tuan K'e-chi (in Taipei), 1 November 1997, No. 159, pp 81-88; translated in FBIS

[9] National Defense Minister, Tang Fei Interview, "Tang Fei: In the Face of War Threats, We Cannot Suffer and not Hit Back", Lien Ho Pao (in Taipei), 28 December 1999 pg.2; translated in FBIS.

[10] See Chang Li-te, "Possible Forms of a Chinese Communist Blockade of Taiwan and Taiwan's Path for Response; Also Discussing International Law's Influence on Such a Blockade", Chien-Tuan K'o-Chi (in Taipei), 1 July 2001 pp 24-33; translated in FBIS. U.S. Department of Defense, Report to Congress on The Security Situation in the Taiwan Strait Washington, D.C. 26 February 1999. <http://www.defenselink.mil/pubs/twstrait> (27 June 2002).

Chinese naval forces currently have a numerical superiority in submarines and large surface ships and possess the capability to blockade Taiwan's major ports. In implementing a blockade, Chinese forces could bring to bear a mix of military ships, submarines, aircraft, commercial ships, fishing ships, and other civilian-use craft. All could do double duty as mine-laying craft, intelligence boats, and amphibious troop carriers.

Barring third-party intervention, the PLA Navy's quantitative advantage over Taiwan's Navy in surface and sub-surface assets would probably prove decisive. Taiwan's military forces probably would not be able keep the island's key ports and sea-lanes of communication open in the face of concerted Chinese military action. Taiwan's small surface fleet and four submarines are numerically insufficient to counter China's major surface combatant force and its anti-submarine warfare assets. The PLA Naval Air Forces' B-6D bombers armed with C-601 anti-ship cruise missiles would place Taipei's merchant ships and combatants at serious risk.

A blockade, while not risk-free, would be far less costly and dangerous to the PLA. The disadvantage of a blockade is that it takes a long time to succeed and the strait is an important and busy waterway used by commercial shipping of many countries: closing it would harm their economies as well as Taiwan's. If successful, it would cripple Taiwan economically without destroying its infrastructure or killing many people. Taiwan is dependent on the freedom of sea cargo transport, which accounts for almost 99 percent of its total cargo transport. Ministry of National Defense (MND) officials estimate that Taiwan would only be able to endure a blockade for 120 days before needing a resupply of essential materials.

Taiwan's Defense Strategy

Taiwan's current military doctrine seeks to address three operational requirements.

- Maintaining air superiority over the strait and the contiguous waters;
- Conducting effective counter-blockade operations;
- Defeating an amphibious and aerial assault on Taiwan.

To meet these objectives Taiwan must maintain a technologically superior qualitative edge over PLA assets. For the past decade, Taiwan's military has been transforming its operational forces by acquiring modern weapons systems and associated equipment in order to deter Chinese aggression. Billions of dollars have been spent on developing both domestic programs like the Indigenous Defense Fighter (IDF) and the *Tien Kung* air defense system, as well as on foreign purchases such as F-16 fighters and French-built Lafayette-class frigates.

However, the current organizational structure of Taiwan's armed forces hinder force modernization. Additionally, Taiwan's defense purchases often appear to be made for political reasons rather than as part of an overall strategy to effectively defend the island from attack. To overcome these definite deficiencies, Taiwan is engaged in a ten-year (2001-2010) modernization, reform, and restructuring plan.

On January 5, 2000, the Legislative Yuan passed the National Defense Law and the Organic Law of the Ministry of National Defense (MND). The main goal of the legislation is to effect greater control over the military services and to better coordinate weapons acquisitions programs. This is being implemented by bringing the operation of the military under one unified system led by a single defense minister. The laws require Taiwan's defense establishment to reorganize the national defense systems and unify its military administration and military command structure. In effect, it mandates requirements necessary for a modern, professional armed force. Taiwan's military services are now under pressure to demonstrate better coordination between competing, independent operating branches and units.

With the exception of some recent systems from Russia, the most modern Chinese conventional weapons are inferior one-for-one with the Western-built equipment in Taiwan. The Chinese military is impressive in size, but lacking in technological sophistication. Taiwan's F-16s and Mirage 2000s, for example, could counter China's SU-27s with Taiwan's pilots better trained than their Chinese counterparts. Taiwan still has a technological edge over the Mainland militarily, but this will disappear without U.S. support. Taiwan's advanced weapons are not being used to their fullest extent.

The most pressing needs of Taiwan's military include improved defenses against cyber attack and incoming missiles, better anti-submarine warfare capabilities, expanded military training programs, and a restructuring that would emphasize naval and air power rather than ground forces.

Officials of the Defense Ministry believe Taiwan will be forced to fight an island defensive war, with little to no early warning time, shallow depth, and a quickly moving field of battle and is modernizing its armed forces to meet those needs. An invasion would run headlong into Taiwan's strong suit of layered shore-based coastal defense, an effective air force and the Asian region's third most powerful navy. For example Taiwan has begun to invest increasing amounts of time and money in developing its own offensive Information Warfare (IW) capabilities but they are believed to be limited. Taiwan's armed forces have also decided that the upgrade of the island's Early Warning (EW) capabilities is a main goal.

U.S. Strategy

Since our official recognition of the PRC, U.S. foreign and defense policy has been designed to ensure continued stability and security of the Asia Pacific region. The overarching U.S. goal is to avoid any use or threat of force by China or provocative behavior by Taiwan to resolve differences in the strait. The "Three Communiqués" and the Taiwan Relations Act provide a political framework to manage the relations between Beijing, Taipei, and Washington. This framework has provided an environment within which China-Taiwan relations can develop without threatening the peace of the Taiwan Strait and the Asia-Pacific region.

U.S. objectives for the cross-strait relationship include:

- Deterring China attacking Taiwan;
- Supporting Taiwan's ability to defend itself without outside assistance; or
- Defending itself long enough to permit U.S. assistance so that the combination of Taiwan and U.S. forces can defeat a PLA attack, should the U.S. decide to intervene.[11]

In 1979 the United States officially recognized the government in Beijing as the legitimate government of China and ceased recognition of Taiwan. In the same year the Congress passed

[11] U.S. Department of Defense, Executive Summary of Report to Congress on Implementation of the Taiwan Relations Act (Washington, D.C.: U.S. Department of Defense, 18 December 2000).

The Taiwan Relations Act (TRA) to ensure that Taiwan's security would not be compromised as a result of the termination of diplomatic relations between Taiwan and the United States. In 1982 President Reagan promised Taiwan that the United States would not negotiate behind its back on Taiwan's status or arms sales.

Since its passage and reconfirmation by successive administrations, the TRA -- together with President Reagan's assurances -- has proved to be a solid foundation for Washington and Taipei relations. It has also been crucial in managing and shaping American policies toward Taiwan and Asia. Since its inception, however, Beijing has simply rejected the TRA as an attempt by the United States to interfere in China's internal affairs and has repeatedly declared the TRA invalid. It continues to insist that the "Three Communiqués" are the only basis for the Sino-American relationship.

While the TRA does not identify specific actions that the U.S. would take in the event that Taiwan's security of Taiwan was threatened, it does provide the option for the U.S. to come to Taiwan's defense. The U.S., however, is obliged by the TRA to help Taiwan defend itself through the provision of such items that it needs for its self-defense.

In assessing Taiwan's defense needs, DoD has dedicated significant resources to monitoring the security situation in the strait and continues to improve these efforts. It continually reevaluates Taiwan's defense posture to ensure that we make available to Taiwan such items as will provide a sufficient self-defense capability.[12]

In 2001, the U.S. approved the largest sale of defensive weapons and services to Taiwan in nearly a decade. Taiwan's legislature now needs to determine if it will fund the purchases. The major items in the proposed sale are:

- Four used Kidd-class destroyers
- 12 P-3C Orion aircraft, land-based, long-range surveillance aircraft, used primarily in anti-submarine or anti-surface warfare
- Eight diesel submarines designed to counter blockades and invasions
- Paladin M109A6 self-propelled artillery system
- MH-53E minesweeping helicopters
- AAV7A1 Amphibious Assault Vehicles
- Mk 48 torpedoes without advanced capabilities (designed to combat fast, deep-diving nuclear submarines and high-performance surface ships
- Avenger surface-to-air missile system (lightweight, highly mobile and air transportable)
- Submarine-launched and surface-launched torpedoes
- AN/ALE-50 self-defense pods for the F-16s (aircraft survivability equipment)
- 40 Maverick, AGM-65G air-to-ground missiles for the F-16s
- 40 Javelin anti-tank missile systems[13]

Earlier, the Congress included a provision in the Defense Authorization Act of 1998 that required the Department of Defense to study ballistic missile defense for Taiwan. In April 2000

[12] Ibid.

[13] "U.S. Offers Arms to Taiwan," ABC News.Com, 24 April 2001, <http://abcnews.go.com/sections/us/DailyNews/taiwan010424.html> (24 April 2001); Shirley A Kan, "Taiwan: Major U.S. Arms Sales Since 1990," CRS Report for Congress, 30 January 2002.

the U.S. approved the sale of sophisticated air-to-air and anti-ship missiles and a Pave Paws long-range radar system that could eventually be linked to a theater missile defense system.

In 2000, the U.S. sold Taiwan advanced AIM120C air-to-air missiles but with the caveat that the missiles be delivered only in the event of a threatened attack by China. U.S. policy is to avoid introducing capabilities that would go beyond what is required for Taiwan's self-defense. The AIM120C would have introduced beyond-visual-range capability into the region. Taiwan pilots, however, are permitted to train with the missiles on U.S. ranges. This decision should be reviewed if the transfer by Russia to China of AA-12/Amramskis is verified.

The Commission notes that the role of Congress in developing U.S. policy towards Taiwan has been sporadic over the years because successive administrations have resisted active consultation as specified under the TRA. Important policy differences between Congress and the Executive Branch, many of which stem from a lack of consultation, have not been conducive to a coherent American policy. That has changed in the past two years in part because of new legal requirements for periodic consultations. This is a welcome evolution.

U.S. policies have been successful over the years because they have injected caution in the Chinese leadership about resort to force in dealing with Taiwan and, at the same time, induced caution in Taiwan about publicly declaring independence, fearful that without a firm U.S. commitment China might retaliate with force. The strategic ambiguity policy also sought to stabilize the status quo while the two resolve their differences. It is important for all sides to avoid miscalculation and for the United States to make it clear to leaders in both Beijing and Taipei that their behavior has consequences that may adversely affect the long-term gains in democracy on Taiwan and the impressive economic gains in both Taiwan and on the Mainland. The Commission believes it must remain U.S. foreign policy and national security objective to convince the parties that only a peaceful resolution of their differences is acceptable.

National Security Implications

Taiwan today has a strong economy and a vibrant, multiparty democracy. The people on Taiwan have demonstrated impressive courage and resilience in their embrace of freedom as they live under dangerous circumstances. Taiwan has achieved remarkable progress in democratic elections, civil liberties, market economic development, and stable, viable governmental institutions.

A strong defense capability is important to Taiwan's security and economic well-being. The current posture of Beijing to pursue economic integration as a peaceful mechanism to asserting its sovereignty over Taiwan could be supplanted by more troublesome strategies and actions in the next three to five years. After that time, the PLA will have sufficient military capability, to pursue forceful unification.

A strong Executive-Congressional consensus on U.S. policy regarding Taiwan needs frequent updating based on regular consultations, given the severe national security implications of this situation and for U.S. credibility throughout the region.

RECOMMENDATIONS

The Commission recommends that Congress work with the Department of Defense to continue its current policies of substantive military dialogue with Taiwan and conduct exchanges covering issues ranging from threat analysis, to doctrine to force planning.

The Commission recommends that the U.S. along with its allies should continue to call upon China to renounce the threat of or the use of force against Taiwan and continue to caution Taiwan about declaring independence.

The Commission strongly recommends those provisions in the FYs 2001 and 2002 Foreign Operations Appropriations Acts, providing for briefings to the Congress by the Executive Branch on the ongoing discussion between any Executive Branch agency and the government of Taiwan on U.S. arms sales and that the defense relationship be included as a permanent requirement.

Chapter 4

CHINA'S OUTWARD FOREIGN DIRECT INVESTMENT IN SOUTHEAST ASIA

***Hsiu-Ling Wu*[*] *and Chien-Hsun Chen*[†]**

ABSTRACT

The main purpose of this paper is to scrutinize the development of China's outward foreign direct investment (FDI) in Southeast Asia, paying particular attention to motivational factors, government support and industry orientation, as well as an examination of the problems encountered. By providing a careful and exhaustive analysis, our aim is to shed some light on China's overall progress.

China's overseas investment began only twenty years ago, but the speed at which it has developed is rather impressive when compared to that of other developing nations. China's strategy is to encourage those enterprises which have adequate funds and a reasonably high level of technology to engage in FDI, so that they can participate in the international division of labor and acquire foreign technology and management techniques. Political and foreign policy considerations are also extremely important; in contrast to the situation in other countries, virtually all Chinese enterprises engaging in transnational operations are state-owned enterprises (SOEs).

Although Chinese investment began earlier in Southeast Asia than in other regions, with the move towards the establishment of an ASEAN free trade zone and ASEAN's influence in the Asia region steadily increasing, China cannot afford to ignore the Southeast Asian market, and thus needs to step up its investment within the region. There are still some problems affecting the overall development of Chinese overseas enterprises, but now that China has gained accession into the WTO, the continued opening, both of China's own markets and the international markets, will provide further impetus for overseas investment by Chinese enterprises.

Key Words: China's outward FDI, Southeast Asia.

---

[*] Associate Professor, Department of International Trade and Graduate Institute of International Business, Tamkang University, #151 Ying-Chuan Rd., Tamsui, Taiwan 251, Tel: 886-2-2621-5656 ext 2567, E-mail: hlwu@mail.cier.edu.tw

[†] Research Fellow, Chung-Hua Institution for Economic Research, 75 Chang-Hsing St., Taipei 106, Taiwan, Tel: 886-2-2735-6006 ext 336, E-mail: chchen@mail.cier.edu.tw

I. INTRODUCTION

The gradual institutional transformation undertaken by China has led to the country enjoying rapid economic growth. Since the late 1980s in particular, China has opened up further to the outside world, attracting foreign capital, technology and management experience as a means of making up for its own inadequacies; this has in turn led to further improvements in productivity being achievable. In response to the trends towards economic globalization, regionalization and the development of overseas markets, Chinese enterprises have recently demonstrated their enthusiastic engagement in overseas investment, and this rapid growth has attracted considerable attention outside of China. The United Nations now rates China as an important new overseas investor nation, and several Chinese companies such as China National Chemicals, the Import and Export Corporation and China State Construction Engineering Corporation are all included in the United Nations' list of the fifty largest multinational corporations in the developing nations.

The first example of overseas investment by a Chinese enterprise came in 1979, when a joint venture was established in Tokyo by Beijing City's Youyi Commercial Services Company and Japan's Tokyo Maruichi Trading Corporation, under the name of Jinghe Ltd. As the implementation of the government's policy on opening up has continued, the number and scale of overseas investment projects has increased dramatically. By the end of 2001, 6,008 Chinese enterprises had been established overseas, involving a total investment of US$12.17 billion, of which US$8.42 billion was provided by the Chinese side. In the early days, most overseas investment was conducted by state-owned enterprises (SOEs), with an emphasis on the provision of labor and contracting projects, but gradually, with the more rapid growth of the economy, the scope of overseas investment has expanded to include resource development and transnational investment controlled by the Chinese enterprises concerned. Trade became the biggest motivator for implementing overseas investment, with the aim being to develop new markets, to boost exports, or to take advantage of advantageous local conditions for commercial purposes.

During the period 1979-1997, when the growth of the Chinese economy became particularly striking, China was in need of considerable amounts of inward investment. Limited national capabilities, and the fact that Chinese enterprises had not yet reached a sufficiently high level of development, meant that although the government did gradually relax its restrictions on overseas investment, its basic policy stressed that companies should not over-extend themselves, with the emphasis being placed on slow and steady progress. However, at the second plenary session of the 15th Central Committee, held in 1998, Jiang Zemin announced that, "while aggressively boosting exports, it is also necessary to direct the systematic provision of support for strong state-owned enterprises which can undertake processing and trade overseas, thereby increasing exports and bringing about the internationalization of mature industries". This demonstrated that China had already formulated a new economic development strategy in response to the changing international political and economic environment and the changes in China's own economic system. This will undoubtedly mean that as time passes, and the economy continues to develop, China will expand its outward foreign direct investment (FDI) and engage in transnational operations in order to enhance the competitiveness of its industries, so as to obtain greater benefits in the international markets.

China's outward FDI began with its SOEs. As private enterprises began to develop in the 1990s, they too began to evaluate the feasibility of overseas investment and to embark on investment projects. However, for the most part, it is still only SOEs that have sufficient capital to expand overseas. China's outward FDI is spread over more than 160 countries around the world, with the regions that have attracted investment by the largest number of enterprises being Asia, Europe and North America. In terms of the amount invested, the main investment destinations are, in order, North America, Asia and Oceania (Wu and Chen, 2001).

Chinese investment in North America and Australia has been very aggressive, largely because both of these countries are rich in natural resources; the development of natural resources is the main focus of China's overseas investment. Furthermore, the abovementioned countries and regions offer a generally superior investment environment, including highly-developed financial and consumer markets, a high level of technological development, advanced management methods, superior infrastructure, and so on. This means that China can use its overseas investment to acquire high technology and learn advanced management methods, in conformity with its own policy objectives underpinning the encouragement of overseas investment (Ma and Li, 1995; Nan, 2001).

Amongst the economies of Asia, whether in terms of the total amount of investment or the number of enterprises established, apart from Hong Kong and Macao, which have received large amounts of Chinese investment for political reasons, the main focus of Chinese investment has been in Southeast Asia, including Thailand, Singapore and Malaysia. Since these countries have large ethnic Chinese communities and are geographically close to China, they have always attracted a significant amount of Chinese investment (Hou, 1997). China has also attached enormous importance to the development of economic ties with the member nations of ASEAN. Following China's accession to the World Trade Organization (WTO) in 2001, it has been aggressively promoting the idea of a free trade area to include China and the ASEAN member nations.

This paper will discuss and evaluate Chinese outward FDI in Southeast Asia, starting in Section II with an examination of China's motivation for investing in the region. Since most of the Chinese enterprises involved in overseas investment are SOEs, the impact of government policy is clearly very important, therefore, Section III explores the ways in which government policy has encouraged overseas investment during the process of institutional transformation. Section IV analyzes the development of Chinese investment in Southeast Asia followed in Section V with a discussion of the problems which Chinese enterprises face during such regional investment. The final section draws together the conclusions of this study.

II. China's Motivation for Undertaking Outward FDI

Overseas investment has become increasingly common since the 1960s, and by the 1980s, various theories had been put forward to explain its attraction, including the monopolistic advantage theory (Hymer, 1960), product life cycle theory (Vernon, 1966), comparative advantage theory (Kojima, 1978) and eclectic theory (Dunning, 1981). From China's standpoint, after being closed to the world for so many years, during the process of institutional transformation, the major emphasis has been on strengthening its global political and economic influence; however, with international competition becoming increasingly fierce, enhancing the competitiveness of domestic enterprises has also become a very important task. China believes that by investing overseas it can exploit foreign resources and capital, whilst acquiring foreign technology and management techniques. In this way, not only will it be able to enhance the international competitiveness of its enterprises, it will also be able to expand China's political and economic influence in the international community.

China's motivation for investing overseas is largely based on the desire to use foreign resources to make up for the inadequacies in China's own resources, to acquire advanced foreign technology and management techniques, to acquire access to foreign capital, to develop new export markets and thus boost exports, to promote industrial restructuring and to earn foreign currency (Liu, 1992; Pan, 1998). These motivating factors are analyzed in more detail below.

Using Foreign Resources to Compensate for China's Own Inadequate Resources

The use of overseas investment by the developing nations in order to exploit foreign resources, takes one of two forms. The first stems from a developing nation's lack of domestic natural resources, leading to the needs of economic development necessitating reliance upon foreign resources. The second involves countries which, despite having considerable domestic resources, recognize that since efficiency is low and consumption is high, the cost of developing these resources is also high; these countries' domestic resources are thus inadequate to meet the needs of a rapidly growing economy.

Although China does have extensive natural resources, these are, for the most part, rather difficult to exploit, and a considerable part of China's mineral resources has already been depleted. By undertaking overseas investment, China can develop other countries' resources, making effective use of these to substitute for its domestic resource deficiencies. Resource development was thus one of the first areas to see extensive overseas investment by Chinese enterprises, with resource-related investment accounting for a very high proportion of China's total overseas investment. The main investment areas include deep-sea fishing, forestry and mining. Taking deep-sea fishing as an example, China has established several dozen joint ventures and wholly Chinese-owned fishing companies in more than twenty countries and regions around the world, including Morocco, Senegal, Gabon, Nigeria, Iran, the USA, Argentina and Indonesia. When exchange reserves are favorable, these companies ship several hundred thousand tons of fish back to China every year.

As far as mining is concerned, China has extensive iron ore resources, but the iron content of most of China's ore is low; extraction is also difficult and thus, mining costs are very high. Chinese domestic production is also insufficient to meet the needs of the domestic iron and steel industry, and indeed, similar problems exist in the production of other metals, such as aluminum. China has therefore invested in iron and copper mining and smelting in Australia, Brazil and Peru, the output of which is then shipped back to China to meet the needs of the domestic iron and steel industry.

As regards forestry, China has invested mainly in countries with extensive forest resources, such as North America, South America, the South Pacific and Africa. Many of the wooden products from these ventures are subsequently shipped back to China.

Acquiring Advanced Technology and Management Techniques

As most Chinese enterprises are short of capital, it is difficult for them to upgrade their technology relying solely on their own R&D efforts. Chinese firms also lack experience in business administration, making it difficult for them to cope with increasingly fierce international competition. China hopes that overseas investment can help it to acquire advanced foreign technology and management techniques, since it believes that whilst it is possible to buy technology and equipment, or obtain new technology through FDI in China, the technology obtained in these ways tends to be second-rate or outdated, as opposed to the cutting-edge technology which China now seeks. Overseas investment is therefore seen as the most efficient way of gaining direct access to such advanced technology. By establishing joint venture companies in the advanced nations, Chinese firms can participate in the development of new products and new technologies and can gain easy access to the latest information on high technology. Thus, the main function of the joint venture companies which have been established by China in the USA and Japan is to acquire the latest technology, and indeed, these joint venture companies have already made an important contribution to the upgrading of technology in China's domestic industries.

Making Use of Foreign Capital

China's overseas investment generally takes the form of joint ventures or acquisitions. This means that Chinese enterprises do not need to pay the full cost of establishing a new enterprise overseas; it also allows them to make use of foreign capital markets for funding. China often uses loans provided by major foreign financial institutions to acquire foreign companies. It is estimated that around one-third of China's total overseas investment is in the form of cash investment, and that the total funds which actually have to be remitted overseas from China are less than one-tenth of the total amount of investment; nine-tenths of the total is therefore provided by the international capital markets. Exploiting international capital markets in this way has clearly allowed China to expand the scale of its overseas investment.

Developing Export Markets and Boosting Exports

Outward FDI can stimulate the exporting of equipment, materials and components; it can thus help in the promotion of international trade, and this has certainly been true in China's case. When China establishes a joint venture in a developing nation, the equipment and technology is invariably provided by China; overseas investment thus helps to boost China's equipment exports. At the same time, much of China's overseas investment takes place in processing industries, thus helping to stimulate China's exports of raw materials and semi-finished products. More importantly, at present, many countries impose high tariffs or quotas on imports from China; however, by investing in overseas production, China can circumvent these obstacles to trade.

Promoting the Reorganization of Domestic Industry

After two decades of institutional transformation, China has entered a new stage of economic transition. Overcapacity is a problem in many industries, including textiles, the electro-mechanical industry, home appliances, and so on, and China's industrial structure is in urgent need of an overhaul. Investing overseas can help to absorb excess capacity and outdated technology, and China hopes that such investment will enable it to divest itself of traditional technologies and equipment, thereby easing the problem of overcapacity. In many hi-tech industries, companies are busy developing new technologies and products on the one hand, whilst on the other hand, they are also using trade and investment to move mature products and technologies to underdeveloped nations and regions, thereby speeding up the process of structural adjustment in China's industrial sector.

Earning Foreign Exchange

Generally speaking, outward FDI involves the exporting of capital, which thus reduces the amount of capital held in the investing nation; however, much of China's overseas investment is in the form of equipment and technology, so the problem of capital exportation is not so serious. Furthermore, as already noted, China's overseas investment enterprises often use capital provided by the nation in which the investment is being undertaken, or by the international financial markets; there is therefore no need for the actual exportation of funds from China, and thus, once the profits from overseas investment start flowing back into China, overseas investment will come to play an important role in the maintenance of China's international balance of payments.

The overall policy of the Chinese government is to encourage those enterprises which possess sufficient capital and sufficiently advanced technology to engage in overseas investment, so that they can participate in the international division of labor and acquire foreign technology and management techniques. The stage of economic development which China has now reached in the process of institutional transformation and the issue of foreign exchange controls means that the motivation for foreign investment, the methods used, and the attitudes taken towards it, all have their own unique characteristics. For example, in stark contrast to the situation in other countries, the Chinese enterprises engaging in transnational operations are mostly SOEs. Political and foreign policy considerations are also very significant (Qiao, 1997; Qi, 1999; Liu, 2001); indeed, prior to the return of Hong Kong to China in 1997, Chinese investment poured into Hong Kong in what was clearly a political move to ensure the social and economic stability of the territory (Bacher, Lorz and Schuknecht, 1992).

III. Government Support and Industry Orientation

In order to encourage enterprises to invest overseas, to participate in the international division of labor, and to engage in transnational operations, the Chinese government has formulated various policies for the provision of necessary support. In the case of negotiations involving large-scale overseas investment projects, senior government leaders may participate directly in the negotiations with the country in which the investment is being undertaken, or, hold talks with the government of the country concerned, whilst on an official visit, in order to further the negotiations. This provides some idea of the kind of support and encouragement which the Chinese government provides for overseas investment (Pan, 1998; Yin, 1998; Yu, 2001; Zhou, 2001).

The main areas in which the government provides support are as follows. Firstly, it provides assistance with regard to funding. Since China's system of foreign exchange controls makes it difficult for Chinese enterprises to implement large-scale overseas investment projects, the government encourages enterprises to make use of a variety of different channels to solve their funding problems. Generally speaking, if a Chinese enterprise wishes to establish a small or medium-sized enterprise (SME) overseas, it will be able to fund the project itself. In the case of a resource development project, or a large-scale manufacturing enterprise, besides providing part of the funding itself, the investing enterprise can also apply to a state-owned bank for a low interest rate foreign currency or a Renminbi preferential loan. Joint venture projects which are deemed to fall under the category of foreign aid can be included in foreign aid plans, in which case funding can be provided from the annual foreign aid budget with additional foreign currency being allocated. These methods have been used for funding deep-sea fishing, forestry, mining and aquaculture investment projects.

Secondly, tax exemptions and remissions are allowed for overseas investment enterprises. In order to support the development of new overseas enterprises, regardless of whether a double taxation agreement has been signed between the Chinese government and the government of the country in which the enterprise is being established, the profits remitted back to China by the enterprise are exempted from SOE income tax for a period of five years from the date on which the enterprise began its operations. In order to ensure that the investing enterprise has more funds available for production expansion, it is allowed to retain all foreign currency earned during the first five years. After the five years exemption period has elapsed, the enterprise is required to pay income tax, and to remit only 20 per cent of its foreign exchange to the government. In the case of resource development projects where the products are shipped back to China, if the project is included within the national importation plan, then the goods can enjoy the same preferential tariff rates as regular imports. Furthermore, machinery, equipment and raw materials shipped overseas for use in overseas investment projects, are also exempted from export duty.

Thirdly, overseas enterprises are allowed to engage in domestic product resale. If the goods produced in an overseas investment project are goods which China needs to import, then, provided they are of the same quality and the same price, application can be made for their inclusion in the importation plan, and priority will be given to their importation by a specialized trading company. In the case of products not included in the importation plan, the investor may sell the goods in China but must bear the profit or loss themselves. In the case of products whose importation is restricted, approval must be obtained from the relevant authorities, and the goods may not be imported into China until an import permit has been secured. In the case of goods obtained in lieu of profits by the Chinese partner in an overseas venture, the goods may be shipped back to China and sold by the investing enterprise.

Fourthly, the Chinese government has signed a number of Investment Promotion and Protection Agreements with foreign countries. Since 1982, the government has signed agreements to avoid double taxation with the governments of more than fifty countries and regions, and has signed Investment Promotion and Protection Agreements with the governments of more than seventy countries and regions. These bilateral agreements have a positive impact on Chinese enterprises' overseas investment and transnational operations.

Finally, there are some stimuli which the Chinese government can provide for overseas investment. In order to encourage the use of domestically-produced equipment and materials in overseas investment projects, application can be made to have the ordering and production of such equipment and materials included in the annual plan. In the case of investing in the export-oriented electro-mechanical industry, the procedures are simplified and restrictions are relaxed.[1] However, the government still needs to formulate a Direct Overseas Investment Law and relevant sub-statutes, such as an Overseas Investment Insurance Law and a Law for the Management of State-owned Assets in Overseas Enterprises.

As regards which industries are involved in overseas investment, China's main considerations are to earn additional foreign exchange for the nation, to participate in the international division of labor, and to promote industrial upgrading and further economic development. At present, the government's encouragement towards overseas investment is focused on certain specific industries. Firstly, it focuses on those processing and assembly industries involving multiple levels of manufacturing, and which have high added value, since these industries can earn significant amounts of foreign exchange and can thus help China to upgrade its industrial structure. Secondly, China's shortage of raw materials and energy is a handicap when it comes to industrial development; thus investment in resource development will help to ease the resource shortage. The Chinese government therefore hopes to use foreign investment to develop productive resources which can then be shipped back to China to ease the domestic shortage of resources. Thirdly, the Chinese government encourages investment in hi-tech industries since this can help the country to acquire much needed technology. Fourthly, the government also believes that establishing contracting firms overseas to undertake contracted projects will thereby boost the export of Chinese machinery, technology and labor services. Finally, it sees investment in the service industries, including foreign trade, finance and insurance, restaurants and travel, medicine and healthcare, real estate, and so on, as a way of helping to stimulate the development of China's own service sector.

IV. CHINESE INVESTMENT IN SOUTHEAST ASIA

Chinese overseas investment began earlier in Southeast Asia than in other regions. During the early stages of overseas investment (roughly 1979-1984), as a result of policy restrictions, only import/export companies and specialized international economic and technical corporations from the provinces and municipalities were permitted to engage in overseas investment.[2] Most of the investment undertaken by the specialized import/export companies was concentrated in areas in which China was already engaging in importing and exporting. For the most part, this meant Southeast Asia. The most common method used was to establish an overseas branch or representative office specializing in a particular commodity. Subsequently, as the pace of overseas investment quickened, the increase was greatest in productive investment items, and

[1] According to Yin (2002), with regard to overseas investment by Chinese enterprises, the government's main role is to establish risk management mechanisms, simplify the approval procedures and strengthen the provision of relevant services.

[2] See: Wu and Chen (2001) which divided the development of Chinese overseas investment into three stages: (i) the exploratory stage (1979-1984); (ii) the early development stage (1985-1991); and (iii) the rapid development stage (1992 to the present).

there was a significant increase in the proportion of investment going to developed nations such as the USA, Australia and Canada.

The overall distribution of Chinese overseas investment was based on different investment objectives. In the case of developed nations such as the USA, Australia and Canada, the main purpose of such investment was to acquire advanced technology and management techniques, and to secure a larger share of the international markets. In the case of Southeast Asian nations, such as Thailand and Malaysia, the purpose of investment was to exploit the economic, technical and cultural links which had been formed with these countries over the centuries, and to develop them as export markets. There have been recent suggestions from Chinese academics that the developing nations in the Asia-Pacific region should become the main focus of China's overseas investment activities, and as a result, the economies of Southeast Asia have once again become targets for investment by Chinese enterprises. The main reasons suggested for such concentration on these developing economies are as follows.

First of all, China is still at a low level of economic development with inadequate capital, thus the Chinese government encourages enterprises to invest overseas in order to obtain resources that are in short supply in China, thereby reducing production costs, boosting exports and developing international markets. Most of the developing nations in the Asia-Pacific region have limited capital available for economic construction, but nevertheless, have extensive resources awaiting development. The cost of both natural resources and human resources in these countries is low, whilst the level of dependency on foreign technology and equipment is high. These countries are thus ideally suited to China's overseas investment objectives.

Secondly, since the reforms began, China has been actively acquiring advanced technology from other countries, and after more than twenty years of development, it has established an advantage over other developing nations in terms of electronics, machinery, metallurgy and chemical engineering technology, whilst also taking major strides in terms of the improvement of management quality. This relatively high level of technology and management puts China in a good position to undertake FDI in the developing nations.

Thirdly, in terms of the level of economic development, industrial structure and consumer preferences, there are major similarities between China and other developing nations in the Asia-Pacific region. There has also been considerable economic and technical collaboration between China and these nations in the past, as a result of which China has become familiar with conditions in these countries. This is beneficial when it comes to undertaking overseas investment (Nie, 1999).

The nations of Southeast Asia are also linked to China by history and culture, and China has generally maintained good relations with the governments of these countries. These nations are home to considerable numbers of ethnic Chinese, which gives China a distinct advantage when it comes to direct investment within the region. Southeast Asia has extensive natural resources and has recently been enjoying rapid economic development; thus, the region has been going through a period of industrial upgrading of its own, which has attracted a great deal of investment from the developed nations and the newly industrializing economies. From the point of view of international competition, therefore, China has more or less been forced to increase its investment in Southeast Asia. Without question, strengthening investment in Southeast Asia is an important strategy for China in terms of protecting and expanding its traditional export markets.

The total amount of Chinese investment in a number of Southeast Asian nations is shown in Table 1. This is followed by an examination of the state of Chinese investment in each of the individual countries listed (owing to the limitations imposed by the available data, the subsequent analysis is limited to Thailand, Singapore, Malaysia, the Philippines and Vietnam).

Table1. Chinese outward FDI stock in Southeast Asia, by country, 2000

Unit: US$ Million

	Approved by Chinese Government	
	Number of Projects	Chinese Investment Value
Thailand	145	7,253
Singapore	91	3,265
Malaysia	80	3,208
Philippines	32	1,446
Vietnam	29	2,928
Indonesia	43	5,728

Note: Data are on an approved basis.
Source: Almanac of China Foreign Economic Relations and Trade, (2001).

Thailand

In the mid-1980s political stability and low labor costs made Thailand an important recipient of foreign investment in Southeast Asia, thus, the official Chinese statistics show that Thailand has received more Chinese investment than any other country in the region. According to the *Almanac of China Foreign Economic relations and Trade*, by the end of 2000, the Ministry of Foreign Trade and Economic Cooperation had given approval for the establishment of 145 joint ventures and wholly Chinese-owned enterprises in Thailand, with the total amount of Chinese investment amounting to US$72.53 million.

In 2000, there were six Chinese investment projects in Thailand, with the total amount of Chinese investment being US$3.26 million. Trading companies accounted for around 65 per cent of these investment projects, and for around half of the total investment amount. Productive enterprises accounted for the remaining 35 per cent of the total projects with the industries concerned including cultivation, light industry, oil exploration, trade and finance, restaurants, hotels, shipping and real estate, most of which are areas in which the Thai government has been encouraging investment. In the last few years the scale of Chinese investment in Thailand has expanded from productive SMEs, to include larger ventures, such as the establishment of Asia Petroleum by Sinopec, and the establishment of joint venture insurance companies by the Bank of China.

Prior to the Asian financial crisis in 1997, the Thai government imposed strict restrictions on those industries in which foreign investment was permitted, and on foreign shareholding. As a result, most of the Chinese enterprises in Thailand were registered as joint ventures. Foreigners were allowed to hold a controlling share in only a handful of hi-tech and import substitution industries; in other industries, only those enterprises where at least 51 per cent of the equity was held by Thais were treated as local companies and afforded the same rights. Thus, in order to expand their scope of operations, most Chinese enterprises opted for joint ventures. Nominally, these companies were controlled by Thais, but in reality, in about 80 per cent of all cases, the Chinese partner held a controlling share.

Overall, the operational performance of Chinese enterprises in Thailand has been poor, and many Chinese companies which were in too much of a hurry to find a joint venture partner ended up being defrauded, with no legal redress. It is estimated that no more than 20 per cent of Chinese enterprises have actually returned a profit, whilst around 10 per cent have been making a loss, and the remaining 70 per cent have been more or less breaking even. The main reason for this is that Chinese enterprises are generally unfamiliar with overseas markets, the legal system and the overall environment in these markets.

A point worthy of note is that Chinese companies have been contracting to undertake an increasing number of construction projects in Thailand over the past few years. Previously, contracts in Thailand were generally awarded to European or American companies, whilst contractors from other Asian countries found it difficult to enter the competition. Recently, however, companies such as China Harbor Engineering and China Civil Engineering have been winning large contracts in Thailand, securing for themselves a sizeable share of the market. For example, by the end of 1999, Chinese companies had signed a total of 1,786 contracts to provide labor services in Thailand. These contracts had a total value of US$1.851 billion, most of which were awarded by government agencies, whilst contracts worth US$888 million had already been completed. One dam contract won by China Irrigation and Hydroelectric Engineering was worth US$109 million, making this the largest construction contract ever secured by a Chinese company in Thailand.

Singapore

Although Singapore has reached a much higher level of economic development than China, it ranks only second in Southeast Asia in terms of the number of Chinese enterprises which have established themselves there. According to China's *Almanac of China Foreign Economic relations and Trade*, at the end of 2000, the Chinese authorities had given approval for the establishment of 91 Chinese enterprises in Singapore, with the total amount of Chinese investment being US$32.65 million. However, according to Singaporean government statistics, there are actually over 150 Chinese enterprises in Singapore.

The majority of Chinese investment in Singapore took place after 1992, when formal diplomatic relations were established between Singapore and China, and when Singapore undertook adjustment to its China policy, relaxing its restrictions on Chinese investment. Since then, Chinese enterprises have been increasingly establishing themselves in Singapore, with their investment being concentrated mainly in the finance, insurance, trade, shipping and construction sectors; indeed, there is only one manufacturing firm.

Four companies which are partly owned by Chinese enterprises have secured stock market listing in Singapore – Zhong Yuan Investment, Guang Da, Northern Industries and China Petroleum Import-Export Company. It is worth noting that Zhong Yuan Investment has achieved quite an impressive level of operational performance in Singapore, having acquired a 61.5 per cent share in a listed Singaporean company in October 1993. Only one year later, the company's net assets had risen sevenfold, from S$17 million to S$120 million.

Those Chinese enterprises that have been established in Singapore include both wholly Chinese-owned companies and joint ventures. Prior to the establishment of formal diplomatic relations between Singapore and China in 1992, Singapore placed considerable restrictions on Chinese investment, with Chinese companies being allowed only to establish joint venture firms within which the Chinese share had to be less than 50 per cent. Since 1992, however, these restrictions have been relaxed, and Chinese companies are now allowed to establish both wholly Chinese-owned and joint venture companies. No restrictions are placed on the Chinese share; the only requirement is that registration procedures must be completed. The restrictions on the nationality of the chairman and president have also been relaxed; hence, the company must now include one Singaporean, but this can be either a Singaporean national or a foreigner with the right of residency in Singapore. With the restrictions on Chinese investment having been relaxed, Chinese investment has been flooding into Singapore since 1992.

As regards the operational performance of Chinese enterprises in Singapore, it is estimated that around one third are making a profit, one third are making a loss and one third are just about breaking even. Most Chinese enterprises in Singapore are small and have failed to undertake sufficient in-depth investigation of the local environment. As a result, they have had difficulty in improving their operational performance. Hence, the Chinese trade office in Singapore has been discussing a plan to establish a Chinese Chamber of Commerce in order to improve the coordination of the service provision and management of Chinese enterprises in Singapore.

Malaysia

Chinese investment in Malaysia got off to a relatively late start, and indeed, it is only in the last few years that China has come to appreciate the importance of Malaysia in Southeast Asia and to increase its investment there. There has been a significant increase in the number of Chinese investment projects in Malaysia since 1988, when an Investment Promotion and Protection Agreement was signed between China and Malaysia. By the end of 2000, the Chinese authorities had approved 80 investment projects in Malaysia, with a total value of US$32.08 million. The main areas invested in were basic industries, industrial machinery and food processing.

The Philippines

In the past, political instability made it difficult for the Philippines to attract foreign investment; for example, in 1989, the Philippines adopted countervailing measures against China which restricted the development of economic ties. It was not until 1995, when the Philippines took China off the list of countries within which trading activities were restricted, that the Philippines began to look more attractive to Chinese enterprises. In the last few years, Chinese investment in the Philippines has gradually increased, and by the end of 2000, 32 investment projects (involving total Chinese investment of US$14.46 million) had either been approved, or were awaiting approval, by China's Ministry of Foreign Trade and Economic Cooperation. Most of these enterprises were trading companies; productive enterprises were mainly involved in the textiles, motorcycle or bicycle industries.

Vietnam

It was as long ago as 1989 that Vietnam began to permit foreign investment; however, owing to the inadequacy of the infrastructural and legal framework, the country found it difficult to attract European and American companies to establish themselves there. The positive aspects of Vietnam's investment environment lies in a workforce which is cheap, hardworking and easily managed; this makes Vietnam very attractive to labor-intensive industries, particularly for a country such as China which is only just getting started in overseas investment. However, there are still relatively few Chinese investment projects in Vietnam, and the total value of these projects is low; furthermore, most of the technology and equipment involved is low level.

By the end of 2000, there were 29 Chinese investment projects in Vietnam, with the actual amount of Chinese investment being US$29.28 million, ranking China 21st in the list of foreign investment sources for Vietnam. Chinese investment is concentrated in restaurants, beverage processing, glass processing, and so on. The largest investment project is located in the Ling Chung Export Processing Zone in Ho Chi Minh City; the agreed investment amount for this project is US$14 million, with the Chinese and Vietnamese partners each having a 50 per cent share. Research in this area indicates that at present, Chinese investment in Vietnam is largely limited to areas where the level of risk is low and where the investment can be recouped as quickly as possible.

Overall, there has been a significant increase in Chinese direct investment in Southeast Asia over the last few years. In particular, there has been a dramatic increase in investment in productive enterprises, as a result of which the scale of such enterprises has grown. As China and Southeast Asia have similar industrial structures, there is considerable overlap in their manufactured products, making them competitors in the international markets. Both China and Southeast Asia hope to exploit foreign investment to speed up their economic growth; consequently, they have both been devising measures to attract foreign capital. It is these factors which represent the main restrictions on investment between the two.

During the last few years, there has been a steady increase in economic collaboration within ASEAN, which is currently working towards the establishment of an ASEAN free trade area, and as a result, its influence within Asia is increasing. This means that China cannot afford to ignore the Southeast Asian market, and has thus been encouraged to step up investment within the region. The main reasons for China attaching so much importance to strengthening investment in Southeast Asia are as follows.

Firstly, the fundamental emphasis is on the development of foreign trade and economic collaboration as part of China's own institutional transformation and economic reforms. This emphasis has led China to attach greater importance to its economic ties with Southeast Asia. Secondly, regional economic collaboration is developing within the Asia-Pacific region. Since close collaboration with the nations of Southeast Asia will be beneficial to China's own economic growth, this has forced China to strengthen its ties with these countries.

Finally, Southeast Asia has a very large ethnic Chinese community which can wield enormous economic power, and China hopes to draw capital from this community into China. It is therefore working actively to improve its relations with the nations of Southeast Asia.

V. Problems Affecting Chinese Enterprises in Southeast Asia

As in other regions, there are certain problems affecting the development of Chinese enterprises in Southeast Asia. First of all, as far as the industrial structure is concerned, Chinese overseas investment has displayed an excessive emphasis on the processing, manufacturing and other primary industries, whereas there has been little investment in hi-tech industries. These processing industries tend to be industries which are labor-intensive with low added value, and faced with fierce international competition, it will be difficult for these industries to develop their markets further.[3]

Secondly, China's overseas investment projects tend to be small-scale, with the enterprises thus far established having low levels of managerial capability and competitiveness. Less than 30 per cent of China's overseas investment projects involve a total investment of US$5 million or more. In addition, China lacks a comprehensive legal framework for overseas investment; for example, China needs an Overseas Direct Investment Law to regulate the activities of enterprises operating overseas (Wang and Xu, 2000; Wang, 2002).

Thirdly, few Chinese enterprises possess well-known international brands. China does not figure at all in the list of the fifty most valuable global trademarks, which is a major obstacle to the development of its overseas operations. Furthermore, there is a tendency for Chinese enterprises not to undertake sufficient research before embarking on overseas investment projects, and government interference is still far too commonplace. Many Chinese enterprises decide on their overseas investment location without having first clarified why they are investing overseas, how the location should be chosen, or how the overseas market can be developed. Different countries have different political and legal systems, different levels of economic development and different customs and practices. If a company fails to carry out sufficient research before deciding on an investment project, the level of risk will clearly be extremely high. In order to turn some of its larger SOEs into conglomerates, the Chinese government ordered these enterprises to establish themselves among the world's leading enterprises within a specified time period. As a result, these companies have rushed blindly into overseas investment in order to achieve the goal of internationalization as quickly as possible; the results have been catastrophic (Lin, 1998; Cai, 1999).

Chinese overseas enterprises are also badly managed, and lack talented personnel. Many Chinese enterprises have simply transplanted their domestic management systems into their overseas operations, without placing any real effort into learning from the experience of other countries. The generally poor management abilities, and the assignment of substandard managers, often results in overseas enterprises incurring losses, and in some cases, the insolvency of an overseas subsidiary has affected the financial health of the parent company. The problem faced by Chinese enterprises in transnational operations is the need to determine ways in which to establish effective corporate governance mechanisms and to strengthen the cultivation of talent, so as to enhance their competitiveness in the international markets (Li and Li, 2000; Xu, 2002).

Finally, China has recently experienced large-scale capital flight. Overseas enterprises can engage in undervaluing overseas investment assets, concealing and retaining the revenue from overseas investment and then re-investing it, or using internal price transfers to increase the price of the equipment, raw materials and intermediate goods that the company has to import from other countries, so as to push down the price of exports, thereby leading to large-scale capital flight. When Chinese enterprises establish overseas subsidiaries in order to circumvent China's foreign exchange controls or other restrictions, then this is also what is normally referred to as capital flight. For example, during the period 1992-1996, there were 35 non-trading Chinese enterprises actually operating in Hong Kong, with a total investment of US$123.1 million; however, there were a total of 179 Chinese

[3] Qiao (2002) noted that Chinese enterprises do not enjoy competitive advantage when it comes to overseas investment in the hi-tech sector.

enterprises registered in Hong Kong, with total investment of US$2.655 billion; this gives some idea of the scale of capital flight (Gunter, 1996; Song, 1999). The establishment of overseas enterprises as a means of capital flight is a very serious problem, which has resulted in the loss of huge amounts of state-owned assets. Over the period 1982-1999, capital flight totaled around US$232.865 billion, or an average of US$12.937 billion per year (Li and Tian, 2000).

VI. Conclusions

China has enjoyed rapid economic growth as a result of its gradual institutional transformation, and has begun to undertake aggressive overseas investment in order to expand its markets, to engage in technological exchange, to obtain access to stable supplies of resources and to enable the companies concerned to develop new markets. The productive activities of multinationals and other foreign companies in China have helped to stimulate economic development in China, which has brought home to China the importance of foreign investment. As China continues to achieve remarkable success through its economic reforms, the government is seeking to expand the scope of overseas investment and transnational operations; overseas investment has thus become an integral part of the strategy of institutional transformation.

China's strategy is to encourage those enterprises which have adequate funds and a reasonably high level of technology to invest overseas, so that they can participate in the international division of labor and acquire foreign technology and management techniques. Owing to the particular tasks that have to be undertaken at this current stage of institutional transformation, and the impact of problems such as foreign exchange controls, there are a number of distinctive aspects to China's motivation for overseas investment, and to its views on such investment.

The motivation for investing overseas is largely based on the desire to use foreign resources to make up for the inadequacies in China's own resources, to acquire advanced foreign technology and management techniques, to acquire access to foreign capital, to develop new export markets, thus boosting exports, to promote industrial restructuring and to earn foreign currency. Political and foreign policy considerations are also very significant. Prior to the return of Hong Kong to China in 1997, Chinese investment poured into Hong Kong in what was clearly a political move to ensure the social and economic stability of the territory. Furthermore, in stark contrast to the situation in other countries, almost all Chinese enterprises engaged in transnational operations are SOEs.

As regards Chinese direct investment in Southeast Asia, China and Southeast Asia both have similar industrial structures, they are competitors in international markets, and both are seeking to use foreign capital to speed up their domestic economic growth, with means that they are also in competition when it comes to securing foreign investment. This situation has placed restrictions on the development of investment between the two. At the same time, with the move towards the establishment of an ASEAN free trade zone and the steadily increasing influence of ASEAN throughout the Asia region, China cannot afford to ignore the Southeast Asian market, and thus, has to step up its investment within the region.

Over the past few years, there has been a significant increase in Chinese direct investment in Southeast Asia which has been particularly marked in productive enterprises, leading to a steady increase in the scale of Chinese enterprises in the region. Thailand currently receives the lion's share of Chinese investment, a level of investment which is nevertheless gradually increasing.

Trading companies currently account for around 65 per cent of all the Chinese enterprises established in Thailand, and around half of the total investment amount, whilst productive enterprises account for the remaining 35 per cent. Most of the Chinese investment in Singapore took place after 1992, when formal diplomatic relations were established between Singapore and China, and when Singapore undertook adjustments to its China policy, relaxing the restrictions on Chinese investment. As a result, increasing numbers of Chinese enterprises began to invest in Singapore. Chinese investment in Malaysia got off to a relatively late start, and it is only in the last few years that China has begun to recognize Malaysia's importance in Southeast Asia, and to step up its investment there.

Overall, whilst Chinese overseas investment is still at a relatively immature stage, and there are still some problems affecting the development of overseas enterprises, some Chinese enterprises have achieved impressive results in their overseas operations. Now that China has joined the WTO, its price system will have to be brought into line with international market prices, eliminating the price distortion effect. Therefore, it will become imperative for SOEs to establish effective corporate governance mechanisms in order to ensure their competitiveness. The further opening of both China's domestic markets and the international markets will encourage enterprises, particularly SOEs, to speed up the process of reorganization and to enhance their competitiveness in order to equip themselves for the fierce competition ahead. It will also provide the further necessary impetus to encourage Chinese enterprises to invest overseas.

REFERENCES

Bacher, B., Lorz O. and Schuknecht, L. (1992), 'Chinese Investment - 'Hostages' for Hong Kong?', *Journal of Institutional and Theoretical Economics*, **148**, (Dec), pp.645-654.

Cai, K.G. (1999), 'Outward Foreign Direct Investment: A Novel Dimension of China's Integration into the Regional and Global Economy', *The China Quarterly*, **160**, pp.857-880.

Dunning, J.H. (1981), *International Production and the Multinational Enterprise*, London: George Allen & Unwin Ltd.

Gunter, F.R. (1996), 'Capital Flight from the People's Republic of China: 1984-1994', *China Economic Review*, **7**, pp.77-96.

Hou, Xiaoqing (1997), 'Chinese Outward FDI in Asian Countries', Guoji Touzi, *Investment Research*, **9**, pp. 48-50.

Hymer, S.H. (1960), 'The International Operations of National Firms: A Study of Direct Foreign Investment', Ph.D. Thesis, M.I.T., published by M.I.T. Press, 1976.

Kojima, K. (1978), *Direct Foreign Investment: A Japanese Model of Multinational Business Operations*, New York: Praeger.

Li, Ji and Li, Lin. (2000), 'Prerequisite to Transnational of Chinese Enterprises: Reformation of Administrative System', Gaige, *Reform*, **2**, pp.49-55.

Lin, Ye (1998), 'Chinese Enterprises are Facing a New Challenge to Adjust their Strategies in Transnational Operation', Guoji Jingji Hezuo, *International Economic Cooperation*, **10**, pp. 37-40.

Li, Qingyum and Tian, Xiaoxia (2000), 'The Re-estimation of the Capital Flight from China: 1982-1999', Jinrong Yanjiu, *Journal of Financial Research*, **8**, pp.72-82.

Liu, Jinyong (2001), 'WTO Entry and China's Outward Business Expansion Strategy', Guoji Maoyi Wenti, *Journal of International Trade*, **6**, pp.1-5.

Liu, Yan (1992), *Multinational Corporation and Internationalization of Chinese Enterprises*, (Quoguogongshi yu Zhongguo Qiyeguojihua), Beijing: China Trust Press.

Ma, Shouye and Li, Jianjun (1995), 'Location Decision of Chinese Outward FDI', Touzi Yanjiu, *Investment Research*, **6**, pp.47-49.

Ministry of Foreign Trade and Economic Cooperation (2000), *Almanac of China's Foreign Relations and Trade 1991-2001*, Beijing: Foreign Relations and Trade Press.

Nan, Zhenghua (2001), 'Issues of Chinese Companies' Globalized Operation and Some Countermeasures', Guoji Jingji Hezuo, *International Economic Cooperation*, **4**, pp.55-57.

Nie, Minghua (1999), 'On the Regional-Choice of China's Foreign Investment', Touzi Yanjiu, *Investment Research*, **12**, pp. 2-7.

Pan, Ye (1998), *The Strategies for China to Develop its Outward FDI*, (Zhongguo Duiwaitouzi Fazhanzhanlue), Beijing: Economic Science Press.

Qiao, Huiping (2002), 'Selection of Development Strategies for Chinese Enterprises' External Investment', Gaige, *Reform*, **2**, pp.64-66.

Qiao, Jinmin (1997), 'Chinese Enterprises' Overseas Investment', Touzi Yanjiu, *Investment Research*, **2**, pp.16-22.

Qi, Chunyu (1999), 'The Situation on Direct Investment Abroad by China and its Reasons: On Investment in Hong Kong from China', Jingji Kexue, *Economic Science*, **2**, pp.34-40.

Song, Wenbing (1999), 'A Study of China's Capital Outflow: 1987-1997', Jingji Yanjiu, *Economic Research Journal*, **5**, pp.39-48.

Vernon, R. (1966), 'International Investment and International Trade in the Product Cycle', *Quarterly Journal of Economics*, **80**, (May), pp.190-207.

Wang, Qin (2002), 'Issue and Countermeasures in Chinese Enterprises' Transnational Business Activities ', Guoji Jingji Hezuo, *International Economic Cooperation*, **2**, pp. 13-16.

Wang, Wen-ju and Xu, Lin (2000), 'The Problems and Countermeasures of Chinese Outward FDI', Caimao Yanjiu, *Finance and Trade Research*, **2**, pp.51-55.

Wu, H. L. and Chen, C. H. (2001), 'An Assessment of Outward Foreign Direct Investment from China's Transitional Economy' *Europe-Asia Studies*, **53(8)**, pp. 1235-1254.

Xu, Lifeng (2002), 'An Analysis on the Strength of State-Owned Foreign Engineering Contractors', Guoji Jingji Hezuo, *International Economic Cooperation*, **3**, pp.9-12.

Yin, Yingkai (2002), 'The Interaction of Developing Countries Utilizing Foreign Investment and Investing Abroad', Guoji Maoyi Wenti, *Journal of International Trade*, **1**, pp.36-39.

Yin, Ziqing (1998), *Twenty Years of Reforms of Chinese Foreign Economy and Trade*, (Zhongguo Duiwai Jingji Maoyi Gaige 20 Nian), Henan: Zhongzhou Press.

Yu, Lingyan (2001), 'Investing Overseas Needs Government Support', Guoji Maoyi Wenti, *Journal of International Trade*, **8**, pp.19-20.

Zhou, Kewei (2001), 'Can China be Among the Big Investing Countries as its Objective?', Guoji Jingji Hezuo, *International Economic Cooperation*, **5**, pp.37-39.

Chapter 5

CHINA AND THE WORLD TRADE ORGANIZATION*

Kathleen J. Michels, et al.

KEY FINDINGS

- The U.S. Government supported China's entry into the World Trade Organization (WTO) as part of its overall national security strategy for relations with China. U.S. support was premised on both commercial and political goals. While enhanced market access for U.S. goods and services was a central goal, equally important were the development of economic, civil, and political reform within China, and the promotion of regional stability in Asia.

- China's leaders pursued WTO membership as a means to continue China's rapid economic growth through increased exports and to attract foreign investment, capital, and technology. They believe that continued economic reform and growth is essential for China to become a preeminent world power.

- China's WTO accession carries high stakes and risks for both the United States and China. Both countries seek China's continued economic reform. The United States hopes such reform will foster a democratic and more open society. The risk to the United States is that China will become economically stronger, but not more democratic. China's leaders hope that WTO membership will bolster China's economic growth, but they will likely work to minimize any accompanying political liberalization. The risk to the Chinese one-party regime is that economic liberalization may lead to political liberalization.

- China's WTO accession may exacerbate economic and social strains and lead to further social unrest, political instability, and an economic downturn, with an uncertain outcome for U.S.-China relations. The future direction of the Chinese economy — whether it is marked by continued growth, stagnation, or collapse — has important implications for U.S. national security and therefore the U.S. Government should be prepared for each of these scenarios.

---

* In: July 2002 - Report to Congress of the U.S. - China Security Review Commission - *The National Security Implications of the Economic Relationship between the United States and China*.

- China's WTO accession agreement is unprecedented in its complexity and scope. China's broad commitments to eliminate its discriminatory and trade-distorting practices have the potential to significantly enhance market access for U.S. goods and services. However, WTO implementation will be a tremendous challenge to China. Localism and provincialism heavily influence the Chinese economy and decision-making process, and the willingness of provincial and municipal governments to comply with WTO commitments is uncertain.
- China's WTO membership is in the national security interest of the United States if it promotes economic reform in China that is accompanied by the development of political and personal freedoms and broadly shared prosperity.

INTRODUCTION

Both Republican and Democratic Administrations strongly supported China's accession to the WTO, arguing that integrating China into the world trading system would economically enrich both countries and, over the long-term, would stimulate development of the "rule of law" and democracy in China and temper regional hostilities in Asia. The writings and public statements of officials in China suggest that the Chinese leadership had significantly different long-term objectives for joining the WTO. China's leaders sought WTO accession as a means to foster continued economic growth, with the goal of both enhancing China's economic wealth and, by so doing, maintaining the Chinese Communist Party's legitimacy and monopoly on power.

The long-term consequences of China's accession to the WTO will not be known for several decades, but clearly the United States has much at stake in the outcome. Accordingly, it is essential that U.S. policymakers carefully assess post-accession developments in China as they unfold, and adequately prepare for the full range of potential scenarios. The U.S. Government must make it a priority to provide bilateral or multilateral support to encourage WTO compliance and broader economic and political liberalization in China, while at the same time preparing for situations where China's actions may be inimical to U.S. interests.

THE U.S. AND CHINESE LEADERSHIP'S GOALS FOR CHINA'S WTO ACCESSION

U.S. Goals

The final stages of China's accession to the WTO were negotiated under the Clinton and present Bush Administrations, both of which strongly supported bringing China into the world trading system. During the run-up to Congress' consideration of legislation in 2000 to grant China Permanent Normal Trade Relations (PNTR), a necessary precursor of U.S. support for China's WTO accession, President Clinton highlighted both PNTR's trade benefits and its importance to U.S. national security. He noted, "even though for me the economic choice is clear

. . . far, far more important to me are the moral and national security arguments."[1] President Clinton explained his arguments as follows (bullets added):

- [B]y forcing China to slash subsidies and tariffs that protect inefficient industries, which the Communist Party has long used to exercise day-to-day control, by letting our high-tech companies in to bring the Internet and the information revolution to China, we will be unleashing forces that no totalitarian operation rooted in the last century's industrial society can control.
- [T]he more China operates within rules-based systems, with us and with other countries, the more likely they are to see the benefit of the rule of law, and the more likely that benefit is to flow down to ordinary people.[2]

President Clinton's National Security Advisor, Samuel Berger, reinforced the national security argument for supporting China's WTO accession:

> [T]his debate should not be defined as economic rights versus human rights — or economic security versus national security. That is a trap, a false choice. This agreement is just as vital "if not more vital" to our national security as it is to our economic security. It is far more likely to move China in the right direction — not the wrong direction — on all of our other concerns. We can't duck these issues by saying we're only interested in talking about economics. If we are going to win this debate, we must be persuasive that it promotes both growth and jobs in America and progress toward change in China.[3]

The policy has been consistent under the current Bush Administration. Following the WTO's decision to admit China at its meeting last November, President Bush echoed his predecessor in lauding the non-economic benefits of China's accession:

> I am confident that China's entry into the WTO will bring other benefits to China beyond the expected economic benefits. WTO membership, for example, will require China to strengthen the rule of law and introduce certain civil reforms, such as the publication of rules. In the long run, an open, rules-based Chinese economy will be an important underpinning for Chinese democratic reform.[4]

As these public statements demonstrate, the U.S. Government's support for China's accession to the WTO was premised not only on achieving immediate commercial benefits for the United States but also on achieving long-term economic and political change in China. As articulated in these statements, not only would China's WTO accession reap economic benefits for U.S. exporters in terms of market access, but also, equally important, it would lead to fundamental civil and political reforms inside China.

The key U.S. goals for supporting China's accession can be summarized as follows:

---

[1] William J. Clinton, "Remarks by the President at Democratic Leadership Council retreat," 21 May 2000, <http://clinton6.nara.gov/2000/05/2000-05-21-remarks-by-president-at-democratic-leadership-council-retreat.html> (17 June 2002).

[2] Ibid.

[3] Samuel R. Berger, "Remarks to The Business Roundtable." 8 February 2000. <http://www.fas.org/news/china/2000/000208-prc-usia1.htm> (17 June 2002).

[4] "President Welcomes China, Taiwan into WTO, Statement by the President: Ministerial Decision to Admit the People's Republic of China and Taiwan Into the World Trade Organization," White House Press Release, 11 November 2001, <http://www.whitehouse.gov/news/releases/2001/11/20011111-1.html> (17 June 2002).

- **Market Access** - The most concrete economic goal U.S. policymakers touted in support of China's accession to the WTO is the market access benefits that would accrue to U.S. firms. Despite the enormous and growing volume of Chinese goods flowing into the U.S. market, U.S. exports have largely been restricted from China's market through a variety of tariff and non-tariff measures. Pursuant to its terms of accession, China has agreed to significantly lower tariffs and other barriers to trade, raising the prospects of greatly enhanced U.S. exports to this market.

- **Economic Reform** - China has made remarkable progress in modernizing its economy in the past two decades; but still has a long road ahead to develop a mature market economy. China's accession to the WTO is viewed by many U.S. policymakers as providing the best opportunity for China to move forward in reforming its economy, by forcing it to open up to foreign competition and investment and by subjecting it to the strictures of the WTO. Supporters of China's accession feared that China's economic development would stall in the absence of these outside influences.

- **Political and Civil Reform -** A belief that political liberalization and development of the "rule of law" will follow China's economic liberalization as a result of joining the WTO underpinned U.S. support for China's membership. The hope is that WTO membership will force China to open up its economy to foreign business and develop new legal institutions and regimes to enforce its WTO commitments, and that these developments will foster broader political and civil reforms.

- **Regional Stability -** With both China and Taiwan joining the WTO, there is optimism that this development will improve cross-strait relations by increasing economic linkages between the two and providing a forum for dialogue between Chinese and Taiwan officials. There is also the hope that it will promote peaceful relations between China and its Asian neighbors as these nations become more economically integrated and thereby vested in avoiding hostilities.

China's WTO accession was not uniformly supported within the U.S. Government.[5] Nonetheless, the statements of President Clinton, President Bush and other Administration officials represent the prevailing rationales and goals that were provided at the highest levels of the U.S. Government for supporting China's WTO accession.

These goals — political and civil reform, market access, economic reform, and regional stability — are key issues discussed in more detailed in other sections of this Report. These goals will serve as important benchmarks that the Commission will use to assess progress in the U.S.-China relationship.

Chinese Leadership's Goals

The Chinese leadership made economic reform and WTO accession a top national priority and persisted in its negotiations to join the trade organization for more than 15 years. Underpinning the Chinese leaders' effort has been a belief that greater economic integration and

---

[5] For example, see Regular Media Availability with House Minority Leader Richard Gephardt, 18 May 2000.

the reforms it would necessitate are essential to China's continued growth and prosperity. Despite apprehensions of U.S. motives and of opening the doors to foreign competition, China's leaders appear to have supported accession to the WTO because of their belief that China's ability to assume the status of a preeminent world power depends on further integration into the global economic system.

Long Yongtu, China's chief trade negotiator for its WTO agreement, cited the following advantages of WTO membership in a presentation to CCP officials in January 1999:

- Facilitate creating a better image of China abroad — especially diminishing the perception that China will become a threat to the West.
- Enable China to participate in formulating new trade rules.
- Instill in Chinese citizens a culture of obedience to law and social responsibility akin to those virtues embraced by the West.
- Take advantage of WTO rules of arbitration and multilateral negotiations to counter the influence of the United States.
- Demonstrate to foreign countries that China is practicing a market economy and should not be treated in a discriminative manner.
- Gain permanent most-favored-nation status from the United States.[6]

On December 11, 2001, the day China formally entered the WTO, *The People's Daily*, the Party's official news outlet, discussed China's goals as a WTO member (bullets added):

- We should take WTO entry as a new starting point to strive to raise our level of opening to the outside world.
- We should make full use of the favorable conditions offered by entry into the WTO, implement diversified strategies and try by every possible means to enlarge exports. While guaranteeing maintenance of our traditional export markets, we should actively explore new export markets and vigorously advance the diversity of markets.
- We should continue to deepen reform of the foreign trade system, make major efforts to foster new growth points of export and promote the diversification of the mainstays of foreign trade management.
- We should continue to stimulate "going out", encourage qualified domestic enterprises to go abroad to engage in the businesses of investment and development and undertake contracted projects as well as labor cooperation, so as to boost the exports of domestic equipment, materials and labor through investing in foreign countries, thereby diversifying the methods of export.
- We should strengthen energy resource cooperation with foreign countries and gradually realize the diversification of channels for the import of important strategic materials.
- We should strengthen and perfect the import management system in accordance with the WTO rules.

[6] "PRC Media Reiterate Standard Line on WTO Entry, Hint at Internal Beijing Tensions on Market Opening," 11 January 1999, translated in FBIS.

- In addition, we should seize the opportunity of joining the WTO to raise the level of the use of foreign capital.
- We should closely integrate the absorption of foreign capital with the upgrading of domestic industries, the coordinate development of regional economies, the reorganization and transformation of State-owned enterprises and the expansion of exports.
- We should further improve the investment environment, particularly the soft environment, maintain the stability and continuity of the policies on attracting foreign investment, strengthen the protection of intellectual property rights and enhance China's attraction to foreign investment.
- We should actively spur foreign capital to flow into high and new technological industries, and encourage transnational corporations to come to China to set up R&D centers and regional headquarters.
- We should gradually expand market access for finance, insurance, commerce and trade, tourism, intermediary and other service trades, at the same time, we should study new situations emerged after opening these sectors and solve new problems, so that these sectors can develop in a healthy and orderly way.
- As a new WTO member, China will, together with other WTO members, play an active and constructive role in promoting the world economic and trading development and establishing and perfecting a multilateral trading system.[7]

In sum, the Chinese leadership views WTO membership as a means to continue economic growth and enhance China's wealth and international standing through the following:

- **Economic Reform** - Despite a growing private sector, China's economy is still dominated by state-owned enterprises (SOEs), many of which have been financially unviable for years. China's leaders embraced WTO accession as a means for imposing outside pressure on the SOEs, through increased foreign competition, to undertake necessary reforms.

- **Attraction of Foreign Investment, Capital, and Technology** - Chinese leaders see WTO membership as a means for attracting the foreign investment, capital and advanced technology necessary for continued economic progress. China's economic growth over the past two decades has been fueled by foreign direct investment (FDI) and such investment will be critical to its future growth as well. The Chinese leadership in particular is seeking FDI in the high-tech sector, since investment in that sector often is accompanied by transfers of technology and know-how. WTO accession is expected to result in a large influx of FDI into China, with some investment banks predicting that FDI could rise from current annual levels of $40-45 billion to $100 billion in the near term. Although China has an exceptionally high rate of savings, and a domestic stock market that has grown dramatically in terms of capitalization over the past decade, it likely will need to tap foreign capital in order to meet its growing capital needs.

[7] "Opening Wider to Outside World with WTO Entry as Opportunity: Commentary," People's Daily Online, 11 December 2001, <http://english.peopledaily.com.cn/200112/11/eng20011211_86382.shtml> (17 June 2002)

- **Expanding/Maintaining Export Markets** - Chinese officials view WTO membership as a means to expand, or at least maintain, their vital export markets. While China's trading partners have focused on China's market opening concessions, China too is looking at its trading partners to lower barriers, or to not raise new barriers, to its products. Given the burgeoning size of China's trade surplus with the United States, it is likely that Chinese officials sought WTO membership as a means to prevent the U.S. Government from reacting to the growing trade deficit with new bilateral restrictions on its products, preferring instead to have disputes handled in the more neutral WTO dispute resolution process. As Long Yongtu's statement indicates, China views its entry into WTO as an opportunity to counter U.S. unilateral trade actions against China, by subjecting U.S.-China trade to the multilateral rules and processes of the WTO.

- **Influencing the "Rules of the Road"** - WTO membership confers on China the opportunity to help develop and shape the rules governing the international trading system. With China now the world's seventh largest trading nation, it has a significant stake in the outcome of these rules, and now will be able to play an active role in their development.

- **Prestige/Legitimacy** - Becoming a member of the WTO is another key component in China's efforts to gain international prestige and legitimacy. China's absence from the most important multilateral organization governing international trade was likely viewed as a loss of face for one of the world's most important trading nations. Just as awarding the Olympics to Beijing for 2008 has elevated its international standing, so too does its WTO membership.

CHINA'S ECONOMY AS IT ENTERS THE WTO

The future direction of the Chinese economy following its entry into the WTO — whether it is marked by continued growth, stagnation or collapse — will have a direct impact on U.S. national security. Consequently, understanding and analyzing the Chinese economy has been, and will continue to be, an important component of the Commission's efforts.

Despite the impressive performance of the Chinese economy over the past two decades, serious structural and fiscal challenges remain. Beijing must overcome these challenges to continue its rapid economic progress. As noted above, China's entry into the WTO was motivated in part by a belief that outside pressures are needed to achieve economic reform and continued economic growth.

The Commission received testimony and briefings from economists and other experts on the Chinese economy about China's economic prospects over the medium or long-term. There were strong differences of opinion among these observers.

Experts who foresee China's continued economic ascendency emphasize the many successful reforms that have been implemented to date, such as:

- The gradual end to central planning in nearly all sectors of the Chinese economy,

- The agricultural production reforms that stimulated peasants to participate in local market economics (the "rural household contract responsibility system"),
- The gradual freeing of some sectors of workers from a strict labor regime that limited their mobility and opportunity,
- The creation of an investment friendly and export-oriented economy, that has resulted in large inflows of foreign investment and technology and spurred China's entrance into the global capital markets,
- And the reduction in import tariffs and other trade barriers.

These observers tend to believe that China's WTO membership will positively influence its economy. They argue that the strictures of the WTO will force China to undertake continued market-oriented reforms and to further open up its economy to trade and investment. Dr. William Overholt, Senior Fellow at the Harvard University Asia Center, told the Commission that China has been more aggressive than its Asian neighbors in opening up its economy and tackling some of its most significant structural problems:

> China, although it has not been commented on much in the press, has gone far beyond most of its capitalist neighbors in opening its economy. Its trade to GDP ratio is now three times that of Japan. It is more welcoming of foreign investment than anybody else in the Third World — I'm talking in terms of institutional structures and rules — than anybody except Hong Kong, Taiwan, and Singapore.[8]

Others in this camp predict that China will continue its rapid economic expansion following WTO accession and may in the foreseeable future become the world's second largest trading economy. Nicholas Lardy of the Brookings Institution testified:

> [W]ithin five years or so, they [China] could easily surpass countries like Canada, France, and the UK and became the fourth-largest trading country within the world; within a decade, they might surpass Germany and Japan and be the second-largest trading economy in the world. It is within the realm of possibility given the very large role that foreign firms in China are already playing in generating exports and the additional liberalization that is coming with their WTO obligations.[9]

Those who believe that China's impressive growth over the past two decades rests on an unstable foundation and that the economy is heading for stagnation or collapse emphasize problems such as:

- The continued misallocation of capital by government planners, through state-owned banks or otherwise, to inefficient SOEs instead of to private, market-driven enterprises
- The reliance on government fiscal spending to maintain high growth levels,

[8] U.S.-China Security Review Commission, Hearing on WTO Compliance and Sectoral Issues, Oral Testimony of William H. Overholt, 18 January 2002, 234-35.

[9] U.S.-China Security Review Commission, Hearing on China's Capital Requirements and U.S. Capital Markets, Oral Testimony of Nicholas R. Lardy, 6 December 2001, 117

- The government's rapidly expanding fiscal burdens, including a state-owned banking sector plagued with bad debt levels significantly higher than reported and "hidden obligations" in the form of underfunded pensions and other social security costs,
- The lack of a social safety net to support the high levels of unemployed and "furloughed" workers that have resulted from the termination of unviable SOEs and other economic reforms, and the rise in large-scale worker protests in response,
- Poor worker and environmental standards,
- Corruption and arbitrary regulation by government officials,
- And the replacement of tariffs with equally restrictive non-tariff barriers.

This group believes WTO membership will exacerbate many of China's underlying economic and social problems as domestic firms are subject to increased foreign competition and the norms of the international trading regime.

The Commission heard dramatic testimony on the precarious state of the Chinese economy from Gordon Chang, an American attorney who practiced law in China for more than twenty years and wrote *The Coming Collapse of China*:

> In the WTO era, the state-owned enterprises, which are the pride of Chinese socialism, will just not be prepared for the enhanced competition that accession will bring. Beijing has essentially deferred structural reform of the SOEs. There has been some window dressing. The SOEs look more profitable, but they are not more competitive. Some analysts say that in the years following accession, only a few of the approximately 1,100 Chinese companies that are listed on Chinese stock exchanges will survive. I don't know if the shake-out will be that horrendous, but certainly, there will be a change. With state-owned banks, the story is similar. They have gone through two major recapitalizations, one in 1998 and the other in 1999 and 2000. Yet even after the recapitalizations, they still are insolvent and they're not prepared for accession.[10]

China's Real Economic Growth

One overarching problem facing all observers of the Chinese economy, and a problem that constrains the ability of U.S. policymakers to accurately assess the situation, is the general unreliability of official Chinese economic statistics. Perhaps the most significant example is China's pronouncements of its official economic growth rates. While official statistics indicate annual GDP growth averaging over 9 percent since 1978, there is a general consensus among economists that have studied China that the actual rates are likely several percentage points less than the announced rates, with some economists concluding that China may in fact have experienced negative growth in recent years.

In particular, the Commission notes the work of Professor Thomas Rawski, an expert on the Chinese economy from the University of Pittsburgh, who briefed the Commission on his assessment of China's real growth rate for the period 1997-2001. Professor Rawski argues that China's actual growth rate during this period is likely in the range of 2 to 4 percent annually at best (with corresponding low-end estimates ranging from —2 to 3 percent) given the country's

[10] U.S.-China Security Review Commission, Hearing on Bilateral Trade Policies and Issues Between the U.S. and China, Oral Testimony of Gordon Chang, 2 August 2001, 67-68.

negative growth in energy consumption, modest employment growth, and falling consumer prices.[11]

A similar sentiment was expressed by the brokerage house Credit Lyonnais in a January 2002 report that concluded that "the data that show China as the fastest growing economy in the world are not worth the paper they are written on" and therefore Credit Lyonnais "lack[s] the basic statistical information to be able to construct even a rudimentary model" to forecast China's future GDP growth.[12]

These assessments demonstrate the difficulty in gaining a clear picture of the current state of the Chinese economy. If the more pessimistic estimates of China's recent growth rates are correct, this analysis would indicate an economy growing modestly if at all.

ECONOMIC CHALLENGES

Reform of State Sector

Among the key constraints on China's continued economic growth are the significant structural impediments present in its economic system, most notably the weakness of its SOEs and state-owned banking system.

The problems of the SOEs and state-owned banks are interrelated, and arise from the continued intervention by the state in investment decisions and allocation of capital. Widespread bankruptcy of the state sector has in part been avoided thus far because the state has propped up many SOEs with so-called "policy loans" from the state-owned banking system, which holds the assets of millions of Chinese who have no other investment alternatives. Instead of confronting the problem of unviable state enterprises, Beijing's policies created insolvent state-owned banks saddled with the bad loans they made to the SOEs. China's leaders have shown little resolve or ability to curtail policies of state-directed lending to SOEs, or to free the domestic capital markets and financial service industry from state dominance.

Financial Challenges

The Chinese Government has pumped billions of dollars into the economy in the past few years, in infrastructure and other projects, to stimulate economic growth. This "pump-priming" spending has contributed to record budget deficit levels, which according to official accounts have risen from $11.1 billion in 1998 to an estimated $37.4 billion in 2002.[13] Both economists and Chinese officials have underscored the importance of this fiscal spending to China's economy.

Finance Minister Xiang Huaicheng recently estimated that fiscal spending contributed 1.5 to 2 percent to GDP growth in the past four years.[14] This represents approximately one-quarter of the official growth rate during that period, and is equivalent or exceeds some economists' estimates of the real GDP growth for those years, as discussed above. In a dramatic assessment

[11] Thomas G. Rawski, "What is happening to China's GDP statistics?" China Economic Review, 2001, 349.

[12] "The Janus Face," Credit Lyonnais Securities Asia Emerging Markets, Hong Kong, January 2002, 3-5.

[13] China Statistical Yearbook 2001 and People's Daily Online, cited in Gordon Chang, China's Capital Needs, Report prepared for the US-China Security Review Commission, 8 May 2002, 4 [hereafter referred to as the Chang Report].

of the key role of fiscal spending to the Chinese economy, Premier Zhu Rongji admitted, "if we hadn't adopted a proactive fiscal policy and a prudent monetary policy, the country would have collapsed."[15]

In addition to stimulating the economy, Beijing faces other formidable financial challenges in the next decade. The SOEs must be restructured so that financially unviable enterprises are shut down and profitable enterprises given the ability to develop. This task has become more urgent given the increased competition China's SOEs will face in the post-WTO accession period. Another major challenge is the need to recapitalize the state-owned banking system. Some estimates put the percentage of nonperforming loans in this sector above 50 percent, well above the officially reported level of 27 percent.[16] China must also address the fiscal costs of its substantially underfunded pension and other social security obligations and invest heavily in infrastructure improvements and energy resources in the coming decade, including its buildup for the Olympics in 2008. Lastly, as discussed in Chapter 9, China's ongoing military modernization program is drawing a growing share of the government's budget resources.

Cost estimates for such capital needs vary. In testimony before the Commission, Stephen Harner, a financial services consultant based in Shanghai, suggested China will invest some $2.5 trillion ($487 billion a year) in fixed assets and major infrastructure projects during its next Five Year Plan period (2001-2005), an amount in line with investment of $1.7 trillion in such assets during its past Five Year Plan period.[17] Harner estimated that China will need $466 billion, equivalent to 43 percent of GDP in 2000, to recapitalize its banking sector.[18] A report on China's capital needs prepared for the Commission estimates the cost of bank recapitalization to be $510 billion and the cost to finance pension and other social security obligations to be nearly $1 trillion.[19] In an attempt to quantify China's total capital needs over the next five years, and China's ability to meet them through revenue generation, the report concludes that China's budget deficit will soar to over $150 billion by 2005.[20]

Projecting the scope of China's financial needs over the next decade involves some guesswork at this point in time. Nonetheless, there appears to be a general consensus that these needs are enormous and that China faces a monumental challenge in meeting them. How China addresses these fiscal challenges and its ability to tap domestic and international capital to assist in this effort will be critical to its long-term economic success.

Corruption

China's endemic corruption poses a formidable obstacle to its future economic growth. Although Beijing has undertaken public anti-corruption campaigns and periodic high-profile trials (and even executions) of corrupt Party officials, large-scale corruption in both the central and regional government and in the commercial sector in general continues unabated. Analysts

[14] James Kynge, "China's Growth Leaps as Fiscal Move Hits Coffers," Financial Times, 17 April 2002.
[15] Owen Brown, "Chinese Premier Zhu Defends Deficit Spending, Criticizes U.S.," Wall Street Journal, 15 March 2002.
[16] Clay Chandler, "Trying to Make Good On Bad-Debt Reform," Washington Post, 15 January 2002, E1. This article references an Ernst & Young study that put the amount of unprofitable loans at $480 billion, or 44 percent of total bank lending.
[17] U.S.-China Security Review Commission, Hearing on China's Capital Requirements and U.S. Capital Markets, Written Testimony of Stephen M. Harner, 6 December 2001, 5.
[18] Ibid.
[19] Chang Report, Chap. 1, p. 7; App. 3, p. 3.
[20] Ibid., Chap. 4, p. 1.

who represent commercial interests in China regularly identify corruption as one of the contributing factors to the possible social backlash against economic reforms.

Instability/Social Unrest

The Commission heard repeated testimony on the social strains that would likely result from China's WTO accession, most notably mass unemployment and an accompanying widening income gap between rich and poor. Many observers predict that unemployment in the rural regions of the country, already at high levels, could escalate markedly as the agriculture sector would be particularly hard-hit by foreign competition. In addition, if WTO accession forces the restructuring or closure of inefficient SOEs, these enterprises will be laying off significant numbers of workers. The Development Research Center of the State Council, a Chinese governmental research institute, estimates high employment losses due to WTO accession in the agricultural and automotive sectors: in rice, wheat and cotton production, it forecasts an aggregate loss of nearly 13 million jobs; in "road vehicle" production, it forecasts a loss of nearly 500,000.[21] Given the official nature of these estimates, they may understate the potential employment impacts.

The expected increase in unemployment following WTO accession will be countered to some extent by new employment opportunities in certain export-oriented industries, including new foreign-invested enterprises. The Development Research Center forecasts significant employment increases in textiles, apparel and other sectors to offset the losses in agriculture and the automotive industry.[22] Even if this assessment proves accurate, China's WTO accession likely will result in large-scale unemployment is certain sectors, particularly in rural areas.

The potential for social instability and unrest and the concerns this raises for U.S. national security, was recognized by Director of Central Intelligence George Tenet in his most recent annual threat briefing before the Senate Select Committee on Intelligence:

> China's entry into the WTO underscores the trepidation the succession contenders will have about maintaining internal stability. WTO membership is a major challenge to Chinese stability because the economic requirements of accession will upset already disaffected sectors of the population and increase unemployment. If China's leaders stumble in WTO implementation — and even if they succeed — they will face rising socioeconomic tensions at a time when the stakes in the succession contest are pushing them toward a cautious approach to problems. In the case of social unrest, that response is more likely to be harsh than accommodative toward the population at large.[23]

If high levels of unemployment materialize in the wake of WTO accession, the possibility exists for a marked escalation of mass protests against government institutions by unemployed workers, which are already occurring on a frequent basis. In some instances, local governments that have a vested interest in the economic status quo may join in the protests. The leadership's response will be a marker for accessing China's progress toward the rule of law and political

---

[21] Development Research Center of the State Council, PRC, The Global and Domestic Impact of China Joining the World Trade Organization, (Washington: Center for China Studies, 1998), 38.

[22] Ibid.

[23] Senate Select Committee on Intelligence, Hearing on Current and Projected National Security Threats to the United States, Written Testimony of George J. Tenet, 107th Congress, 2nd Session, 6 February 2002 <http://www.cia.gov/cia/public_affairs/speeches/dci_speech_02062002.html> (17 June 2002)

reform. If the response is characterized by enhanced repression, as Director Tenet predicts, this will signal backward movement on these important U.S. goals for China's WTO accession. Similarly, if the leadership responds by protecting its SOEs against competitive market forces, thereby minimizing employment losses, economic reform (and the hoped-for U.S. commercial benefits) will be undermined as well. At the same time, unchecked social unrest could lead to a breakdown in the current political system and an accompanying period of instability, with uncertain implications for China, Asia and U.S.-China relations.

Market Access and Compliance

China's WTO accession could yield substantial economic benefits for the U.S. economy. But for this to occur, China must comply with its WTO obligations, a massive undertaking that will require fundamental changes to its economic system. The Commission held hearings on the potential impact of China's WTO membership on certain key U.S. industry sectors and on China's prospects for compliance. Set forth below is an overview of these topics, as well as a discussion of the mechanisms and tools available to the U.S. Government to monitor and enforce China's implementation of its WTO obligations.

China's WTO Commitments

China's accession documents are unprecedented within the WTO or its predecessor, the General Agreement on Tariffs and Trade (GATT), in terms of their complexity, range of specific commitments, and number of deviations permitted at the time of accession. As Peter Davidson, General Counsel of USTR, explained to the Commission, the major market access concessions under the agreement are (bullets added):

- China will reduce average tariff levels on goods of interest to the United States from 24% to 7%
- China will phase-out all tariffs on Information Technology Products by 2005;
- China will broadly open up its services sectors, such as insurance, banking, securities, telecommunications, express mail, legal, accounting and computer-related services; and
- China will permit U.S. companies to operate wholesale, retail, and franchised distribution networks.[24]

In addition, China has agreed to considerable non-tariff concessions, to join WTO agreements regarding areas such as law reform, import licensing, and subsidies for SOEs, and to assume the obligations of more than twenty existing multilateral WTO agreements, such as the GATT, General Agreement on Trade in Services (GATS), Technical Barriers to Trade (TBT), Trade-related Investment Measures (TRIMs), and Trade-related Aspects of Intellectual Property Rights (TRIPs). China has also committed to reforming its state trading enterprises and SOEs and the elimination of price controls.

[24] U.S.-China Security Review Commission, Hearing On Bilateral Trade Policies and Issues Between the United States and China, Written Testimony of Peter Davidson, 2 August 2001, 1.

Market Access

U.S. officials touted the market access benefits that would accrue to U.S. firms as a result of China's accession to the WTO, and this became an important factor motivating U.S. support for China's WTO membership. The Commission heard testimony during its first year from representatives of several key industry sectors of U.S.-China trade — aerospace, agriculture, automotive, electronics and information technology products, entertainment and communications, financial services, and steel. There certainly are other important sectors in U.S.-China trade, and the Commission intends to hear from them in future years.

The industry representatives that came before the Commission during the past year discussed both the potential market access benefits they foresee as well as the challenges they face in achieving these benefits.[25]

- **Aerospace** — China's WTO accession agreement requires it to reduce average tariff rates on civil aircraft products from 10.5 percent to 7.2 percent and to immediately eliminate all non-tariff measures, including quotas and licenses, for all items listed in the Agreement on Trade in Civil Aircraft (though China is not a signatory). Moreover, China has agreed not to condition import or investment approvals on technology transfer, research and development, or production offsets. In testimony before the Commission, John Douglas, President and Chief Executive Officer of the Aerospace Industries Association of America (AIA), estimated that China's demand for commercial aircraft would be $144 billion over the next twenty years, making it the world's second largest market for commercial aircraft after the U.S. market, and that China will purchase at least $3 billion in communications satellites and related equipment over the next ten years.[26]

- **Agriculture** — China has committed to reduce tariffs on agricultural products from an average of 22 percent to 17.5 percent, with the average duty on certain U.S. priority agricultural products falling from an average of 31 percent to 14 percent. In addition, China has agreed to utilize only scientific-based sanitary and phytosanitary standards on agricultural goods and to otherwise eliminate non-tariff barriers in this sector. A representative of the U.S. Department of Agriculture (USDA) testified that "[w]hen fully implemented, USDA estimates that by 2005, China's WTO commitments could add approximately $2 billion a year to U.S. agricultural exports due to tariff reductions."[27]

- **Automotive** — China has agreed to lower tariffs on imported automobiles from current levels of 80-100 percent to 25 percent by July 2006, and to eliminate quotas by 2005.

---

[25] Unless otherwise indicated, the references in this section to China's specific WTO commitments are drawn from "China in the WTO: What it means for U.S. business," U.S. Commercial Service, U.S. Department of Commerce, October 2001, and U.S. Department of Commerce industry fact sheets for "Civil Aircraft" and "Steel," China Gateway, U.S. Department of Commerce, December 2001. <http://www.mac.doc.gov/China/Docs/industryfact sheets/> (20 June 2002).

[26] U.S.-China Security Review Commission, Hearing On Bilateral Trade Policies and Issues Between the United States and China, Written Testimony of John W. Douglas, 2 August 2001, 1-2.

[27] U.S.-China Security Review Commission, Hearing on WTO Compliance and Sectoral Issues, Oral Testimony of Patricia Sheikh, 18 January 2002, 36.

Tariffs on auto parts will be reduced from an average of 23.4 percent to an average of 10 percent. In addition, foreign firms will be permitted to operate their own sales and service networks within three years of accession.

- **Electronics and Information Technology Products** — China has agreed to join the WTO's Information Technology Agreement (ITA) upon accession, thereby committing to eliminate tariffs on all products covered by the ITA, including semiconductors, computers, peripherals, and telecom equipment. China's WTO commitments also provide for greater foreign ownership and market access for foreign firms in telecommunications services and enhanced protection of intellectual property rights through adherence to the TRIPs Agreement. Dave McCurdy, President of the Electronic Industries Alliance, told the Commission that "China is the single most promising emerging market in the world today, and this fact is especially true for the U.S. electronics industry."[28]

- **Entertainment and Communications** — Under its WTO obligations, China has committed to allow at least 20 foreign films into the country annually on a revenue-sharing basis, reduce tariffs on films from 9 percent to 5 percent and on home videos from 15 percent to 10 percent, and permit greater levels of foreign ownership in video distribution ventures and cinemas.[29] Bonnie Richardson of the Motion Picture Association of America noted to the Commission that "[i]t is our good fortune in the film industry to have reached a level of mutual respect and communication with our Chinese partners that we can now speak with total candor about how to expand our cooperation to the benefit of both industries. The WTO framework with its clear predictability in legal and trade terms adds immeasurably to the success of this process."[30]

- **Financial Services** — China's WTO negotiations resulted in key market opening commitments for foreign banking, insurance, and securities firms, including broadening the scope of permitted services, phasing-out of geographic restrictions, and establishment of transparent and prudential criteria for awarding licenses. A financial services industry representative testified that "[T]he development of the financial service industry in China will offer many exciting opportunities for banks, insurance companies, securities firms and other players in the industry. China has the potential to emerge during the next fifty years as one of the largest markets in the world for a wide range of products."[31]

- **Steel** — China's WTO agreement calls for a reduction in tariffs on steel and steel mill products from an average of 7.5 percent to 6 percent and the elimination of restrictions on the number of enterprises permitted to import or export steel products. Although

[28] U.S.-China Security Review Commission, Hearing On Bilateral Trade Policies and Issues Between the United States and China, Written Testimony of Dave McCurdy, 2 August 2001, 2.

[29] U.S.-China Security Review Commission, Hearing On WTO Compliance and Sectoral Issues, Written Testimony of Bonnie Richardson, 18 January 2002, 1.

[30] Ibid.,4.

[31] U.S.-China Security Review Commission, Hearing on WTO Compliance and Sectoral Issues, Written Testimony of David Hale, 18 January 2002, 6.

skeptical about China's prospects for complying with these commitments, Thomas Usher, Chairman and CEO of USX Corporation, explained that "[i]f China fully adheres to its WTO commitments upon accession, most of the principal restrictions which limit access to the Chinese market will be eliminated — most importantly, the quota/licensing system. The result will be an increase in imports from nearby Asian countries as well as producers in the former Soviet Union. This will relieve pressure on the U.S. market and will subject inefficient Chinese producers to intensified competition."[32]

The industry representatives acknowledged the considerable challenges they face in realizing the potential market access benefits discussed above. They identified the following cross-cutting areas of concern:

- **Legal Reform -** One of the most crucial issues facing foreign companies in China is the country's lack of a functioning legal system. Transparency of laws, uniform application of the law, and impartial review are the three most glaring deficiencies. The WTO addresses these three areas, and the Commission will closely monitor them. The Commission is highly skeptical that China can comply with this obligation, particularly given the country's lack of a truly independent adjudicative body.

- **Trade-Related Investment Measures (TRIMs) -** Under the TRIMs agreement China will not be able to condition the award of contracts on requirements such as technology transfers or offsets. While the TRIMs agreement is clear in this regard, the Commission is concerned that it will prove ineffective in practice, as companies are pressured into technology transfer or offset contracts in order to remain competitive.

- **Trade-Related Aspects of Intellectual Property Rights (TRIPs) -** In evaluating China's compliance with the TRIPs agreement, the Commission heard testimony from representatives of the Motion Picture Association of America, the International Intellectual Property Alliance, the International Anti-Counterfeiting Coalition and that of an independent film producer. The consensus was that China's record on IPR enforcement has improved, but that violations still continue on a wide scale. In part as result of U.S. pressure, the Chinese Government has shut down many production facilities for pirated audio-visual products, which has halted the problem of China being a major exporter of such products. But with the production base of pirated goods shifted to Southeast Asia, China's domestic market for U.S. audio-visual products remains closed. The Commission heard from independent film producer Larry Spiegel that despite these improvements "China, it appears, is condoning robbery on a grand scale...The loss in real dollars is staggering."[33] The International Intellectual Property Alliance estimates that U.S. firms lost $1.5 billion in 2001 due to the piracy of audio-visual products and software, and that piracy levels for such products were around 90 percent that year.[34]

---

[32] U.S.-China Security Review Commission, Hearing On Bilateral Trade Policies and Issues Between the United States and China, Written Testimony of Thomas Usher, 2 August 2001, 6.

[33] U.S.-China Security Review Commission, Hearing on WTO Compliance and Sectoral Issues, Written Testimony of Larry Spiegel, 18 January 2002, 1-2.

[34] International Intellectual Property Alliance, "2002 Special 301 Report, People's Republic of China," 2002, 2.

China's record for trademark protection has been even worse. With techniques such as "salting," in which the top layer of goods in a container are authentic while the products below are counterfeits, China remains a major exporter of pirated trademarked goods, with its products reaching markets throughout Asia and Europe. China's own Development and Research Center has issued a report indicating that counterfeiting in China is a $16 billion industry.[35]

A major obstacle to effective enforcement of IPR is the lack of criminal penalties that would make IPR violations a serious matter, as opposed to a pre-calculated cost of business. As a member of the WTO TRIPs Agreement, China is now required to impose criminal penalties for such violations. To date, China's laws treat IPR violations as a criminal offense but rarely do authorities enforce them as such. In its 2002 Special 301 decision on China, the USTR noted "administrative penalties have failed to deter further infringements. Criminal investigations and sanctions are rare (i.e. administrative fines imposed are nominal), and very few cases are referred to criminal prosecution."[36]

The recognition by Chinese business interests and the Chinese Government that China itself has potentially lucrative intellectual property worth protecting has been the most significant impetus in fostering improvements in IPR. The United States should encourage this domestic drive by Chinese entrepreneurs and business people to protect their burgeoning market for intellectual property by providing education and legal assistance programs in this area. Such programs are discussed in greater detail below.

- **State Owned or Invested Enterprises -** Foreign businesses are concerned that China will not comply with its WTO obligation to force SOEs or state-invested enterprises (SIEs) to operate on a commercial basis, thus allowing an uncompetitive situation to continue. Discrimination between foreign and domestic suppliers to these enterprises is also a concern. Because of the complex cost structures and accounting systems used, a major obstacle to assessing China's compliance is the difficulty of evaluating whether SOEs and SIEs are profitable or subsidized.

- **Areas Outside the WTO -** Outside of the Trade-related Investment Measures (TRIMs) Agreement, which deals with investment tied to trade flows, the WTO generally does not address investment restrictions. With the exception of dumping and subsidization, anticompetitive practices (e.g., price-fixing and cartels) are also not restricted by the WTO. These two issues are part of the Doha Development Agenda of the WTO. China is currently an "observer" of the WTO's Government Procurement Agreement (GPA) and has pledged to join the agreement. China's participation in the GPA is necessary to allow U.S. companies to compete fairly when selling to China's large stated-owned sectors.

Only time will tell whether the hoped-for market access gains for U.S. firms in China will materialize. This will depend on whether China has both the will and institutional capacity to adhere to its broad commitments under the WTO. Surely some U.S. industry sectors will enjoy

---

[35] U.S.-China Security Review Commission, Hearing on WTO Compliance and Sectoral Issues, Written Testimony of David Quamm, 18 January 2002, 3.

[36] Terence P. Stewart, "Accession of the People's Republic of China to the World Trade Organization: Baseline of Commitments, Initial Implementation and Implications for U.S.- PRC Trade Relations and U.S. Security Interests," Report prepared for U.S. China Security Review Commission, 30 April 2002, 50.

expanded market access, but how broadly beneficial China's accession will be to the U.S. economy as a whole remains to be seen. Moreover, China's accession may open the door more to U.S. investment than to U.S. goods and services, which could have a deleterious impact on U.S. employment if such investment flows into export production that displaces U.S.-based production.

China's Prospects for Compliance

China's record of compliance with past U.S.-China bilateral agreements has been inconsistent and raises questions about its prospects for complying with its broad WTO commitments. The following is a description of China's adherence to its most significant bilateral trade agreements with the United States over the past decade.[37]

1992 Memorandum of Understanding (MOU) on Market Access

In 1991, the USTR carried out its most sweeping market access investigation involving China. The investigation cited product-specific prohibitions, restrictive import licenses, technical barriers to trade, and a lack of transparency of laws. After negotiations broke down, USTR threatened $3.9 billion in sanctions. Under mutual challenges of sanctions, the United States and China reached an agreement in 1992. By signing the 1992 MOU on Market Access, China agreed to specific measures in return for U.S. support for China's bid to enter the GATT. Despite tense negotiations in 1993, due to China's poor implementation of the agreement, and again in 1994, due to China's anger at the United States for blocking entry to the WTO, the USTR reported in 1994 that China was "substantially in compliance" with the 1992 MOU.

During Congressional testimony in 1996, former USTR Charlene Barshefsky described the nature of China's compliance and the remaining frustrations for USTR:

> To its credit, China has done much to implement the agreement...While China has removed a substantial number of non-tariff barriers, we are concerned with China's tendency to give with one hand and take away with the other. In some instances, China had substituted new barriers in the place of those removed... China must live up to its agreements and eliminate those impediments to free trade...If I could pick one area under it where we are dissatisfied, seriously dissatisfied, I would say it is in the agricultural sector.[38]

In its 1998 Foreign Trade Barriers report, USTR listed non-tariff barriers, transparency, import substitution laws, and sanitary and phytosanitary issues as the key areas in which China's compliance was lacking.

1992 and 1995 MOUs on Intellectual Property Rights (IPR)

The 1979 Agreement on mutual nondiscriminatory treatment required both countries to provide copyright, patent, and trademark protection equal to that offered in the corresponding country. Despite talks in 1985 and 1987, China made no progress in protecting IPR. After placing China on the "priority watch list" in 1989 and 1990, the USTR listed China as a "priority foreign

---

[37] Unless otherwise indicated, the following discussion on China's compliance with past bilateral agreements is drawn from Wayne M. Morrison, "China-U.S. Trade Agreements: Compliance Issues," Congressional Research Service Report, 1 September 2000.

[38] Ibid., 7.

country" in 1991. After carrying out a Section 301 investigation, the USTR threatened $1.5 billion in sanctions, which China avoided by signing an MOU on IPR on January 16, 1992 in which it promised to strengthen patent, copyright, and trade secret laws and increase protection of U.S. intellectual property.

Although China's leadership was successful in ratifying the new laws, they failed to enforce them. In 1994, USTR placed China back on the "priority foreign country" list and threatened import tariffs of 100 percent on $1.1 billion worth of Chinese imports. China again avoided such sanctions by signing another MOU on IPR on March 11, 1995. In the 1995 MOU, China pledged to step up enforcement as well as eliminate hidden barriers, which kept U.S. audio-visual products out of the China market and therefore encouraged piracy. But the cycle of failed compliance continued and, in April 1996, USTR again put China on the "priority foreign country" list and threatened $2 billion in sanctions. China again avoided them by signing an accord on June 17, 1996. The accord laid out an action plan towards proper enforcement of IPR law, which has meet with success. In its 2002 National Trade Estimate Report, USTR explained, "China has made substantial progress in some aspects of intellectual property rights protections since it signed agreements in 1992, 1995, and 1996...however, significant problems remain, particularly in the area of enforcement."[39]

1997 U.S.-China Textile Agreement

The United States and China have established quotas under a series of bilateral agreements, the most current of which is the February 1997 MOU that restricts Chinese textile and apparel exports to the U.S. market.[40] By transshipping products through Hong Kong and Macau, among other countries, China has at times bypassed U.S. textile quotas. Estimating that transshipment violations amounted to $2 billion of product annually, the USTR negotiated enforcement provisions into the U.S.-China textile agreements. The provisions allow U.S. officials to inspect factories and impose penalties in the forms of reducing future textile quotas or even fining the Chinese an amount equal to triple the value of the transshipped products. The United States has acted on these provisions on a number of occasions. The 1997 U.S.-China textile agreement contained market access provisions for U.S. textile products. Despite China's compliance with this agreement, there has been no discernable benefit to U.S. textiles.

China has a mixed record of compliance with its bilateral trade agreements. One consistency has been the repeated need for the USTR to renegotiate agreements to incorporate more specific implementation requirements and to resort to sanctions, or threat of sanctions, to push China to comply.

Protectionist policies, under-resourced enforcement agencies, corruption, local protectionism, and lack of an effective legal system have contributed to China's problems with compliance. As well, differences between U.S. and Chinese officials over what qualifies as compliance has been a constant point of friction. As a result, USTR has learned to avoid loose agreements with China. Detailing how the WTO accession agreement differs from past bilateral agreements, former USTR Charlene Barshefsky explained:

> China's compliance with tariff changes has always been absolute because that's a known obligation, it is a knowable obligation and compliance can be judged. When we negotiated the

[39] United States Trade Representative, "2002 National Trade Estimate Report on Foreign Trade Barriers, People's Republic of China," 14.

[40] The U.S. will be forced to abandon this quota system under the WTO in the year 2005.

> WTO accession agreement, it was with that example in mind leading to an agreement, which as you know, doesn't read like an agreement. It reads more like about 150 pages of grid work. So that China in every year at every point knows exactly what the obligation is and we know exactly what our rights are.[41]

However, while the agreement does involve explicit "grid-work" obligations on tariff rates, it also includes numerous commitments designed to reduce trade-distorting practices. A number of witnesses testified that China will simply replace WTO-identified barriers with new ones.

China's accession to the WTO is part of a larger economic reform effort that has been taking place for the past two decades, and the success of WTO implementation largely rests on the success of the reform effort as a whole. There was strong domestic opposition in China to joining the WTO, with many officials outside the central leadership expressing concern about the increased foreign competition it would bring and arguing that China had given in to conditions that benefited the Americans more than the Chinese.[42] This opposition is likely to intensify as China begins the difficult process of implementing its WTO commitments. U.S. and international support for China's economic reforms, and pressure on China to comply with its WTO commitments, may be essential to the reform effort. To this end, some witnesses suggested that the Chinese leadership is counting on U.S. pressure to help further the reform process in domestically painful areas such as the restructuring of SOEs and state-owned banks.[43]

Localism and provincialism may be stronger forces than centralism for the Chinese economy and economic decision-making process. While the central leadership has signed onto the WTO, it remains to be seen whether the provincial and municipal governments will comply. David Bleyle, Consul General of the American Consulate in Chengdu, told the Commission that compliance in the provinces is on "a line of sight from Beijing" basis in which the central leadership exerts paltry influence over provinces' protectionist policies. WTO compliance will therefore largely be a matter of the central leadership's ability to put in place and enforce a strong legal system that will hold up in the face of localism and provincialism.

WTO implementation will be a tremendous challenge to China in the social dislocation of expected layoffs and company failures. Chinese companies in the manufacturing and service sectors are still in their formative stages and have little exposure to the competitive market forces that WTO-entry will unleash. Massive layoffs could bring protests and even violent uprisings, and the provincial governments can be expected to make every effort to protect their home industries.

Initial Areas of Noncompliance

China's membership in the WTO is only several months old and many of its most far-reaching obligations will not be phased in until later years. Nonetheless, many significant commitments were required to take effect upon accession. To date, there have been a number of

---

[41] U.S.-China Security Review Commission, Hearing on U.S-China Current Trade and Investment Policies and Their Impact on the U.S Economy, Oral Testimony of Charlene Barshefsky, 14 June 2001, 169.

[42] Seth Faison, "China Seeks to Win over Dissenters on Joining Trade Group," New York Times, 8 June 1999, Section C, p. 4.

[43] Overholt, Written Testimony, 12.

areas where China has failed to meet its commitments, including several that have become sources of bilateral trade tensions.[44]

The Information Technology Agreement (ITA)

Despite its commitment to participate in the ITA agreement upon accession to the WTO, China has denied ITA tariff rates to 15 tariff items unless those products are imported for domestic production. USTR Robert Zoellick stated that the "benefits [China] has accrued from the zero tariffs" of the ITA "will evaporate if it attempts to distort the basic intent of the agreement...We will make this point as often as necessary- and it will have to be made often- to the Chinese."[45] Because of this dispute, the United States blocked China's application to join the ITA at the February 15, 2002 meeting of the ITA working group in Geneva.

Tariff-Rate Quotas (TRQs)

One of China's early commitments under the WTO is to increase market access for certain agricultural products by granting TRQs to end-users in China. The agricultural products subject to such TRQs are wheat, corn, rice, soybean oil, palm oil, rapeseed oil, sugar, grain rice, wool, and cotton. Although in September of 2001 China promised that it would allocate agricultural TRQs by the end of 2001 or the date of accession, it has delayed issuing TRQ regulations and those they have released have been deemed inadequate by the USTR. Problems with TRQ allocation have also arisen for automobiles and fertilizer. The agricultural product TRQ delays are most likely due to interagency disputes in China between the Ministry of Foreign Trade and Economic Cooperation (MOFTEC), the Ministry of Agriculture, and the State Development Planning Commission.

Genetically Modified Organisms (GMOs)

In January 2002, China released GMO regulations scheduled to take effect on March 20, 2002. The regulations required a lengthy process of inspections, safety assessments, and labeling that could take 9 months to complete. With the regulations threatening all U.S. soybean exports to China (America's largest agricultural export to China) and with the possibility that the regulations were not WTO-compliant because they were not "science-based", the U.S. trade officials came close to taking the case to the WTO. By March, China offered an interim proposal to accept U.S. safety certificates as long as U.S. exporters had begun the approval process in China. Despite a temporary hurdle that required interim licenses for U.S. exporters, China began granting these licenses in April. While the dispute has been diffused, USTR has openly stated that it is on the lookout for new hurdles to exporting soybeans to China.

Insurance Services

In November and December of 2001 China issued new insurance regulations covering foreign-invested insurance companies that have caused concern among the U.S. insurance industry. The regulations' deficiencies lay primarily in the areas of branching, transparency, and

[44] The following discussion on initial areas of noncompliance is drawn from Terence P. Stewart, "Accession of the People's Republic of China to the World Trade Organization: Baseline of Commitments, Initial Implementation and Implications for U.S.- PRC Trade Relations and U.S. Security Interests," Report prepared for U.S. China Security Review Commission, 30 April 2002, 112.

[45] "Zoellick Outline Concerns Raised by Lags in China's WTO Compliance," BNA's Daily Report for Executives, 1 February 2002, A-27.

capital requirements. As well, insurance companies continue to face unnecessary obstacles when pursuing insurance licenses. Chinese officials say that the matter is complex and should be addressed via the WTO's annual transitional review mechanism.

Courier Services

China generally agreed that conditions on ownership, operation, and scope for existing foreign courier service providers will not be made more restrictive. Following accession it issued new regulations on courier services which imposed new licensing requirements, anticompetitive pricing restrictions, and weight restrictions on what companies could deliver. All of these regulations restrict market access and therefore are directly in violation of China's WTO commitments. The regulations appear to be protective measures by China as the country attempts to protect the State Postal Bureau (China Post), which is facing severe competition in the profitable express delivery market. Similar to the dispute over insurance regulations, Chinese officials have refused to discuss the problems at the WTO Services Council meeting and insists that the proper forum is the WTO's annual transitional review mechanism.

Export Subsidies

China agreed to stop all export subsidies on industrial and agricultural goods upon accession, but U.S. industry and agriculture representatives' state that China has continued subsidizing exports. These subsidies can be difficult to identify and quantify because of their myriad forms in a socialist economy. Subsidies can take the form of shifted assets, credit allocations, low-interest loans, or guaranteed provisions of energy and raw materials. The USTR's 2002 National Trade Estimate Report on Foreign Trade Barriers identifies soda ash, wood products, fiberglass, auto glass, steel, flat glass, cotton, and corn as areas of particular concern.

MONITORING AND ENFORCEMENT MECHANISMS

Monitoring

The U.S. Government has established an interagency group, coordinated by USTR and overseen by the Bush Administration's Trade Policy Staff Committee (TPSC), to monitor China's progress in implementing its WTO commitments. This China-specific group has a three-tiered system, in which staff and sub-committees comprise the first level, a deputy-level Trade Policy Review Group forms the second level, and the cabinet-level National Economic Council Deputies Committee or the NEC make the third level. The Committee will rely on information gathered and assessed by the Departments of Commerce, State, Agriculture, Treasury, Labor, and the U.S. Patent and Trademark office.

In addition to their involvement on the TPSC, the Commerce and State Departments are also taking the lead in organizing on-the-ground efforts in China. Shaun Donnelly, Acting Assistant Secretary of State, Bureau of Economic Business Affairs, testified:

> Ambassador Randt has made China WTO implementation one of his top priorities for his mission. In Beijing, the Embassy has established a WTO Implementation Coordination Committee chaired by the Embassy Economic Minister to coordinate the efforts of the Departments of State and Commerce and other agencies, Agriculture and Customs attaches. They are responsible for tracking and analyzing the changes in these laws, obviously requiring Chinese language capability

> and so on. The Embassy has also formed a special IPR working group to monitor China's WTO intellectual property legislation and enforcement. Our consulates in Shanghai, Guangzhou, Chengdu, Shenyang, and Hong Kong, are also key players in WTO compliance efforts.[46]

The Commerce Department will take the lead, in coordination with the USTR, in investigating market access and compliance problems as they arise. William Lash, Assistant Secretary of Commerce for Market Access and Compliance, outlined the Department's five-point "Compliance Plan", the components of which are to (1) concentrate enforcement efforts; (2) help China reform; (3) promptly address market access problems; (4) give U.S. companies a head start; and (5) aggressively monitor trade flows.[47] As part of this process, the Commerce Department intends to seek input from a variety of sources, such as the U.S. Chamber of Commerce, the U.S.-China Business Council, and organized labor, and to meet with U.S. small and medium size enterprises to assess whether they are gaining proper market access to China.[48]

Separate from the review and monitoring efforts of the U.S. Government, the WTO will conduct an annual review of China's compliance record as part of the Transitional Review Mechanism (TRM) provided for under Article 18 of China's Protocol of Accession. China is the only country in the WTO subject to an annual review, and the TRM process will continue for eight years, after which there will be a final review in the tenth year. Pursuant to the TRM process, the subsidiary bodies of the WTO that have mandates covering China's commitments — e.g., Council for Trade in Goods, Committee on Subsidies and Countervailing Measures, Committee on Antidumping Measures — are to review China's compliance, with China providing relevant information "in advance" of these reviews. The results of these reviews will be reported to the WTO General Council, which will conduct the final review. Annex 1A of China's accession Protocol sets forth a detailed list of specific information China must provide, including economic data in ten fields ranging from foreign exchange to pricing policies, as well as copies of laws and regulations on issues ranging from import licensing to government procurement.

U.S. trade officials recently attempted to have a discussion on TRM procedures placed on the agenda of several WTO committee meetings. China blocked these efforts on the grounds that discussions of this nature go beyond its Article 18 requirements. There now appears to be a process in place to have all the appropriate WTO subsidiary bodies take up TRM matters in October. It remains unclear how far in advance of these discussions China will provide members with documentation, how substantive such documentation will be, and whether China will formally respond to members' questions regarding the information provided.

During meetings in Geneva with WTO officials, U.S. trade officials, and representatives of various member country delegations, the Commission was told that WTO members are concerned that the TRM process, at least for the first year, may not yield a thorough review of China's compliance if the process is truncated to a limited review period at the end of the year. Some noted that the TRM process, which was an important component of U.S. and other member country support for China's accession package, will only be valuable if it is robust enough to

[46] U.S.-China Security Review Commission, Hearing on WTO Compliance and Sectoral Issues, Written Testimony of Shaun Donnelly, 18 January 2002, 4-5.

[47] U.S.-China Security Review Commission, Hearing on WTO Compliance and Sectoral Issues, Written Testimony of William Lash, 18 January 2002, 2-3.

[48] U.S.-China Security Review Commission, Hearing on WTO Compliance and Sectoral Issues, Oral Testimony of Jeffery Bader, 18 January 2002, 47.

function as an early warning system of potential trade disputes and thereby encourage China's compliance to avoid such disputes.

As the U.S. Government and the WTO monitor China's compliance with its WTO commitments, it will be important for both to assess China's broader economic practices, as some may effectively circumvent its WTO obligations. For example, the Commission is concerned about reports that China has adopted a policy of granting subsidies to its steel companies that use domestic rather than imported inputs.[49]

Enforcement

The U.S. Government has a variety of means to address Chinese noncompliance with its WTO commitments, including the WTO dispute settlement process, the WTO China-specific safeguards, and U.S. trade law provisions:

WTO Dispute Settlement Understanding

By joining the WTO, China has agreed to submit to binding external adjudication of trade disputes, therefore giving the WTO dispute settlement process precedence over its own domestic courts in trade-related matters. The Dispute Settlement Understanding (DSU) requires an initial 60-day consultation period followed by the additional time requirements of establishing a panel and selecting panelists. Although the briefing and hearing phases can be quick, the panel customarily takes several months to make a decision. If the decision is appealed, which is quite common, and the appellate decision can take three or four months. In its entirety, the DSU process generally takes 18 months, and therefore is viewed as a time consuming mechanism for resolving trade disputes.[50] In meetings with representatives of various WTO member country delegations, the Commission was told that many countries likely will initially pursue disputes with China through bilateral discussions (or plurilateral discussions as appropriate), then through the TRM process, and lastly through the WTO's formal dispute settlement processes.

Non-Market Economy Antidumping Methodology

Although application of non-market economy (NME) antidumping has long been a part of U.S. trade law, it has never been a part of WTO law. China's accession agreement includes a provision allowing the U.S. (and any other WTO-member country) to use the NME methodology for assessing China's cost of production in antidumping cases for the 15 years following China's accession.

The ability of WTO members to use NME evaluations of China when prosecuting antidumping cases could be extremely important to the protection of American industries, if strongly enforced by the Commerce Department. Currently the Department has the discretion of determining whether China is a non-market economy.

---

[49] "U.S. Official Warns China Against Taking WTO Action Against U.S. Steel Safeguard," Inside U.S.-China Trade, 27 March 2002.

[50] Bader, Oral Testimony, 17.

Product Specific Safeguard

The inclusion of Product Specific Safeguards into the Chinese accession agreement will allow WTO members to defend against import surges from China for the next 12 years. These safeguards extend well beyond normal WTO laws because they allow more lenient standards that call for finding of "market disruption" rather than "serious injury", and because they allow WTO members to single out China-specific products as opposed to addressing all imports of a product, regardless of origin. U.S. law already contained such a remedy against imports from China prior to accession under Section 406 of the Trade Act of 1974, however, it was used sparingly. The new Product Specific Safeguard tracks Section 406 and was agreed to by China in recognition of the numerous areas where immediate compliance was unlikely. The Commission believes that Congressional action under this safeguard is completely appropriate.

Textile Safeguard

Under China's accession agreement, WTO members can impose restrictions on Chinese textile imports using a "market disruption" rather than a "serious injury" standard. This safeguard is available through 2008.

GATT Article XXI Security Exception

Article XXI of the GATT, to which all WTO members are subject, provides for national security-related exceptions to a member country's WTO obligations. The language of Article XXI seeks to define what constitutes a legitimate national security concern and to discourage commercially inspired abuse. The United States has taken the view that Article XXI is self-judging, whereby if a country invokes Article XXI, its actions are not subject to adjudication by a third-party dispute settlement mechanism such as that of the WTO. Either branch of government- the Congress by statute, or the President by executive order - can declare the exemptions.

Article XXI(b) defines what qualifies as a national security interest as follows:

i. Relating to fissionable materials or the material from which they are derived;
ii. Relating to the traffic in arms, ammunition and implements of war and to such traffic in other goods and materials as is carried on directly or indirectly for the purpose of supplying a military establishment;
iii. Taken in time of war or other emergency in international relations.

Because of its broadness, Article XXI has been the subject of much debate among international trade law specialists. However, the WTO has not yet seen a case where the Article XXI exemption is cited before its dispute resolution body. The propriety of its use was raised in 1997 by the European Union with regard to U.S. legislative efforts (the Cuban Liberty and Democratic Solidarity Act and the Iran and Libya Sanctions Act), but the issue was resolved between the United States and EU before proceeding to the WTO.[51]

---

[51] Jeanne J. Grimmett, "GATT Article XXI Security Exceptions," Congressional Research Service Memorandum, 8 June 2001. (This memorandum was requested on behalf of the U.S.-China Security Review Commission by Senator Robert C. Byrd).

U.S.-China Bilateral Communications

Although currently there are many U.S.-China bilateral cooperative programs in place, many initiated by the Carter Administration in 1979, there is no centralized mechanism for coordinating, reporting on, or funding these meetings.[52]

Following his summit with President Jiang Zemin this past February, President Bush announced that the United States and China had agreed to increase cooperation and exchanges in areas including trade, energy, science and technology, and law enforcement. They also agreed to continue the annual meetings of the Joint Commission on Commerce and Trade (JCCT), the Joint Economic Committee (JEC), and the Joint Commission on Science and Technology (JCS&T). Following the April 2002 meeting of the JCCT in Beijing, Undersecretary of Commerce Grant Aldonas announced that he will visit China every six months to consult with the Chinese Ministry of Foreign Trade and Economic Cooperation (MOFTEC) Assistant Minister Ma Xiuhong on China's WTO implementation efforts.

While these meetings are beneficial and productive, the Commission notes that meetings with higher-level Chinese officials would likely be more helpful. In the JCCT the Commerce Secretary meets with Minister of MOFTEC; in the JEC the Treasury Secretary meets with the Minister of Finance. While these annual meetings are commendable and should continue, ministers are not always the functional equivalents of U.S. cabinet secretaries, and U.S. cabinet-level officials could more effectively meet with State Council members, who would have the power to respond to U.S. concerns.

In addition to more frequent meetings between central government officials, the United States would benefit from encouraging the use of existing bilateral mechanisms at the state and municipal levels to promote and monitor WTO compliance. These take place in the form of state government-to-provincial government and city-to-city meetings.

Technical Assistance

The Commission heard from numerous witnesses that one of the most effective measures the U.S. Government could employ to promote China's compliance with its WTO obligations is the funding of technical assistance and legal education programs in China. China's development of a functioning commercial legal system is vital to the country's ability to comply with its WTO obligations. Developing such a system is a massive undertaking for which the Chinese Government has asked for international help.

The Commerce Department funds a variety of technical assistance programs in China, in coordination with the U.S. embassy and consulates.[53] The funding levels of these programs have been modest and represent only a fraction of the amounts provided for similar programs in Central and Eastern Europe and the former Soviet republics. Moreover, the U.S. Government's assistance programs for China are not coordinated with other countries' efforts and are almost exclusively done using a top-down approach of educating government officials (as opposed to the arguably more effective bottom-up approach of educating Chinese students and attorneys).

---

[52] Kerry Dumbaugh, "The early infrastructure of U.S. relations with the People's Republic of China (PRC) during the Carter Administration," Congressional Research Service Memorandum, 23 April 2002. (This memorandum was requested on behalf of the U.S.-China Security Review Commission by Senator Robert C. Byrd).

[53] Lash, Oral Testimony, 24.

The U.S. Agency for International Development (USAID) is restricted under U.S. law from providing assistance to China.

The EU, the UK, Australia and Japan have also developed capacity-building programs for China. The WTO has been administering some modest programs of technical assistance and capacity building in China to facilitate compliance with its accession commitments and has been participating in similar programs sponsored by member countries. The WTO has begun a long-term project to build a comprehensive database of technical assistance/capacity building programs for developing countries that would encompass international organization, individual government, and private-sector initiatives. The hope is that this database will help better coordinate such programs and avoid overlap and duplication.

Most technical assistance programs supplement existing and internally supported PRC-government and think tank programs such as the Shanghai WTO Affairs Consulting Center, which is one of China's leading WTO research centers. Numerous nongovernmental institutions such as the Ford Foundation, Asia Foundation, Temple University and Harvard University and international financial institutions such as the World Bank and Asian Development Bank also support capacity building.

National Security Implications

China's accession to the WTO carries high stakes for both the United States and China. While they have some complementary goals for supporting China's WTO accession — e.g., promoting market-oriented economic growth and reform — they have very different long-term objectives: the United States seeks a democratic and more open China, while the Chinese leadership seeks an economically strengthened nation that continues to be governed by one-party communist rule. The national security implications for the United States of a more economically prosperous China governed by an authoritarian regime are very serious. An economically powerful, non-democratic China may use its wealth and regional influence to enhance its military power projection, bolster its alliances with rogue states, and otherwise undermine U.S. regional, if not global, interests. If China's WTO membership leads to economic growth and reforms that are accompanied by the development of political and personal freedoms, worker rights, and broadly shared prosperity, China may become a strategic partner for the United States that shares similar long-term objectives. There is no guarantee, however, that a more economically prosperous China will *necessarily* be a more democratic China.

At the same time, China enters the WTO with a rapidly growing, yet potentially unstable economy burdened with significant fiscal and structural problems. If, as some observers predict, China's economy stagnates or even collapses under the weight of its WTO commitments, the United States would face a new spectrum of security risks. Consequently, an understanding of the Chinese economy and how the Chinese leadership is handling its important economic challenges should be central to U.S. strategic planning. The U.S. Government needs to prepare for negative contingencies regarding the Chinese economy as a result of WTO accession and have appropriate policy options in place before a crisis occurs. The Commission remains concerned by the limited preparedness of our government for various scenarios.

China's WTO agreement is unprecedented in terms of its complexity and scope. There is considerable uncertainty at the present time as to whether China has the capacity, or the Chinese leadership has the will, to comply with its broad obligations. China's success in adhering to its

WTO commitments will determine not only whether U.S. firms enjoy enhanced access to the Chinese market for their goods and services, but may also determine whether China is on track to move in a positive direction toward greater economic, and hopefully political, liberalization. Consequently, the U.S. Government should be prepared to provide technical assistance to China where appropriate to facilitate its WTO compliance efforts and to aggressively employ its WTO and U.S. trade law tools to enforce compliance when necessary.

The Commission plans to monitor, through continued hearings, briefings, and research, China's progress in implementing its WTO commitments, and the health of the Chinese economy. The Commission also plans to use the stated U.S. objectives for supporting China's accession as benchmarks for assessing the success or failure of U.S.-China policy with respect to China's economic integration.

RECOMMENDATIONS

- The Commission recommends that the U.S. Government clearly and publicly articulate, in both multilateral and bilateral settings, the importance of China's compliance with its WTO commitments and provide technical assistance to this end. Current technical assistance programs would benefit from greater resources and coordination. Due to the restrictions placed on USAID's involvement in China, the Commission recommends that Congress appropriate and authorize funds directly to technical assistance programs such as the Commerce Department's Commercial Law Development Program (CLDP).

- The Commission recommends that Congress require that the Department of Commerce obtain Congressional approval before implementing any determination that a non-market economy (NME) has achieved market economy status.

- The Commerce Department currently interprets the countervailing duty (CVD) law to be inapplicable to NMEs. The Commission recommends that Congress amend the CVD law to specifically state that it applies to NMEs and thereby can be used to protect U.S. industries from unfair competition from the imports of these economies.

- The Commission recommends that the U.S. Government encourage the use of existing U.S.-China state government-to-provincial government and city-to-city bilateral mechanisms to help promote and monitor WTO compliance.

- Congress currently charges the Commerce Department to submit annually a report on U.S. trade promotion activities in the form of the Trade Promotion Coordination Committee (TPCC) report. In addition, the Secretary of Commerce is charged to testify to Congress on that report. During Secretary Evans' recent testimony on that report he discussed the importance of China complying with its WTO obligations and noted that a senior Commerce official would travel to China once a month to evaluate China's compliance efforts. The Commission recommends that Congress request that each annual TPCC report assess China's WTO compliance progress and recommend any additional resources or other initiatives to facilitate compliance, and that this report include a survey of the market access attained by key U.S. industry sectors in China, including agriculture. The report should compare actual market access results with the initial estimates made by the Executive Branch in support of granting China Permanent Normal Trade Relations status and compare U.S. market access in those key sectors with that gained by the European Union and Japan.

- China's WTO accession agreement includes three important China-specific safeguards: the ability of WTO members to use a non-market economy methodology in anti-dumping cases, a product specific safeguard that allows WTO members to restrain Chinese imports that disrupt their domestic markets, and a textile safeguard. Inclusion of these safeguards was a key component of U.S. support for China's accession as they provide important tools to combat unfair trade practices or import surges. The Commission recommends that USTR and the Commerce Department make aggressive use of these safeguards during the limited time period for which they will be available.

- With regard to the WTO China-specific textile safeguard, the Commission recommends that Congress request the Commerce Department to prepare an annual report on the U.S. textile industry addressing whether "market disruption" is occurring with regard to any products in this industry as a result of imports from China. A determination of "market disruption" would trigger the textile safeguard mechanism.

- The Commission recommends that Congress encourage USTR to request consultations at the WTO on China's noncompliance with its obligations under the TRIPs Agreement, in particular the lack of adequate enforcement to reduce and deter counterfeiting and piracy of U.S. motion pictures and other video products. If China's noncompliance in this area is not adequately resolved through such consultations, Congress should encourage USTR to request that a WTO dispute settlement panel be convened on this matter.

- Congress mandated the Commission to evaluate and make specific recommendations for the U.S. Government to invoke Article XXI of the GATT (relating to security exceptions) as a result of any adverse impact on U.S. national security interests. Current trends indicate that China's rapid growth as a steel producer may have an adverse impact on the U.S. steel industry. The Commission believes that the steel industry is a likely candidate for using Article XXI, as demonstrated by the Bush Administration's decision to impose temporary safeguard measures on key steel products and President Bush's statements on the importance of the U.S. steel industry to our national security. The Commission therefore recommends that Congress consider using Article XXI to ensure the survival of the U.S. steel industry, if the Administration's current safeguard measures prove ineffective.

- The Commission recommends that Congress renew the Super 301 provision of U.S. trade law to address unfair trade practices that have the greatest impact on U.S. export market opportunities in China and elsewhere.

- The Commission recommends that Congress examine the tools available to the U.S. Government to address market access-limiting practices by China not covered by its WTO obligations, and direct U.S. trade officials to make full use of these tools to protect U.S. export opportunities.

Chapter 6

CHINA'S GROWTH AS A REGIONAL ECONOMIC POWER*

Carmen Arleth, et al.

KEY FINDINGS

Cross-Strait Economic Relations

- Trade and investment between the Mainland and Taiwan have grown dramatically in recent years. Estimates of the cumulative level of investment by Taiwan firms in China are as high as $70 billion (far in excess of officially reported levels).
- The level of cross-strait business linkages is particularly significant in the computer electronics sector, with Taiwan manufacturers increasingly transferring production to the Mainland to remain competitive in the global supply chain. There is an ongoing debate within the Taiwan Government regarding whether to loosen existing restrictions on investment and technology transfers to the Mainland in its flagship semiconductor industry.
- Cross-strait economic linkages are likely to accelerate in the future now that both China and Taiwan are members of the WTO, and over time could help ameliorate political tensions between the two.
- The growing reliance of Taiwan firms on the Mainland as a manufacturing center raises concerns about Taiwan's vulnerability to Chinese economic leverage, and correspondingly to U.S. dependence on items made in China for its computer electronics and other high-technology sectors.

---

* In: July 2002 - Report to Congress of the U.S. - China Security Review Commission - *The National Security Implications of the Economic Relationship between the United States and China*.

Regional Impact

- China received nearly 40 percent of the foreign direct investment (FDI) inflows into Asia from 1995 — 2000. Cumulative U.S. FDI into China during this time period exceeded U.S. investment into any other Asian destination, except Japan, Hong Kong, and Singapore. Hong Kong reinvests a significant portion of its inward FDI in the Mainland.
- China far outpaced most of its Asian neighbors in terms of export growth over the past decade. Among Asian countries, China led the region in terms of export growth to the United States and now ranks second behind Japan as a source of U.S. imports.
- In addition to Taiwan, other developed countries in Asia, most notably Japan, are relocating significant manufacturing and research and development (R&D) capacity to China to take advantage of lower production costs.
- China's enhanced economic standing in Asia has given it new political influence in the region as its trade with neighboring countries has increased rapidly in recent years.
- WTO accession may accelerate all of the above trends, enhancing China's attractiveness as a destination for FDI, stimulating export production, and expanding intra-Asian trade.

INTRODUCTION

China's rise as a global economic power has significant implications for its neighbors in Asia and for U.S. interests in the region. The trends that have already begun in this regard appear likely to accelerate as a result of China's accession to the WTO. The intra-Asia balance of power, and U.S.-Asia relations will be a focal point of U.S. economic and military strategic planning for the foreseeable future. Accordingly, it is essential that U.S. policymakers accurately assess how China's emergence as a major player in the global economy will impact the region as a whole.

Subsumed in this topic, but in many regards a separate issue from a U.S. strategic planning perspective, is the developing nature of cross-strait economic relations. The China-Taiwan economic relationship is undergoing fundamental change. Economic linkages are proliferating despite the ongoing political and military tensions. Moreover, both entities are now members of the WTO, a development that introduces a new structure to their economic relationship. Given the United States' direct stake in cross-strait relations, any new dynamic in the China-Taiwan relationship must be carefully monitored and planned for by U.S. strategic planners.

CROSS-STRAIT ECONOMIC RELATIONS

Growing Cross-Strait Economic Integration

Cross-strait economic linkages, in both investment and trade, have expanded dramatically over the past decade. Despite ebbs and flows in the political relations between the two sides over that time, their economic relationship has grown steadily.

China today stands as Taiwan's third largest trading market, with total two-way trade valued at over $30 billion.[1] As reflected in Figure 6.1, Taiwan exports to China — which the Taiwan Government calculates as a composite of its direct exports to China plus 70 percent of its exports to Hong Kong — have increased from around $6 billion in 1990 to over $26 billion in 2000, while Taiwan's imports from China have expanded from approximately $342 million in 1990 to $6.2 billion in 2000, resulting in significant trade surpluses for Taiwan.

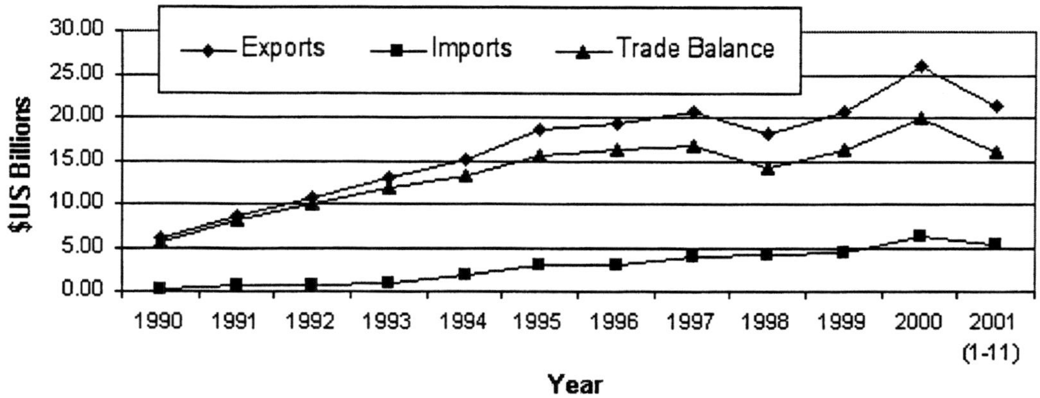

Note: Export figures include direct exports to China plus 70 percent of exports to Hong Kong
Source: U.S.-Taiwan Business Council/Taiwan Board of Foreign Trade

Figure 6.1 Taiwan's Trade With China

On the investment side, there is a great disparity between official and unofficial estimates of Taiwan investment in the Mainland. The Taiwan Government places significant restrictions on such investment, but Taiwan businesses have proven adept at circumventing them by, for example, investing in the Mainland via Hong Kong, the Cayman Islands and other third-party countries. While official Taiwan Government figures place Taiwan firms' investment in the Mainland at $17 billion at the end of 2000, Taiwan officials readily admit that actual investment could be as high as $60-70 billion, which would account for 40 percent of Taiwan's outward investment.[2] Mainland investment in Taiwan is negligible as a result of Taiwan's strict prohibitions on such investment.[3]

The most significant sector for cross-strait trade is computer electronics. Taiwan has been a dominant player in this industry for the past decade and its success has been one of the key drivers of its economic growth and development. More than half of Taiwan's top ten manufacturing firms in 2000 were computer electronics manufacturing firms and Taiwan now supplies 60 percent of the world's motherboards and is the world's leading supplier of notebook computers, monitors, mice, keyboards, video cards, sound cards, on-off switches, LAN cards, graphic cards, scanners, and laser disk drives.[4]

[1] Ing-wen Tsai, Ph.D., "A New Era in Cross-Strait Relations? Taiwan and China in the WTO," Heritage Foundation Lectures, No. 726, 14 January 2002 (lecture delivered 13 December 2001): 63.
[2] Ibid.
[3] U.S.-China Security Review Commission, Hearing on China Sectoral and WTO Issues, Written Testimony of Rupert J. Hammond-Chambers, 14 June 2001, 1.
[4] U.S.-China Security Review Commission, Hearing on Bilateral Trade Policies and Issues Between the United States and China, Written Testimony of Merritt Todd Cooke, 2 August 2001, 1.

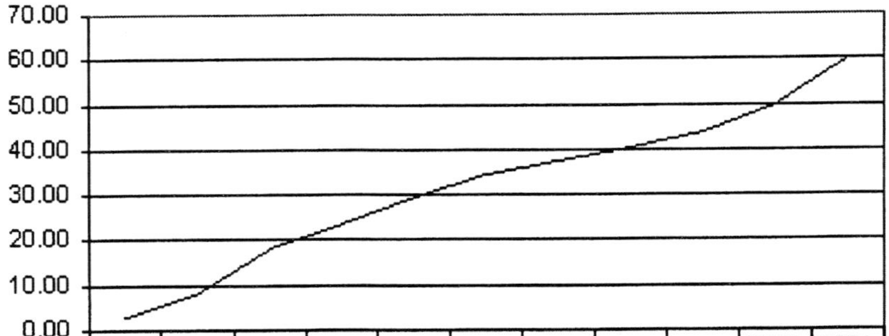

	1991	1992	1993	1994	1995	1996	1997	1998	1999	2000 (Est.)	2001 (Est.)
$US Billions	2.78	8.32	18.29	23.69	29.47	34.61	37.42	40.40	43.77	50	60

Source: U.S.-Taiwan Business Council/Taiwan Board of Foreign Trade

Figure 6.2 Taiwan's Pledged Cumulative Investments into China

To maintain its competitive position in the computer electronics industry, Taiwan has increasingly looked to the Mainland as a low-cost manufacturing center. The degree of cross-strait integration in this sector is striking. As Meritt Todd Cooke of the American Institute in Taiwan testified:

> The Taipei Computer Association reported in the same month [Feb. 2001] that 30 percent of Taiwan's 411 high technology companies had established major investments in Mainland China and that fully 90 percent of those 411 companies planned to be invested in China by the end of 2001. Lastly, China edged out Taiwan in 2000 for the first time for the number three slot in world IT [information technology] production value. China came in behind the US and Japan with $25.5 billion of production value against Taiwan in fourth place with $23 billion. The key point to note, however, is that Taiwanese companies generated fully 70% of that $25.5 production value in Mainland China.[5]

Another significant element of cross-strait economic linkages is the growing number of Taiwan businessman residing and traveling to the Mainland. During its trip to China this past November, the Commission visited Kunshan, a city near Shanghai that has become an enclave of Taiwan-invested businesses, including high-tech manufacturers producing circuit boards, computers, and telecommunications equipment. The Commission members were told that 32 of the top 100 Taiwan firms had invested in Kunshan, which has attracted around $11 billion in foreign investment in the three pillar industries of precision machinery, chemicals, and information technology. During the Commission's visit to Taiwan in January, we were informed that some 400,000 to 700,000 Taiwan nationals live and work on the Mainland (representing 7-10 percent of Taiwan's entire labor force), concentrated in the high technology and high economic growth areas of Shanghai and Shenzhen.

[5] Ibid., 2.

New Developments

Accession to the WTO

Taiwan followed China into the WTO by officially becoming a member of the organization on January 1, 2002, three weeks after China's formal admission. Although Taiwan's accession negotiations generally had been concluded ahead of China's, Taiwan's formal admission was delayed until after China formally joined due to political considerations within the WTO. The Chinese Government ultimately did not contest Taiwan's separate WTO membership on the grounds that this membership only recognized Taiwan as a separate trading entity, like Hong Kong, rather than a separate sovereign entity. Taiwan officially joined the WTO under the designation of the "Separate Customs Territory of Taiwan, Penghu, Kinmen and Matsu," also referred to as "Chinese Taipei".

During these early days of China's and Taiwan's membership in the WTO, there is a sense of optimism that it will improve cross-strait relations by increasing economic linkages and providing a forum for dialogue. This hopeful outlook was recently articulated by Dr. Ing-wen Tsai, Chairwoman of the Mainland Affairs Council of the Executive Yuan of the Republic of China (Taiwan):

> I would see the accession to the WTO as presenting a great opportunity for both sides to interact in a more structured and systematic manner, which is very much needed after more than a decade of exchanges between the two sides in trade, investment, and tourism. It would also help stabilize bilateral relations, which is very much needed for both sides to engage in their respective internal reforms. What is more significant, hopefully, is the possibility of both sides to use the WTO as a venue to open bilateral discussions on WTO issues and a bridge for discussions on a wider spectrum of issues in a separate context.[6]

At the same time, however, WTO membership creates new possibilities for bilateral tensions. As noted, China's acceptance of Taiwan's membership did not signal a new position by the Mainland on the political status of Taiwan. For example, if China refuses to recognize a formal trade dispute initiated by Taiwan or to otherwise accord Taiwan's representatives to the WTO equal treatment with other members, this could become a new source of conflict.[7]

The WTO membership of China and Taiwan in the WTO will likely accelerate the growing levels of Taiwan investment into China. While increasing economic linkages between the two could help ameliorate political tensions, it also has the potential to increase Taiwan's economic dependence on China, and the security implications that go along with that dependence.

Easing of Restrictions on Cross-Strait Investment

To counter concerns about Taiwan's growing economic integration with China, the Taiwan Government in 1996 instituted a "no haste, be patient" policy regarding investment in the Mainland, which, among other things, restricted investment in certain industries, including high-tech and infrastructure projects, and required special approval for individual investments greater than $50 million. The goal was to limit investment in the Mainland and thereby minimize Beijing's ability to exert economic leverage. However, this policy did not effectively stem the flow of investment as Taiwan businesses found numerous ways to circumvent the restrictions.

---

[6] Tsai, "A New Era in Cross-Strait Relations," 62.

[7] Mainland Affairs Division Economic Development Advisory Conference, "Final Summary Report," 26 August 2001. <http://www.gio.gov.tw/taiwan-website/4-oa/20010826/2001082602.html> (30 May 2002).

In August 2001, the Economic Development Advisory Conference (EDAC), an influential group of Taiwan business, academic, and government leaders convened by the Taiwan Government, recommended relaxing the "no haste, be patient" policy in favor of one characterized as "vigorous liberalization and effective management" (also referred to as "active opening, effective management"), which would allow greater flexibility for investments in the Mainland. The EDAC further recommended opening up the "three links" across the Strait — trade, transportation, and communications.[8] Taiwan President Chen Shui-bian promptly endorsed the Conference's recommendations.[9] The main drivers of this shifting approach to cross-strait economic relations appear to be pressure from Taiwan's business community and the need to address the island's current economic slowdown. Taiwan businesses, particularly in the information technology sector, see expansion of their operations in China as vital to remaining competitive in international markets. This is compounded by Taiwan's current economic downturn, its worst in decades.

It is presently unclear how these new policies will be implemented in practice and what impact they ultimately will have on cross-strait investment. Taiwan's political leaders likely will try to strike a balance between their country's need for China as a production and export market and the security concerns raised by this economic integration. This is reflected in statements from Taiwan officials, such as Mainland Affairs Council Chairwoman Ing-wen Tsai:

> On investment, we have developed a new investment review system that is transparent and flexible — a system to suit the needs of businesses and emphasizing macro rather than micro aspects of the investment flows. At the same time, we stress partnership between the government and business in managing risks associated with investment in China, which despite the opportunities offered, is still highly risky for investors and their home countries.[10]

As Taiwan Government officials wrestle with the challenges of cross-strait economic ties, new business relationships are developing apace. In the past year, numerous new ventures were announced, including several in the strategically important energy and semiconductor sectors. The following are some of the most significant:

- **Chinese Petroleum Corp. (Taiwan) — China National Offshore Oil Corp. (China)** - These two state-owned firms controlled by their respective governments signed an agreement in May 2002 to set up a $25 million joint venture to conduct oil and gas exploration in the Taiwan Strait. Executives of the two companies have expressed an interest in expanding the venture to conduct joint oil and gas development in the future.[11]

- **China Airlines (Taiwan) — China Eastern Airlines (China)** - China Airlines, Taiwan's flagship carrier, negotiated to buy a 25-percent stake in China Eastern

[8] Ibid.
[9] Chen Shui-bian, "Address at the Closing Ceremony of the Economic Development Advisory Conference," 26 August 2001, <http://www.gio.gov.tw/taiwan-website/4-oa/20010826/2001082601.html> (30 May 2002).
[10] Tsai, "A New Era in Cross-Strait Relations," 63.
[11] Jason Dean, "Oil Firms From China, Taiwan Sign Joint Exploration Deal," Asian Wall Street Journal, 17 May 2002, A3.

Airlines' cargo subsidiary (China Cargo). China Eastern is one of the Mainland's largest domestic passenger carriers.[12]

- **Sampo Group (Taiwan) — Haier Group (China) -** The biggest consumer appliance makers in Taiwan and China have formed an alliance to sell each other's products. Sampo will sell Haier-made refrigerators, television sets and washing machines under its own brand name in Taiwan, while Haier will sell Sampo DVD machines and flat-screen TV sets in China. Sampo may eventually manufacture products for Haier on a contract basis in its mainland factory.[13]

- **Taiwan Power Co. -** Taipower signed one-year contracts for the purchase of 1.2 million tons of mainland coal — roughly 10 percent of the company's total demand. Taipower has also been in touch with mainland authorities on storing low-level waste from Taiwan's three nuclear power plants.[14]

- **Taiwan Semiconductor Manufacturing Co. and United Microelectronics Corp. -** Taiwan's two largest semiconductor manufacturers have both indicated intent to build plants on the Mainland to produce eight-inch wafers if the Taiwan Government loosens current cross-strait investment restrictions in this sector (see discussion below).[15] Former United Microelectronics Corp. executives have reportedly been involved in the establishment of a semiconductor plant that broke ground on the Mainland earlier this year.[16]

- **Grace Semiconductor Manufacturing and Semiconductor Manufacturing International Co. -** These two firms, which have Taiwan investors, have already set up shop on the Mainland to produce eight-inch wafers. Grace is a joint venture between Winston Wang, son of a powerful Taiwan industrialist, and Jiang Mianheng, son of PRC President Jiang Zemin.[17]

The semiconductor industry has been the pride of Taiwan's high-technology sector and Taipei's deliberations over how to address mainland investment in this industry illustrate the conflicting pressures facing Taiwan in its ongoing efforts to manage cross-strait economic relations. Taiwan semiconductor manufacturers are pushing for a loosening of constraints on their ability to set up manufacturing facilities on the Mainland, while there are conflicting concerns that this would lead to a "hollowing out" of Taiwan's manufacturing capabilities in this industry and would give the Chinese access to cutting-edge technology that could pose a security risk. During the Commission's trip to Taiwan this past January, Morris Chang, President of Taiwan Semiconductor Manufacturing Company (TSMC), told the delegation that his interest was to

[12] Eric Ng, "Cross-strait pact takes off," South China Morning Post, 30 August 2001; Joseph Lo, "China Air buys stake in Eastern Cargo," South China Morning Post, 7 September 2001.

[13] Jason Dean, "Sampo, Haier Forge Appliances Deal," Asian Wall Street Journal, 21 February 2002.

[14] Tyler Marshall, "Cross-Strait Trade Poses a Question," Los Angeles Times, 4 September 2001, sec. A1.

[15] Shu Shin Luh, "Taiwan Strait just Wafer-Thin," South China Morning Post, 27 March 2002; "Taiwan: Plans to Move Fabs to China Delayed," Taipei Times, 15 May 2002.

[16] Mark Landler, "From Taiwan, A Fear of China Technology," New York Times, 3 October 2001, sec. C, p. 1; Jason Dean and Terho Uimonen, "Taiwan Chip Makers Set Their Sights on China," Wall Street Journal, 1 April 2002, sec. A, p. 8.

[17] Landler, "From Taiwan, A Fear of China Technology," sec. C, p. 1; Luh, "Taiwan Strait just Wafer-Thin."

produce only older generation 8-inch wafers on the Mainland, and not any of the advanced 12-inch wafers.

On March 29, 2002, Taiwan Premier Yu Shyi-kun announced a new policy regarding investment by Taiwan firms in semiconductor manufacturing facilities on the Mainland. The new policy would allow up to three Taiwan firms to set up 8-inch wafer plants on the Mainland by 2005 provided they transfer only second-hand equipment to these plants and only if they have constructed more advanced 12-inch wafer foundries in Taiwan that have reached "stable levels of basic production."[18] This policy has not been finalized and reportedly is still being hotly debated within the Taiwan Government.[19]

National Security Implications

The expansion of cross-strait economic linkages is a dynamic that may operate to minimize the prospects for hostilities by developing commercial relationships that give both sides a vested interest in peaceful relations and by opening new channels for dialogue. But this dynamic raises corresponding concerns about economic dependence and the possible leverage this may give China over Taiwan. The future direction of cross-strait economic relations is of enormous significance to U.S. national security given that the state of cross-strait relations is a potential flashpoint in the U.S.-China relationship. Moreover, given the growing integration between China and Taiwan in the global supply chain for high-technology goods, the state of their relations has a direct impact on an industry key to U.S. economic health.

The following are key indicators the Commission will continue to examine to assess the impact of cross-strait economic integration on U.S. national security:

Taiwan's Economic Dependence on the Mainland

By all accounts, Taiwan sees trade and investment with the Mainland as a key to its future economic growth, particularly with regard to high-technology goods. China offers Taiwan a low-cost production center for manufactured goods, an increasingly essential need in order for Taiwan companies to stay internationally competitive in this sector, as well as an enormous potential market for these goods.

But this economic strategy comes with risk, as it links Taiwan's economic well-being to the shifting currents of cross-strait relations. Deterioration in these relations could lead China to exercise economic leverage over Taiwan by threatening to restrict or cut off Taiwan's trade and investment with the Mainland. China might even take (or threaten to take) the provocative step of seizing Taiwan assets located on the Mainland. It is more likely, however, that China will seek to exercise its economic leverage in indirect ways, including attempting to influence the Taiwan business community (which wields substantial political clout in Taipei). To this end, the Commission has learned of instances where China has exerted pressure on Taiwan businessmen operating, or seeking to operate, on the Mainland to support pro-Beijing policies.[20]

---

[18] Premier Yu Shyi-kun, "Policy Statement on the Liberalization of Mainland-bound Investment in Silicon Wafer Plants," 29 March 2002, <http://www.gio.gov.tw/taiwan-website/4-oa/20020329/2002032901.html> (13 June 2002).

[19] "Taiwan: Plans to Move Fabs to China Delayed," Taipei Times.

[20] John Tkacik, "Taiwan Dependence: The Strategic Dimension of Cross-Strait Trade and Investment," The Costs of Conflict: The Impact on China of a Future War (SSI: 2001), p. 56.

The presence of hundreds of thousands of Taiwan businessmen resident on the Mainland presents another security risk for Taiwan as these individuals might be at risk in the event cross-strait relations took a turn for the worse. Further, if the community of Taiwan businessmen on the Mainland was forced by the Chinese Government (or otherwise felt compelled) to return home, Taiwan could face a significant employment crisis.

China's Economic Dependence on Taiwan

China reaps substantial economic benefits from its trade and investment relationship with Taiwan. As noted above, Taiwan's cumulative investment into China is estimated to be around $70 billion and it is increasingly focused on the production of high-technology goods. The Commission again notes the testimony it received that 70 percent of China's $25.5 billion in information technology production value in 2000 was attributable to Taiwan-invested firms. Further, Taiwan officials estimate that Taiwan investment on the Mainland has contributed to the creation of at least 3 million jobs.[21] It seems clear that an increasing number of Chinese businesses are becoming vested in the cross-strait economic relationship, creating a growing force within China for moderating tensions with Taiwan. The extent to which these economic benefits factor into China's posture toward Taiwan may be modest at present, but may become an increasingly important component of Beijing's political calculations should the economic relationship continue to grow.

U.S.-China-Taiwan Triangular Relationship

The integration between Taiwan and China in the high-technology goods supply chain creates a triangular relationship with the United States that presents both economic benefits as well as strategic challenges. In terms of economic efficiency, this triangular relationship allows the three parties to maximize the efficient use of their resources: U.S. research and development, Taiwan manufacturing, management and marketing know-how, and Chinese low-cost labor and production. High-technology goods and services have been a key driver of the U.S. economy over the past decade or more, with the United States leading the way in the innovation and development of these items. During this same time period, Taiwan established itself as a preeminent manufacturer of semiconductors and other high-technology products. The latest development has been the outsourcing of production by Taiwan businesses of these products to the Mainland.

Through this triangular relationship, the U.S. high-technology industry is becoming increasingly reliant on mainland production, heightening the economic stakes of any cross-strait hostilities. Any disruption in this supply chain could reverberate through the U.S. economy via a slump in the technology sector. To illustrate this point, Merritt Cooke of the AIT told the Commission that when a severe earthquake hit Taiwan in September 1999, the tech markets in New York dropped more in percentage terms than in Taipei.[22] Tellingly, news reports indicate that representatives of Dell Computer, a U.S. firm that is the largest buyer of laptop computers from Taiwan companies, have been pressuring Taiwan officials to establish direct trade and transportation ties with the Mainland.[23] This may be indicative of a larger trend of U.S. businesses joining many in the Taiwan business community in pressuring Taiwan's leaders toward more economic integration with the Mainland.

---

[21] Tsai, "A New Era in Cross-Strait Relations," 63.

[22] Cooke, Written Testimony, 1.

The WTO accession of China and Taiwan and the expected expansion of economic linkages between the two might well make the U.S. economy even more vested in peaceful cross-strait relations. Rupert Hammond-Chambers, President of the U.S.-Taiwan Business Council, testified:

> The opening of cross-strait trade and the accession of Taiwan and China to the WTO will highlight this trend and further strengthen the economic inter-dependency between them and with the United States, but that will make the U.S. that much more reliant on an improvement in cross-strait relations for its own economic well-being as American technology products are increasingly produced in one of the world's most potentially dangerous areas.[24]

China and Taiwan in the WTO

The entry of both China and Taiwan into the WTO provides a new forum for dialogue as well as disputes between these parties. At the outset, there have been some positive indications about how the two may interact within the organization. As discussed above, the GATT/WTO made a decision to allow China to formally enter the organization ahead of Taiwan, regardless of the status of their respective accession negotiations. Some observers feared that China would use this sequential accession to block or otherwise hold up Taiwan's accession. In the end, China took no such action and Taiwan formally joined the WTO three weeks after China. Another positive sign was that neither side chose to invoke WTO Article XIII, a provision allowing a member to opt out of the WTO agreement with regard to another member. Nonetheless, China and Taiwan are likely to have an uneasy coexistence in the organization, particularly during the early years of their membership.

WTO accession likely will accelerate cross-strait economic linkages as trade barriers between the two sides are reduced. Trade disputes inevitably will arise that will test their relationship within the organization. If China engages Taiwan in a formal dispute, thereby recognizing Taiwan as an independent member of the organization, China would be demonstrating a willingness to separate its political conflict with Taiwan from its economic relationship. However, China may refuse to formally recognize disputes initiated by Taiwan or work to prevent such disputes from reaching formal dispute settlement in order to avoid such engagement.

The WTO offers China and Taiwan a forum for dialogue outside of the formal government-to-government arena. Under the umbrella of a discussion between two "trading partners" rather than two governments, the two sides may be able to make positive progress on both trade and, potentially, non-trade matters.

Based on discussions the Commission had in Geneva with WTO officials and representatives of various member country delegations, the Commission understands that there have been some initial tensions between China and Taiwan in the early months of their WTO membership. China has apparently admonished WTO officials for inadvertently referring to Taiwan's representative to the organization as "ambassador" and is protesting Taiwan's use of the term "ministries" to reference its governmental entities in documents it submitted to join the WTO's Government Procurement Agreement.

---

[23] Mark Landler, "China Feud Has New Risks for Taiwan," New York Times, 28 July 2001, sec. C, p. 1.
[24] Hammond-Chambers, Oral Testimony, 241.

The United States has a national security interest in a stable cross-strait relationship. The growing economic linkages between China and Taiwan may help to achieve this goal. Nonetheless, if China attempts to exercise its considerable economic leverage over Taiwan in an aggressive manner, the result will likely be a heightening of tensions between the two. The Commission will continue to closely monitor the nature and status of cross-strait economic integration and to assess its implications on broader cross-strait relations.

FUTURE OF HONG KONG

For decades, Hong Kong played the role of gateway to the mainland market, a role many believed might expand following its transfer to mainland control in 1997 as a Special Administrative Region. The past few years, however, have seen the rise of Shanghai as an important business center and with that concerns about Hong Kong's long-term role. The Commission believes it is important to monitor the economic future of Hong Kong as a barometer of the Mainland's development as a sophisticated business and financial center and as an indicator of the success or failure of the "one country, two systems" policy governing its integration into the Mainland.

Hong Kong remains an important flow-through point for mainland trade and investment. According to Hong Kong data, nearly 90 percent of Hong Kong's exports to China during the past few years (1998-2000) were "re-exports" (i.e., goods that were imported by Hong Kong and then exported to the Mainland, often after receiving some additional processing in Hong Kong).[25] More significantly, while specific data is unavailable, it is believed that the vast majority of China's exports to Hong Kong are "re-exported" by Hong Kong to other countries after packaging or further processing since the bulk of these imports are electrical and other machinery, toys, sporting equipment, apparel, and footwear.[26]

Hong Kong's inward FDI flows increased dramatically in 1999 and 2000, surpassing the amount going into China by more than $20 billion in 2000.[27] Chinese statistics indicate that over the past several years around 40 percent of China's inward FDI came from Hong Kong, suggesting that a significant portion of that FDI likely was destined for the Mainland from the outset.[28] This mechanism is used by Taiwan businesses to circumvent Taiwan's mainland investment restrictions, by Chinese investors "round tripping" their money to obtain the favorable treatment available on the Mainland for foreign investment, and by investors in other countries who may be seeking to conceal that the Mainland is their actual investment destination.

Many observers see the expansion of direct trade and investment flows to the mainland market, with no bypass through Hong Kong, as a sign that its role as a gateway may be diminishing. Moreover, the Chinese leadership has made it a priority to develop Shanghai into a preeminent Asian business and financial center, as witnessed by the development of the Pudong

[25] World Trade Atlas, cited in Allen Lenz, Statistical Summary of China's Trade Patterns, Report prepared for U.S.-China Security Review Commission, October 2001, Table 2.5.

[26] Ibid., 4.

[27] UNCTAD World Investment Report 2001, Annex Table B.1, cited in Allen Lenz, The Role of Foreign Investment in China's Trade and Economic Development, Report prepared for U.S.-China Security Review Commission, March 2002, Table 1, 7.

[28] China Statistical Year Books 2000 and 2001, Table 17-15, cited in Allen Lenz, The Role of Foreign Investment in China's Trade and Economic Development, Report prepared for U.S.-China Security Review Commission, March 2002, Table 10, 25.

financial district. China's leaders have made no secret of their desire to see Shanghai overtake Hong Kong as the key financial hub for Greater China. In fact, Premier Zhu Rongji told reporters in 1999 that he saw Shanghai as China's New York and Hong Kong as its Toronto.[29]

Hong Kong's status as a Special Administrative Region of China and the dynamic of the "one country, two systems" structure has allowed the city to remain for the most part an independent economic entity that is still ranked by some as the world's "freest economy."[30] Nonetheless, as Hong Kong's economy stagnates in the wake of the Asian financial crisis and the current global economic slowdown, it has been seeking greater integration with the Mainland, including preferential treatment for its firms over other "foreign" competitors, through the establishment of a free-trade arrangement with the Mainland — the so-called Closer Economic Partnership Agreement (CEPA).[31]

The future role Hong Kong will play in a Greater China and in Asia is still uncertain. The Commission will continue to monitor economic developments in Hong Kong and assess the implications for U.S.-China trade relations and for the region as a whole.

IMPACT ON ASIAN REGION

Asia is a region of vital importance to U.S. national security as it is home to key U.S. allies and trading partners. One of the stated U.S. goals for supporting China's WTO accession was that it would enhance regional economic prosperity and foster peaceful intra-Asia relations. The Commission intends to test this assumption, as there have been some indications that China's growing economic dominance in the region could have negative implications for neighboring economies.

Several key questions must be examined to assess China's economic impact on its neighbors. First, to what degree is China attracting needed capital and export markets away from other Asian economies and how have U.S. investment and import patterns in Asia changed over the last decade? Second, will China grow to the point where it becomes a major investor and trade partner for its neighbors? In other words, the Commission will examine whether the growth of China as an economic power represents a zero sum game for other Asian nations in terms of their own economic growth or an economic engine that adds to the region's economic prosperity. If China becomes a more significant trade and investment partner with the Association of Southeast Asian Nations (ASEAN) and other Asian nations, the dominant role the United States and Japan have played in this regard may diminish, which may lessen their political influence in the region as well.

In beginning to examine these questions, it is helpful to look at some of the basic trends that have emerged over the past decade. Figure 6.3 below indicates that China received nearly 40 percent of total FDI inflows into Asia ($245.1 billion out of $643.3 billion) from 1995-2000. China and Hong Kong together received nearly 60 percent of total FDI inflows into Asia during that period. China's significant levels of inward foreign investment have in part been driven by investment from Hong Kong, which, as discussed above, accounts for around 40 percent of China's annual inward FDI (thereby making any summing of China's and Hong Kong's inward

[29] "Clouds over Hong Kong," The Economist, 14 August 2001, 57.
[30] Gerald, P. O'Driscoll, Jr., Kim R. Holmes and Mary Anastasia O'Grady, "Index of Economic Freedom," The Heritage Foundation and The Wall Street Journal, 2002.
[31] Vanessa Gould, "Chamber Seeks Open Trade Gates," South China Morning Post, 13 March 2002.

FDI levels involve a certain measure of double-counting). FDI inflows into China increased to $46.8 billion in 2001, and are expected to grow significantly in future years in the wake of its accession to the WTO.

Figure 6.3 World FDI Inflows into Asia, 1995-2000 (Billions of U.S. Dollars)

	1995	*1996*	*1997*	*1998*	*1999*	*2000*	*1995-2000*
Asia	75.3	94.6	110.4	98.9	112.4	151.7	643.3
China	35.8	40.2	44.2	43.8	40.3	40.8	245.1
Hong Kong	6.2	10.5	11.4	14.8	24.6	64.4	131.9
China + Hong Kong	42.0	50.7	55.6	58.6	64.9	105.2	377.0
Japan	0.0	0.2	3.2	3.3	12.7	8.2	27.6
Indonesia	4.3	6.2	4.7	(0.4)	(2.7)	(4.6)	7.5
Korea, Rep. of	1.8	2.3	2.8	5.4	10.6	10.2	33.1
Malaysia	5.8	7.3	6.5	2.7	3.5	5.5	31.3
Philippines	1.5	1.5	1.2	1.8	0.7	1.5	8.2
Singapore	8.8	10.4	13.0	6.3	7.2	6.4	52.1
Taiwan	1.6	1.9	2.2	0.2	2.9	4.9	13.7
Vietnam	2.3	2.5	2.8	2.3	2.0	2.1	14.0

Source: World Investment Reports, UNCTAD, 2001

As shown in Figure 6.4, cumulative U.S. FDI flows into China of $6.8 billion for the period from 1995 through 2000 exceed U.S. FDI flows into other Asian markets, with the exception of Japan, Hong Kong, and Singapore. Combined U.S. FDI into China and Hong Kong exceeded U.S. FDI into any of China's neighbors, with the exception of Japan. Notably, these figures suggest that U.S. investment in China remained fairly steady through the Asian financial crisis in 1997-98, while it dropped off in those years to some of the ASEAN nations, particularly Indonesia, Malaysia, and Thailand.

Figure 6.4 U.S. FDI Inflows into Asia, 1995 — 2000 (Billions of U.S. Dollars)

	1995	*1996*	*1997*	*1998*	*1999*	*2000*	*1995-2000*
Asia/Pacific	14.3	15.4	13.7	14.7	21.0	21.0	100.1
China	0.3	0.9	1.3	1.5	1.6	1.2	6.8
Hong Kong	0.6	1.7	3.8	1.9	2.6	3.1	13.7
China + Hong Kong	0.9	2.6	5.1	3.4	4.2	4.3	20.5
Indonesia	0.5	1.0	--	0.5	2.2	1.2	5.4
Japan	2.3	(0.3)	(0.3)	6.4	5.2	8.1	21.4
Korea, Rep. of	1.1	0.8	0.7	0.6	1.2	1.2	5.6
Malaysia	1.0	1.3	0.7	(0.5)	--	0.3	2.8
Philippines	0.3	0.7	0.1	0.3	(0.3)	--	1.1
Singapore	0.9	2.8	3.7	0.3	3.0	2.7	13.4
Taiwan	0.4	0.3	0.7	(0.6)	0.6	1.1	3.2
Thailand	0.7	0.8	--	0.4	1.1	0.5	3.5

Source: BEA, U.S. Dept. of Commerce

China's growth in merchandise exports over the past decade far exceeded most of its neighbors, with the exception of the Philippines and Vietnam (whose export values were only a fraction of China's total). Changes in export value and growth rates for the Asian economies are shown in Figure 6.5

Figure 6.5 Growth in Merchandise Exports of Asian Countries, 1990-2000 (Billions of U.S. Dollars)

	1990	*1995*	*% Growth 1990-1995*	*2000*	*% Growth 1990-2000*
China	62.1	148.8	140%	249.3	301%
Hong Kong	82.4	173.9	111%	202.4	146%
Indonesia	25.7	45.4	77%	62.1	142%
Japan	287.6	443.1	54%	479.2	67%
Korea, Rep. of	65.0	125.1	92%	172.3	165%
Malaysia	29.4	73.9	151%	98.2	234%
Philippines	8.1	17.5	116%	39.8	391%
Singapore	52.8	118.3	124%	137.9	161%
Taiwan	67.1	111.6	66%	148.3	121%
Thailand	23.1	56.4	144%	69.1	199%
Vietnam	2.4	5.4	125%	14.5	504%

Source: WTO 2001, Table A-5

As indicated in Figure 6.6, China led the Asian region in terms of growth in merchandise exports to the U.S. market over the past decade, with such exports growing more than six-fold (Vietnam grew by a higher percentage, but is not yet a significant trading partner of the United States). Japan began and ended the time period as the leading Asian source of U.S. merchandise imports; however China's rapid growth in exports to the United States during that period allowed it to significantly close the gap.

Figure 6.6 Growth in U.S. Merchandise Imports from Asia, 1990-2000 (Billions of U.S. Dollars)

	1990	*1995*	*% Growth 1990-1995*	*2000*	*% Growth 1990-2000*
China	15.2	45.6	199%	100.1	557%
Hong Kong	9.5	10.3	8%	11.5	21%
Indonesia	3.3	7.4	122%	10.4	211%
Japan	90.4	123.6	37%	146.6	62%
Korea, Rep. of	18.5	24.2	31%	40.3	118%
Malaysia	5.3	17.5	232%	25.6	385%
Philippines	3.4	7.0	107%	13.9	312%
Singapore	9.8	18.6	89%	19.2	95%
Taiwan	22.7	29.0	28%	40.5	79%
Thailand	5.3	11.4	114%	16.4	210%
Vietnam	0.0	0.2	---	0.8	---

Source: USITC Dataweb

The implications of China's emergence as a regional trade and investment powerhouse are well understood by its neighbors. In a recent speech, Singapore Trade and Industry Minister George Yeo explained that "[i]n 1990, China accounted for less than 20% of total foreign investments in developing Asia, while Southeast Asia took 60%. Today, the numbers are reversed."[32] Jin Nyum, South Korea's Economic and Finance Minister, remarked that China is becoming a "juggernaut in the global economy, turning itself into the world's manufacturing plant, which will suck all manufacturing facilities into it like a black hole."[33] South Korea's Trade Minister, Hwang Doo-yun, noted that "[w]e are losing competitiveness (to China) in areas of light manufacturing industries that are at the lower end of the market, and they (China) are also very rapidly coming up in areas that are technology-intensive. That is a serious problem."[34]

In addition to seemingly drawing investment dollars and export markets away from its Asian neighbors, China is drawing jobs as well. Taiwan's transfers of manufacturing facilities to the Mainland were discussed above. Japan is also shifting segments of its manufacturing industry to China to take advantage of China's lower production costs and market potential. Japanese electronics manufacturers, including Toshiba, Sony, Matsushita Electric Industrial, and Canon have all announced plans to expand manufacturing operations in China.[35] In many instances research and development activities are following to access China's growing pool of low-cost engineering talent. According to news reports, Matsushita has opened a research and development laboratory for household appliances in Suzhou, the Nomura Research Institute has begun outsourcing software projects to China, and Toshiba is planning a tenfold increase in the number of engineers at its chip development center in Shanghai[36] Hitachi, Sony Pioneer, Fujitsu, and NEC reportedly are among other major Japanese firms that have announced plans to establish research and development units in China as well.[37]

While there are indications that China may be diverting trade and investment away from some of its neighbors, there are also indications that China is expanding its own trade with many of these countries. According to a report issued by the Singapore Government, bilateral trade between China and the ASEAN-5 (Singapore, Indonesia, Thailand, Malaysia, and the Philippines) has expanded at an average rate of 16 percent per year, growing from $7.1 billion in 1990 to $29.6 billion in 2000, with ASEAN-5 imports from China generally running only modestly ahead of exports.[38] The report further noted that while China has not been a significant investor to date in the ASEAN region, "[w]ith the PRC continuing its economic reform and its transition to a market economy, it will play an increasingly important part as a key exporter of capital to Asia."[39] In January 2002, CNOC, China's state-owned offshore oil company, reportedly paid $585 million to a Spanish firm to acquire its assets in a major Indonesian oil company.[40]

---

[32] Richard Borsuk, "Southeast Asia Makes Plans to Join China's Party," Wall Street Journal, 7 March 2002, sec. A, p. 20.

[33] Mark O'Neill, "Even Winners Worry Over World's Workshop," South China Morning Post, 30 October 2001.

[34] Amit Prakash, "South Korea Must Form Economic Alliance with China," Dow Jones Newswire, 15 October 2001.

[35] Clay Chandler, "A Factory to the World," Washington Post, 25 November 2001, sec. A, p. 1.

[36] James Brooke, "Japan Braces for a 'Designed in China' World," New York Times, 21 April 2002.

[37] Ibid.

[38] "China's Rising Investment In Southeast Asia: How ASEAN And Singapore Can Benefit?" Singapore Ministry of Trade and Industry, 2001 Annual Report, 99. <http://www.mti.gov.sg/public/PDF/CMT/NWS_2001Annual_China.pdf?sid=92&cid=1034> (17 June 2002).

[39] Ibid., 100.

[40] Sadanand Dhume and Susan V. Lawrence, "Buying Fast into Southeast Asia," Far East Economic Review, 28 March 2002.

In addition to its WTO entry, China is expanding its economic integration with its Asian neighbors through other arrangements. At the ASEAN summit in November 2001, ASEAN leaders endorsed a proposal to create a free-trade area with China over the next 10 years.[41] This arrangement suggests both a desire by the ASEAN countries to take advantage of China's economic growth through expanded market access and a strategy by China to prevent its Asian trading partners from throwing up protective barriers. A report prepared by an ASEAN-China joint experts group predicts that an ASEAN-China free-trade agreement would increase ASEAN's exports to China by 48 percent and China's exports to ASEAN by 55 percent, and would increase ASEAN GDP by 0.9 percent and China's GDP by 0.3 percent.[42] Such an arrangement would establish China as the leader of an economically powerful Asian trading block, one that can be expanded to cover a broader area of Asia in the future.

National Security Implications

Loss of Trade and Investment

There are a number of reasons that the leading Asian economies are presently undergoing economic slowdowns and experiencing financial instability. Many of these economies have never fully recovered from the Asian financial crisis of the late 1990s and are still struggling to implement necessary structural economic reforms. Compounding these problems is the global economic slowdown, particularly in the United States, which is impeding their ability to export their way back to financial health.

It is clear, however, that these countries are becoming increasingly concerned about how their economies are being impacted by China's emergence as a regional economic power. China is garnering levels of FDI well in excess of its neighbors and its export growth is ahead of most as well. In addition, many Asian economies can no longer compete against China as a low-cost manufacturing center and their manufacturers consequently are moving significant facilities there. While continued analysis is needed to assess the extent to which China's increasing FDI and export production levels are displacing trade and investment in other Asian countries, it seems evident that China's emergence as a major trading nation has to some degree been at the expense of its neighbors.

China's WTO entry likely will accelerate these current trends. China's attractiveness as a destination for FDI should be enhanced post-accession. Moreover, as trade barriers to Chinese goods are lowered by WTO members, China's export production may surge as well, displacing exports from its neighbors and potentially lowering world market prices for many of these items. At the same time, however, a more open Chinese market may create new export opportunities for its neighbors and China's economic growth may lead it to become a significant source of investment capital for its neighbors.

China's entry into the WTO will not impact all of its neighbors equally. Those countries whose economies are the most dependent on labor-intensive exports (e.g., textiles, electronic goods) can be expected to be the most negatively impacted as they compete directly with Chinese exports, while countries that produce higher-end goods, or produce exports for which China is

[41] John Burton, "Asian Leaders Look to Free Trade Area with China," Financial Times, 7 November 2001.

[42] 42. "ASEAN Secretary-General Calls For ASEAN Economic Integration To Compete With China" ASEAN Press Release, 7 March 2002 <http://www.aseansec.org/%5Cnewdata%5Casean_compete.htm> (17 June 2002).

a significant importer (e.g., certain electrical components, mineral/natural resource products), are more likely to be positively impacted.

The United States has a clear strategic interest in the financial stability and continued economic development of its key Asian allies. Promoting Asian economic integration was a stated goal of U.S. support for China's WTO membership. However, as the foregoing discussion highlights, it is not clear whether China's WTO accession will have positive or negative economic implications for its Asian neighbors over the long-term. If China's future economic growth comes at the expense of its neighbors, the consequences could include a more severe Asian financial crisis coupled with social and political instability in the region.

Growing Regional Influence

China's influence in Asia has been enhanced as a result of its growing economic clout. Many of the Asian economies that have traditionally seen the United States as their major trading partner are now looking to strengthen their trade ties with China. The decision by ASEAN leaders last November to pursue a free-trade area with China demonstrates this trend. At the ASEAN summit where the proposal was approved, Singapore Prime Minister Goh Chok Tong noted that "[f]or us to depend on the U.S. alone as a market for growth for east Asia will be much more difficult in the future, because the U.S. economy is going to slow down."

Japan has become increasingly wary of China's growing influence in the region and reportedly was shocked when it learned of the proposed China-ASEAN free-trade area.[43] During Japanese Prime Minister Koizumi's trip to the ASEAN region in January, he floated the concept of establishing a broad-based Asian "economic community," that would include China, perhaps to counter China's attempts to forge its own regional free-trade relationships.

The United States has a critical interest in China's economic integration in Asia because it gives all parties a vested interest in avoiding hostilities. At the same time, China's economic integration with its neighbors raises the prospect of an Asia economic area dominated or significantly influenced by China. If so, the United States may find that its leverage and influence in the region, even with its traditional Asian allies, may wane to some degree, particularly with regard to economic and trade matters.

RECOMMENDATION

- The Commission recommends that the Congress should encourage the Administration to initiate consultations with other Asian countries to assess and make recommendations on the impact of the "hollowing-out" phenomenen with respect to China on regional economies and on U.S. economic relations with the region.

[43] 43. Barry Wain, "Japan's Push to Counter China's Sway in Southeast Asia Runs into Difficulty," Wall Street Journal, 14 January 2002.

Chapter 7

THE DEFENSE BUDGET AND THE MILITARY ECONOMY*

Quentin G. Koffey, et al.

KEY FINDINGS

- China's defense spending is growing rapidly, funding a strategic buildup that is aimed at U.S. interests in the area. The budget and budget process are opaque, and our understanding of them is inadequate. We believe that the announced defense budget is only about a third to a fourth of real defense spending.
- Chinese leaders assert that advances in defense capabilities must parallel those of its economic development and modernization.
- China's aggregate defense spending is modest compared to the U.S. defense budget and similar in size to some major European powers; yet it is significant in areas that could challenge U.S. and allied security interests in the area.
- The People's Liberation Army's (PLA) role in the economy has been significantly reduced since 1998, but it retains a sizable number of commercial ventures from which it derives economic benefits and uses as fronts to acquire military and dual-use technology.

INTRODUCTION

China's military modernization has enormous significance to the United States and regional countries. Although China has emphasized economic expansion and development, its leaders recognize the benefits for military capabilities that can flow from a growing economy. Opinions

* In: July 2002 - Report to Congress of the U.S. - China Security Review Commission - *The National Security Implications of the Economic Relationship between the United States and China.*

differ whether the leadership has chosen to simply modernize the armed forces or undertake a threatening military buildup. There is general agreement that China is a growing military power and is expanding its involvement in regional and global affairs. China has the world's largest standing military, and its actual defense spending is second highest in the world according to the U.S. Department of Defense.[1]

While China currently lacks a conventional ability to attack the United States, it is implementing a ten to fifteen year program to build a modern military. The data show that China seeks to gain a tactical superiority over Taiwan, to narrow the gap with the U.S. and the West in certain sectors, including advanced military technology, and to at least reach parity with the United States in some systems.

How much money it will take to accomplish these objectives is unclear. No one outside top leadership circles in China fully understands the Chinese budget or has confidence in the numbers that are published. The published budgets have significance for the United States only insofar as they inform us of China's official priorities, goals, and needs. Much of China's defense spending is off-budget and concealed in secret accounts, sometimes in the national budget and sometimes through other means.

This chapter explores the relationship between China's growing economy and its defense budget, including the relationship between the official and real defense budgets. The officially announced 2002 defense budget is $20 billion; the latest U.S. Department of Defense estimate of actual 2002 defense expenditures is $65 billion.[2]

CHINA'S BUDGET

The central government is severely limited by its low tax collections and must resort to deficit financing to meet the country's burgeoning demands. Testifying before the Commission, Richard N. Cooper stated that two-thirds of China's budgetary expenditures reside at the state and local levels, and only one-third at the central government level. The budgeted revenues collected at all levels of government amount to roughly 15 percent of GDP, which is low by international standards. The U.S., by comparison, collects 33 percent at all levels of government, and typical European total tax revenues are over 40 percent of GDP. The 15 percent PRC figure excludes so-called "extra-budgetary" revenues (various fees and charges) that are collected at the local levels and are roughly equivalent in amount to one third of the budget. When these extra-budgetary collections are added to the budgeted revenue, China's total collected revenue approaches 20 percent of GDP. That is the aggregate of central, provincial and local revenue collections. However, the PRC central government collects only one third, roughly the equivalent of about 6 percent of GDP. Cooper refers to a World Bank list of 70 countries which notes that China is seventh from the bottom in central government revenue collection. His conclusion is that "the central government is strapped for funds". By comparison, the U.S. federal government collects 22 percent of GDP.[3]

---

[1] U.S. Department of Defense, Annual Report on the Military Power of the People's Republic of China, 1 May 2002, 28.

[2] Ibid.

[3] U.S.-China Security Review Commission, Hearing on Chinese Budget Issues and the Role of the PLA in the Economy, Oral Testimony of Richard N. Cooper, 7 December 2001, 26.

Experts conclude that, over the past four years, China has been buying its way out of trouble with deficit financing — staving off signs of deflation, boosting demand, and countering the slowing economy. The result has been rapid, but diminishing, growth at the expense of fast rising deficits and government debt. Premier Zhu argued at the March 2002 National People's Congress (NPC) that the ratio of national debt to GDP (16.3 percent in 2001) was "still in safe limits" and that there was "still room" for issuing more long-term treasury bonds to finance construction projects. China's credit is good today, and it is still able to finance the record deficits domestically.

China's limited central government revenue collections, even though supplemented by its ability to raise additional funds with deficit financing and other means, set limits on government expenditures. If China's looming debt crisis becomes more severe because its expenditures are consistently exceeding its revenues and because of excessive borrowing, as observers have noted, defense spending will also be constrained.[4] Substantial increases in official funding for the PLA would, under such circumstances, indicate a growing prioritization of the military goals and missions; conversely, a decline or stagnant growth rate would reveal a lower or lesser national and party priority. As Cooper noted:

> It is in this context that PLA modernization has to be viewed, and in my judgment, the major battles that the PLA will be fighting during the next 10 years will be in Beijing over what it considers its rightful share of the budget. It will not be an easy battle to win.[5]

THE OFFICIAL DEFENSE BUDGET

China's published defense budget is only a part of the real total. Furthermore the published budget contains only three major line items, so it is difficult to learn from the official data how actual expenditures relate to the announced targets and capabilities.

For 2001, the official figure for defense expenditures is $17 billion, about 1.5 percent of GDP, and about one-fourth of central government tax revenue.[6] While the military budget has increased in nominal terms during the last two decades, in real terms (adjusted for inflation) such increases have occurred only since 1997. Official annual defense expenditure averaged 16.7 percent of the central budget over the last fifty years, but over the last fifteen years, it amounted to about 8.5 percent of the central budget. The share of official military expenditure as a percentage of GDP has decreased from 6.35 percent for the last fifty years, to 2.3 percent in the 1980's, and to 1.4 percent in the 1990s.[7]

The Defense Budget Process

The purpose of the introduction of Zero Base Budgeting (ZBB) reforms in 2001 was to decentralize the system to increase overall accountability, give total discretion to PLA

---

[4] Gordon Chang L.L.C, China's Capital Needs, section 1(8 May 2002), 3.

[5] Cooper, Oral Testimony, 31.

[6] U.S.-China Security Review Commission, Hearing on Chinese Budget Issues and the Role of the PLA in the Economy, Oral Testimony of Cheng Xiaonong, 7 December 2001, 46.

[7] U.S.-China Security Review Commission, Hearing on Chinese Budget Issues and the Role of the PLA in the Economy, Written Testimony of David Shambaugh, 7 December 2001, 4.

headquarters, and prevent local units from accumulating off-budget revenues. The ZBB reforms left the internal budget bidding process unchanged. Central allocations are still made to all levels of the PLA. The central government's General Logistics Department (GLD), the Central Military Commission (CMC), and the Ministry of Finance (MOF) together establish aggregate annual expenditure targets. Then a budget bidding process by the military regions and districts begins, and budget requests are submitted to the center. The center sets final district and regional budget amounts and the aggregate military budget.[8] ZBB affects the process of PLA budgeting, requiring the unit level to draw up projected expenditures for the coming year from zero up, rather than from the prior year's expenditure levels.

As with the rest of China's economy, the military fiscal system is characterized by double accounting, hidden assets, and a variety of off-budget and extra-budgetary expenditures, as well as corruption.[9]

2000 White Paper

According to "China's National Defense in 2000", published in October 2000 by the Information Office of the State Council, defense expenditures fall into the following three roughly equal categories: personnel expenses, costs for maintenance of activities, and costs for equipment. Beyond active force expenditures, analysts believe the official budget also includes militia, reserves, and various defense-related social costs. The published defense budget reveals very little about China's intentions, strategic priorities, directions, or missions.

Figure 7.1 Composition of China's Defense Expenditures (2000 White Paper, USD — Billions, $1 = 8.28 Yuan)

	1998	1999	2000
Personnel	$3.89	$4.21	$4.89
Maintenance	3.59	4.59	5.04
Equipment	3.79	4.20	4.70
Total	11.28	13.00	14.64

The 24 percent rise in announced equipment expenditures in the three years of published data is significant. It reveals that China's acquisition of technology and weapons is accelerating to support its military modernization program.

The White Paper compares the size of the official defense budget to those of other countries. At $14.6 billion, the official 2000 defense budget was five percent of U.S. defense spending, 30 percent of Japan's, 40 percent of UK's, 48 percent of France's, and 64 percent of Germany's. As a percent of the official national budget, the announced defense budget was 9.33 percent in 1995, 9.07 percent in 1996, 8.8 percent in 1997, 8.66 percent in 1998, 8.2 percent in 1999, and 8.29 percent in 2000. As a percentage of GDP, the United States spent three percent on defense, South Korea 2.8 percent, India 2.7 percent, United Kingdom 2.6 percent, France 2.15 percent, while China spent 1.31 percent.

---

[8] Ibid., 13-15.
[9] Ibid., 3.

The 2002 Budget

The official military budget presented in March 2002 is $3 billion or 17.6 percent larger than last year's military budget. At the same time, the announced national budget contains a projected deficit equivalent to three percent of GDP, "dangerously close to what the International Monetary Fund considers unsafe levels of debt."[10] If, as announced in the White Papers, the priorities behind the military budget are for general defense requirements, it is notable that the defense budget contains such huge increases, especially in fiscally hard times. Added to the 2001 increase, the 17.6 percent 2002 increase will amount to a one-third increase in the acknowledged military expenditures over the last two years. Some of the budgeted increases will pay for increased personnel costs and for losses incurred by the PLA's divestment from its commercial enterprises, while the rest will be allotted to modernization. According to one account, these substantial increases are more understandable if China's "goal, according to Pentagon reports, is to become a 'regional hegemon', project Chinese power into every corner of Asia, protect sea lanes for Chinese oil, replace the United States as the preeminent power in the region, and use Chinese power to guarantee reunification with Taiwan."[11]

The Real Defense Budget

"China's published budget substantially understates its total expenditure on national defense, although there is no consensus as to where its 'hidden resources' of military financing lie and how large its actual defense spending really is."[12] The missing money is either hidden in other budgets or simply not calculated.[13] The official budget does not cover several areas, including: indigenously made weapons and equipment production; some Research Development Test and Evaluation (RDT&E) costs; funding the People's Armed Police (PAP) and reserves; funds for large foreign weapon systems procurement; funds directly allocated to military factories under control of the General Armaments Department (GAD); and foreign military aid.[14]

Additional resources are provided to the PLA by state and local jurisdictions through cost-sharing arrangements, by profits generated through PLA-run enterprises not yet divested, from the production and sale of products and services, through funding allocations from other ministries, and from receipts generated by foreign military sales and transfers. As a result, the official budget is vastly understated; the range of annual estimated defense funding runs from $20 billion to $140 billion. The most recent Department of Defense estimate puts the real defense budget at about $65 billion, which is roughly three times the official claims[15] or just under 5 percent of the GDP.

The PLA complains that the recent budget increases are still not rapid enough. Finance Minister Xiang Huaicheng announced that the 17.6 percent increase in 2002 is for "high technology, to raise our army's defense and combat capabilities"; but according to General Song Qingwei, one of 250 PLA delegates at the March 2002 National People's Congress, "many

---

[10] Winston Yau, "China Faces Record Budget Deficit", South China Morning Post, 4 March 2002

[11] John Pomfret, "China Raises Defense Budget Again," Washington Post, 5 March 2002, sec. A , p.10.

[12] Wang Shaoguang, "The Military Expenditure of China, 1989-98," SIPRI Yearbook 1999, Appendix 7D, 334.

[13] U.S.-China Security Review Commission, Hearing on Chinese Budget Issues and the Role of the PLA in the Economy, Written Testimony of Cheng Xiaonong, 7 December 2001, 2.

[14] Ibid., 7.

[15] Defense Department, Annual Report on Military Power of China, 28.

barracks in cold areas don't have heating, (and the) (t)roops and officers have to eat, live and repair equipment".[16] PLA officers are increasingly urging a more accelerated pace of defense spending. Two Chinese military experts conclude that China's present 'gradual' budget increase model is no longer in line with the military's real needs, and state "the model for defense budget increase should be transformed from a 'gradual' to 'leaping' pattern."[17] These experts believe China is in a military preparatory period and the budget must be significantly increased. Another PLA official says that "China's defense expenditure has come to a point where it has to expand, and the first ten years into the 21st Century should be grasped as the most opportune to increase its defense budget."[18] On the assumption that GDP will grow at an average rate of 8 percent and defense spending increase at 20 percent per year, this official holds that China's official defense budget should reach seven times the 1999 level by 2010, or $100 billion.[19]

A different way to assess the size and trends of the military budget is to look at expenditure per soldier. Based upon the $65 billion DOD estimate of China's military spending and the assumption that PLA downsizing from 2,470,000 to 1,970,000 personnel has been completed, the expenditure per soldier in 2002 would be closer to $33,000. The comparable U.S. and Japan's published expenditures are $213,208 for United States and $192,649 for Japan.[20] Based upon the $65 billion defense spending estimate, the optimistic projections of sustained average GDP growth of 8 percent and average annual defense budget increases of 20 percent, spending per soldier in the downsized PLA in 2010 would be a respectable $170,220. It should be noted that these static expenditure comparisons ignore what the money is being spent on, for example, how much is for modernization and buildup and how much it buys in the local economy.

THE PLA AND THE ECONOMY

Between 1978 and 1998, the PLA became an important actor in the Chinese economy, controlling a multi-billion dollar international business empire that ran the gamut from large farms to world-class hotels, local airlines, and transnational corporations.

Initially to compensate for declining central government defense budgets, the defense industry and military-run units branched out into civilian commercial activity. The PLA-run enterprises in the 1990s began to operate under a different set of rules and policies than the rest of the economy. In the mid-1990s, "a loose network of some 20,000 companies operated as an integral part of China's military establishment and routinely existed above the law. Military units engaged in business enjoyed privileges which often gave them commercial advantages, such as tax breaks and access to state-subsidized raw materials."[21]

PLA business activity included agribusiness, food processing, electronics, transportation, hotels, construction, real estate, tourist attractions, medical services, karaoke lounges, even

---

[16] Taiwan Security Research, "China's Military Grumble Over 17.6 Percent Budget Increase," Associated Press, 7 March 2002.

[17] Liu Yang and Wang Cong, "Military Preparation and Possible Models for Defense Budget Increase," Military Economics Study (PLA Institute of Economics, November 2001).

[18] Xia Jiren, "Circumstances Affecting China's Defense Budget Increases," Military Economics Study (PLA Institute of Economics, December 2000).

[19] Ibid.

[20] U.S.-China Security Review Commission, Hearing on Chinese Budget Issues and the Role of the PLA in the Economy, Written Testimony of Luke Colton, 7 December 2001, 3,4.

[21] Tai Ming Cheung; "Can PLA Inc. be Tamed?," Institutional Investor (July 1996): 41.

smuggling. It first engaged in profit-making activities in 1985. Because of problems of discipline, loss of mission, and corruption, the central government decided to clamp down, and by 1995, 40 percent of these activities had been closed down. In 1998, President Jiang Zemin ordered the PLA and the People's Armed Police (PAP) to divest themselves of their commercial enterprises and, beginning in 1999, to rely almost entirely on the central government's budget for their funds.

Total profits from PLA's domestic commercial activities amounted to about "10 percent of the published defense budget from 1989 to 1991, 15 percent for the two years 1992-93, and 12 percent in the five years 1994-98."[22] It is unlikely that the contribution of PLA's business earnings ever exceeded 20 percent of the official defense budget.[23] PLA analyst Tai Ming Cheung estimated the annual revenues of PLA companies to be between $7 billion and $9 billion, with a profit of $480 million to $720 million.[24] Profits in this range would have been equivalent to less than two percent of actual defense expenditures.

The PLA's income from arms export earnings is no longer a significant source of extra-budgetary revenue. China's arms exports have experienced a severe decline from the peak volume of $3.75 billion in 1988 to $.58 billion in 1996; it is estimated the PLA accounts for only a half of these sales. Finally, when manufacturing and other real costs are subtracted, "(i)t is unlikely that the PLA's net earnings exceeded 20 per cent of the income from arms exports." It is doubtful that PLA's arms trade earnings could have financed China's arms imports.[25]

Following the 1998 order removing the PLA and PAP from most commercial enterprises, many businesses were privatized or transferred back to the control of a civilian ministry. Some enterprises, however, remain only one step removed from the military. Many former active-duty military officers who ran them were offered the opportunity to return to the military or to stay with the enterprise, and many officers retired to run the companies. Some have been controlled by the so-called "princelings" - the children of influential high officials.

Moreover, the Chinese government decided to allow the PLA to retain a number of production units and enterprises, proving the "notion that the PLA is out of business is not true."[26] Observers estimate the PLA has held onto 8,000 to 10,000 such enterprises and units of which "a vast majority were subsistence" units like farms and food-processing units.[27] Militarily useful enterprises were retained for national security reasons, most notably telecommunications, space and satellite-launch services, radar technologies and opto-electronics, lasers, civil aviation and railways. Some enterprises that provided cover for intelligence gathering, national security, foreign affairs, and front operations were only partially divested.[28]

PLA ownership and management of businesses, often referred to as commercialization, has had important indirect effects on the military budget. Commercialization allowed the PLA to use assets from its business enterprises for its own purposes. It has helped fund the construction of military ports, bases, warehouses and channel resources to the state sector. One Commission

[22] Wang, "The Military Expenditure of China," 345.
[23] Cheng, Written Testimony, 3.
[24] Banking, Housing and Urban Affairs Committee, Hearing on S.1315 - "The U.S. Markets Security Act of 1997," Written Testimony of Richard Fisher, 5 November 1997, quoting Tai Ming Cheung, "The Chinese Army's New Marching Orders: Winning On The Economic Battlefield," in Jorn Bromelhorster and John Frankenstein, eds. Mixed Motives, Uncertain Outcomes, Defense Conversion In China. (Boulder: Lynne Rienner, 1997), 195.
[25] Wang, "The Military Expenditure of China," 347.
[26] U.S.-China Security Review Commission Hearing on U.S.-China Current Trade and Investment Policies and Their Impact on the U.S. Economy, Oral Testimony of Charlene Barshefsky, 14 June 2001, 207.
[27] U.S.-China Security Review Commission, Hearing on China's Budget Issues and the Role of the PLA in the Economy, Oral Testimony of James Mulvenon, 7 December 2001, 111.
[28] Ibid., 112.

witness noted that infrastructure and the supply of logistics equipment, and natural resources have been adversely affected, because a good deal of such PLA infrastructure resources is being monopolized for PLA commercial use.[29] The commercial elements of China's most profitable military conglomerates, such as Xinxing, Songliao, and Sanjiu, were not handed over to local governments, but were placed directly under the control of the State Economic and Trade Commission in Beijing.[30] Many PLA headquarters units, such as the General Armament Department (GAD), General Staff Department's Equipment Department (GSD/ED) and the General Logistics Department (GLD) still control private corporations, which use defense factories to produce weapons for the PLA and goods for export, including weapons

The military-run production units and the Chinese defense industrial complex remain heavily subsidized by the state. They are overstaffed, plagued with overcapacity, poor management, ineffective R&D, and a declining customer and product base. The Chinese have not been able to develop and manufacture military technologies in many key industries. Twenty years of reform efforts aimed at creating state-owned enterprises capable of providing technological support to Chinese military modernization have only met with limited success, notably in the very important sector of missile technology.[31] This has forced the military to buy from foreign suppliers and forced defense and PLA-run enterprises to actively pursue foreign technologies and capabilities.[32]

The PLA command is working to make up for these shortfalls. Military scientific research currently emphasizes smaller-scale products incorporating increasingly advanced levels of technology. By emphasizing the strengthening of key science and technology foundations, China is making progress on revitalizing its military production capability.[33] Currently, Chinese companies with deep military ties are producing state-of-the-art or near-state-of-the-art equipment and systems. In some sectors there is no longer a need for China to "steal" advanced technologies from the United States and other Western countries as was allegedly done in the 1980s, because they have achieved cutting edge technology.[34]

PLA-Run Enterprises in the United States

As part of the larger push by the PLA into civilian goods production, PLA-run companies have sought international markets for their products. Many PLA firms have long had representative offices in the United States, and goods made under subcontract or in joint-ventures are commonly sold in United States.

The Chinese trading offices or representative offices identified in the 1990s may no longer be active or may be operating under different names or in different locations. The Commission heard testimony from one researcher that he had not been able to locate any Chinese military enterprise's international subsidiary operating in the United States since 1997.[35] Efforts by the

[29] U.S.-China Security Review Commission, Hearing on Chinese Budget Issues and the Role of the PLA in the Economy, Oral Testimony of Andrew Marble, 7 December 2001, 165.

[30] U.S.-China Security Review Commission, Hearing on Chinese Budget Issues and the Role of the PLA in the Economy, Written Testimony of James Mulvenon, 7 December 2001, 15.

[31] U.S.-China Security Review Commission, Hearing on Chinese Budget Issues and the Role of the PLA in the Economy, Oral Testimony of Colonel John Corbett, 7 December 2001, 149.

[32] U.S.-China Security Review Commission, Hearing on Chinese Budget Issues and the Role of the PLA in the Economy, Oral Testimony of John Frankenstein, 7 December 2001, 144.

[33] Marble, Oral Testimony, 168.

[34] Mulvenon, Oral Testimony, 117.

[35] Ibid., 115.

Commission to obtain data from the Executive Branch on Chinese companies in the United States have not been successful. To date, the Executive Branch has not complied with legislation that requires an official report on Chinese companies operating in the United States. Specifically the legislation requires that the Secretary of Defense "shall make a determination of those persons operating ... in the United States ... that are Communist Chinese military companies and shall publish a list of those persons in the Federal Register."[36]

Trade Surplus and the Military Budget

The Commission is required under its Charter to examine "the extent to which the trade surplus of the People's Republic of China with the United States enhances the military budget of the People's Republic of China." It is difficult to document any direct co7nnection between China's bilateral trade surplus (over $80 billion in 2000 and in 2001) and the PRC military budget. A few preliminary observations may be useful in clarifying some of the considerations that need to be addressed.

China's economic reforms and integration into the world trading system have contributed significantly to its economic growth over the last two decades. The expansion of its export industries has boosted employment in some sectors, attracted vast sums of foreign investment, and made millions of people better off than before. This prosperity has also made more resources available for the government to spend for various purposes, including the military. In this broad sense, trade has not only helped make China richer, it has also helped make China stronger.

The accumulation of dollar reserves, which are needed for PLA modernization (specifically but not exclusively for foreign military purchases), is one important aspect of China's trade surplus with the United States.[37] These cumulative foreign exchange reserves have skyrocketed to about $212 billion at the end of 2001. While the hard currency reserves accumulated by China from its trade surplus with the United States may not directly track to the revenue side of the military budget, not least because the published budget is so unreliable, they have made it possible for China to buy foreign weapons, technology and other components for its modernization program, as detailed in Chapter 10 of this Report. Since the early 1990s, China has spent some $10 billion on purchases from Russia, with Israel's sales to the PLA trailing close behind.[38]

In a growing, export-driven economy with a positive trade balance, the accumulating foreign currency reserves can be utilized for different national objectives, including defense. China's huge foreign exchange reserves, now second only to Japan's, are the result not only of its bilateral trade surplus with the United States, but also of substantial inflows of world foreign direct and portfolio investment. World FDI into China was about $47 billion in 2001, of which nearly $5 billion was from the United States according to Chinese data. World equity investment into state-owned firms has been running at around $7.5 billion (except for the $20 billion spike in 2000) of which the U.S. share has been around a third. Clearly, the major source of China's foreign exchange reserve accumulation remains its annual trade surplus with the United States.

[36] Strom Thurmond National Defense Authorization Act for Fiscal Year 1999, Public Law 261, 105th Cong., 2nd sess. (17 October 1998), sec 1237.

[37] U.S.-China Security Review Commission, Hearing on Chinese Budget Issues and the Role of the PLA in the Economy, Oral Testimony of Charles Wolf, 7 December 2002, 72-4.

[38] Fisher, Written Testimony, Hearing on S.135, 1997.

The Commission heard testimony from one expert, who noted that 40 percent of China's foreign reserves were invested in U.S. Treasury securities, rather than in the Chinese economy. "It is silly for China to be a net capital exporter at this stage in its development," this observer concluded.[39] The benefits to China of the growing foreign exchange reserves may be other than economic.

National Security Implications

China's strong and steady economic growth has enabled it to implement an ambitious military modernization program that, if successful, will catapult China forward as the leading military power in East Asia and a rival to U.S. interests in the region. It has been able to allocate increased resources to its defense budget to achieve this status because of increased revenues generated from its unprecedented economic expansion, access to international capital markets, substantial financial inflows, including foreign direct investment, and accumulated foreign exchange holdings, most of which have been derived from its very favorable trade balance with the United States.

The implications of China's military modernization for the United States and regional states are enormous. We need to know more about China's national budget and its defense budget because miscomprehension, whether due to underestimation or overestimation of the size and purpose of China's defense budget, could be dangerous and lead to miscalculation. Although China's defense budget is small in the aggregate when compared to that of the United States, China allocates significant funds to its missile buildup opposite Taiwan, to preparing for possible conflict in the Taiwan Strait, to modernizing its nuclear-capable ballistic missiles, and to developing capabilities for conducting electronic information and other forms of asymmetrical warfare against the United States and other technologically superior forces.

Given the disparities in the PRC and U.S. military budgets, the question remains: does China's growing military budget reflect a hostile buildup inimical to U.S. and allied interests or is it merely a normal upgrading? The decade of the 1990s was generally peaceful for China, yet its defense spending rose sharply. Some observers conclude that the "PLA is undertaking a complex and long-needed process of modernization", not a hostile buildup.[40] The Commission heard testimony that the pace of this military modernization may be "moderate" and "deliberate". According to that view for China to undertake a hostile buildup, the pace of military modernization would have to be "rapid" and "massive", and the military expenditure would have to increase to hundreds of billions per year.[41,42]

Others disagree and cite China's military spending as one of fastest expanding defense budgets in the world. According to the DoD, it is the "second largest defense spender in the

---

[39] U.S.-China Security Review Commission, Hearing on China's Capital Requirements and U.S. Capital Markets, Oral Testimony of James A. Dorn, 06 December 2001, 322.

[40] U.S.-China Security Review Commission, Hearing on Chinese Budget Issues and the Role of the PLA in the Economy, Oral Testimony of David Shambaugh, 7 December 2001, 194-205.

[41] Colton, Written Testimony, 4.

[42] During the Commission's 7 December 2001 hearing on the Chinese budget an exchange between the Commission and Dr. Shambaugh (194-205) about what constitutes a military build-up prompted this response from Dr. Shambaugh: "Well, it would be, in terms of external purchases of arms, in the range of probably five to seven times what they are buying now per year from Russia. It would be probably a quadrupling of the internal allocation for procurement of equipment and indeed, investment into R & D. It would be procurement particularly of ships to acquire "blue water" capability, a submarine force as well, and in other categories of conventional equipment."

world...and the largest defense spender in Asia."[43] They further point to the increasing allocation of resources devoted to military programs and missions which affect U.S. interests in Asia, prominent among which are to threaten and intimidate Taiwan and project China's growing power.

The latest DoD estimate of China's 2002 actual defense spending at about $65 billion is clearly above a "moderate" level while not yet explosive in size. The allocation of just a moderate part of the $65 billion to a narrow objective could result in the deployment of large forces and other assets on specific targets. That could challenge U.S. interests in the region. It is not simply the issue of how much China is spending, but what China is buying, what it plans to achieve, and how doing so affects its economic growth rate.

RECOMMENDATIONS

- The Commission recommends that the Congress direct the Congressional Budget Office and the Congressional Research Service to enhance monitoring of PRC central government's fiscal and financial activities. Particular emphasis should be placed on China's military budget.

- The Commission recommends that the Congress request the Intelligence Community to conduct an annual "output analysis" of China's defense budget to assess its impact on and relation to China's military capabilities.

[43] Defense Department, Annual Report on Military Power of China, 28

Chapter 8

INTEGRATION OF CHINA AND ASIA: ECONOMIC REFORM AND POLICY SHIFTS

Eddie Chi-Man Hui

ABSTRACT

China looks set to change much in the next five years as in the past ordinary 20. The first two decades of its reform have in essence been catch-up growth, gains that came from disbanding the agricultural communes and from allowing capital and particular labor to be poured into low-end manufacturing and processing, a lot of it for export. The government did not really have to do anything to foster growth. Recently, the norm of double-digit growth rates has seemed disappearing. According to head of the World Bank's mission in China, growth is not only lower these days, but its "labor intensity" has also slowed. Now, China has reportedly committed itself wholeheartedly, irrevocably and unambiguously to creating a market economy at home, tied to the world at large. Particularly in the next five years, China is bound to reshape in a new, different dimension integrating itself more with other economies, particularly in the Asian Pacific region.

This chapter looks at the most recent economic reforms towards marketization in China and the policy shifts necessary for its further integrating into the Asia Pacific economy from the viewpoint of economics and politics. It specifically discusses the salient aspects associated with these reforms and policy shifts: such as economic co-operation, reform of its financial sector and state enterprises and the regional imbalances. The first part of this chapter addresses a number of key questions: such as the way China should improve its financial structure and state-owned enterprises that depress competition, cause corruption and increasingly burden the government financially. The second part looks at urban land reform in China, with particular reference to Shanghai, the most vibrant and cosmopolitan city in the Mainland. It is believed that a more liberalized market regime would be conducive to the pace of economic growth in China. And such a regime is an effective way to integrate the Chinese mainland into the global economy. While this chapter focuses on China, it should be of interest to policy-makers and academics worldwide.

Keywords: Economic cooperation, reform of financial sector and state enterprises, regional imbalances, urban land reform, China

1. Introduction

China's communist regime remained closed to the outside world after it took power in 1949. Nevertheless, its early years saw solid economic achievement as it consolidated its rule over the previously divided country. The Great Leap Forward from 1958 forced agricultural production into a system of communes that led to a collapse in output. Up to twenty million starved over the Cultural Revolution was launched in 1966. The Cultural Revolution died with Mao Zedong in 1976. By 1978 Deng Xiaoping had consolidated this power and the process of economic reform began, over ten years before the collapse of the Soviet Union and the other command economies of Eastern Europe.

China has a population of approximately 1.3 billion people, making it the most populous country in the world. It is also the second largest, after Canada, with a land area the size of the whole Europe. It makes up to one-fifth of the world's population, but they live on only one-fifteenth of the world's land. In fact, because of a large part of its land is inaccessible and inhospitable, the density in the main population center is much higher than those figures suggest. Two-thirds of mainland Chinese live in the fertile eastern fifth of the country. Estimates of GDP per capita range from exchange rate based calculations of US$470 to purchasing power parity calculations ranging from US$1,000-US$2,000. Basic levels of education are high and there is a workforce of nearly 600 million of which over 60% work in agriculture. Politically, China is a one party state, though there are free elections with more than one candidates at the township level and district congresses.

China looks set to change much in the next five years as in the past ordinary 20. The first two decades of its reform have in essence been catch-up growth, gains that came from disbanding the agricultural communes and from allowing capital and particular labor to be poured into low-end manufacturing and processing, a lot of it for export. Recently, the norm of double-digit growth rates has seemed disappearing. According to head of the World Bank's mission in China, growth is not only lower these days, but its "labor intensity" has also slowed. Now, China has reportedly committed itself wholeheartedly, irrevocably and unambiguously to creating a market economy at home, tied to the world at large. Particularly in the next five years, China is bound to reshape in a new, different dimension integrating itself more with other economies, particularly in the Asian Pacific region.

2. Economic Reforms and Policy Shift towards Marketization

The first two decades of reform have in essence been catch-up growth towards "marketization" with substantial policy shift. The 1978 reforms began with the introduction of the "responsibility system" in agriculture and small-scale rural industries. This allows people to keep surplus output for personal gain. The system was extended to some industrial sectors from 1984. Throughout the period, price controls have been gradually lifted so that now most prices are market determined.

Table 1: Major Economic Indicators

	1999		Jan-Sept 2000	
	Value	Growth (%)	Value	Growth (%)
Area (sq km, million)	9.6		9.6	
Population (million)	1,259.1	0.9	1,259.1	0.9
Gross domestic product (yuan billion)	8,205.4	7.1*	6,212.4	8.2*
Added-value (yuan billion)				
primary industry	1,421.2	2.8*	na	2.2*
secondary industry	4,080.6	8.1*	na	9.8*
tertiary industry	2,703.6	7.5*	na	8.1*
Urban per capita income (yuan)	5,854.0	9.3*	4,719.0	8.4*
Rural per capita income (yuan)	2,210.0	3.8*	1,500.0	2.5*
Fixed-assets investment (yuan billion)	2,987.6	5.2	1,347.0	12.9
Added-value of industrial output	3,535.7	8.5	1,706.1	11.6
Consumer goods retail sales (yuan billion)	3,113.5	6.8	2,433.6	9.9
Consumer price index (%)		-1.4		0.2
Urban unemployment (%)	3.1		3.1	
Exports (US$ billion)	194.9	6.1	182.3	33.1
by FIEs (US$ billion)	88.6	9.5	74.6#	36.8
Imports (US$ billion)	165.8	18.2	163.1	38.7
by FIEs (US$ billion)	85.9	11.9	74.4#	40.9
Trade surplus (US$ billion)	29.1	-30.6	19.2	-1.0

Figure for January-August
* Real growth
Sources: The State Statistical Bureau, the Ministry of Foreign Trade and Economic Co-operation (MOFTEC), the General Administration of Customs, and Hong Kong Trade Development Council

The government did not really have to do much to foster growth, other than to keep out of the way. Double-digit growth rates were the norm, and fast growth created new jobs for workers made redundant by inefficient state-owned enterprises, migrants from the countryside to urban areas, and young people looking for their first job. Although state owned enterprises still dominate industrial output, a large number of collectively owned and private sector businesses have mushroomed and are now becoming more significant, accounting for nearly half industrial output overall.

The first special economic zones were created in 1980 in selected coastal states and later extended to several coastal cities. These areas have experienced very far more rapid reform; and very rapid growth with substantial foreign direct investment. There has been total foreign direct investment actually received of nearly US$96 billion, some 30% of all direct investment into developing countries. A further US$2000 billion has been contracted.

Most recently, the mainland's entry into the World Trade Organization (WTO) will be one of the most important events in the communist era. Beijing has concluded bilateral agreements with all but one of the 137 members of the WTO - Mexico. The two most important deals it signed were with the United States in November and the European Union in May.

WTO entry will constitute the biggest milestone since Deng Xiaoping abandoned Maoism in 1978 and launched the open-door and reform policies. Under the two deals, Beijing has committed itself to major liberalization, including cuts in tariffs, an end to the ban on foreign firms doing trading and distribution, opening its telecommunications service sector for the first time and giving foreign banks better access to the local currency market.

On September 19, 2000, the US Senate approved the agreement by giving the mainland permanent normal trade relations, thus ensuring US firms will enjoy the benefits of the mainland's WTO membership along with the companies of its other trading partners. Democratic Daniel Patrick Moynihan of New York called it one of the most important votes in the Senate since World War II. WTO entry will mark the end of a process that began in 1986 when the mainland applied for membership of the organization's predecessor, the General Agreement on Tariffs and Trade. Agreement has taken so long because of the wide gap between international trading practices and the reality of the Chinese economy - in a transition between Maoist planning and the market.

They have been the strongest supporters of the nation's WTO entry, seeing it as a way to bring business practices in line with those abroad, to give them better access to the market and make the legal and regulatory system more fair and transparent. Throughout the 1990s, the mainland ranked as the country attracting the most foreign investment of any developing nation. But only about 25 per cent of those investors have made profits. They complain about illegal taxes and levies, lack of regulatory transparency, corruption, counterfeiting and a playing field that is tilted in favor of Chinese companies.

In November 2000, Mr. Zhu said he expected "economic growth at a rate of 8 per cent for 2001, with the help of accession to WTO in March 2002". Economists believe that, while the mainland will benefit greatly in the long term from WTO membership, it will be a painful transition. One newspaper, the Beijing Youth Daily, estimated membership will result in nearly 10 million farmers losing their livelihood and a net loss of 1.54 million jobs. The following will discuss in turn significant issues in China: i.e. economic cooperation; reform of its financial sector and state enterprises; and balance between rural and urban regions.

2.1 Economic Cooperation

Beijing's policy toward regional economic cooperation has not been explicitly pronounced in the form of policy statements. Yet, through an examination of China's domestic and international interests, and through reports in publications which act as government mouthpieces, it is possible to speculate about the gains the Chinese expect to receive from their membership in APEC, and possibly from greater cooperation with the East Asian economies.

China has been diversifying its economic interests and to establish market niches in the dynamic Asian economies (DAEs). This partially accounts for the improved economic relations between China and Taiwan, and South Korea. On the other hand, U.S. direct investment in China covers a wide range of manufacturing sectors, several large hotel projects, and a heavy concentration in offshore oil and gas development in the South China Sea. U.S. companies have entered agreements establishing more than 20,000 equity joint ventures, contractual joint ventures, and wholly foreign-owned enterprises in China. More than 100 U.S.-based multinationals have projects, some with multiple investments. The 1999 trade deficit of $68.7 billion with China was the United States' second-largest.

Table 2: China's Exports to 10 Major Trading Partners (US$ 100 million)

Country/region	Exports Oct 2000	Exports Jan-Oct 2000	Change (%) Oct 2000	Change (%) Jan-Oct 2000
US	49.2	433.7	21.5	27.2
Hong Kong	37.6	365.0	8.7	23.9
Japan	39.6	337.3	30.7	32.4
EU	30.7	314.9	16.3	31.6
Asean	17.7	141.7	53.9	45.3
Korea	11.4	93.1	64.0	54.2
Taiwan	4.6	41.7	23.7	31.6
Australia	3.4	28.5	31.8	32.1
Canada	2.6	26.5	15.6	35.8
Russia	2.6	17.5	66.7	68.7

Sources: The State Statistical Bureau, the Ministry of Foreign Trade and Economic Co-operation (MOFTEC), the General Administration of Customs, and Hong Kong Trade Development Council

China's vision for the structure of APEC has its limits. As a *Beijing Review* article asserts, "the actual conditions that exist in the Asia and Pacific region will strongly impede, in the remaining years of this century, the formation of contract-like economic cooperation that is being practiced in Western Europe and North America." (Beijing Review 1989) Thus, Beijing's model of economic cooperation eschews any notion of market sharing in the form of a trade union. Similarly, the supranational characteristics of an economic community are anathema to the Chinese, who consistently find themselves defending their domestic policies against the interference of others. Yet, because they are faced with greater protectionism in the European Community and the United States, the Chinese are more willing to harmonize economic and trade policies provided that the sovereignty of each individual government is not violated (Shen 1987).

Lardy (1990) attributes this apparent desire to be instrumental in shaping the Asia-Pacific economic environment, while remaining ambivalent toward institutionalizing the economic cooperation process further, to several factors. First, China fears that Japan will become the dominant power in any regional cooperation mechanism. While the Japanese represent a significant threat, the Chinese value Japan's role as an important economic leader. By forming a strictly economic forum for economic cooperation, Beijing hopes to reap the benefits of closer economic relations while avoiding any threat to its security and sovereignty.

Second, China has not abandoned the North-South framework of international relations, and believes that the North still has obligations to the South. Economic assistance is welcomed and the structure of regional cooperation should take on a form which can integrate formal equality among its members with the extension of aid and mixed credits specially from Japan and its developing economies in the South.

Finally, reforms have not progressed to the extent that the Chinese economy can be more fully opened to the regional market. China remains a socialist, semi-planned economy in which many components of trade are under the influence of the central and provincial governments. Until reforms of China's trade regime and other relevant domestic economic reforms such as loosening controls over prices proceed further, the country's trade regime will continue to differ significantly from those of regional partners, making formal cooperation impossible.

The dynamics of Beijing-Taipei relations is a factor which will inevitably influence APEC and other regional cooperation proceedings. Given that direct shipping, aviation, and communications between the two sides of the straits are still by and large restricted, it would be unrealistic to envision comprehensive economic integration within the region. Nevertheless, the mere fact that China, Taiwan, and Hong Kong all became members of APEC at the same time at the Seoul summit in November 1991 is indicative of the direction of relations between the two former adversaries, and how they relate to the region.

Although direct trade and investment in China by Taiwan residents have technically been illegal—and thus official statistics are difficult to come by—economic relations between the two have become significantly extensive. China's two-way trade with Hong Kong—the conduit for Taiwan-China trade—grew significantly in the 1980s, from US$9.4 billion in 1984 to just over US$44.2 billion in 1990; to some US$50 million in 2000. Similarly, Taiwan's total trade with Hong Kong grew from US $3 billion to more than US$12 billion during the same period. Growth in consumer spending among Hong Kong's 6 million people has certainly not accounted for this growth.

Taiwan investment in China has been funnelled through Hong Kong toward Guangdong and Fujian provinces in particular, where the effects have been seen in double-digit growth rates since 1987. In April 1991, when it became legal, more than 2,500 Taiwan companies registered their investments in China, with a declared total value exceeding US$660 million (Lardy 1990). Taiwan has also become important to other economies in the region. This has especially been the case since the latter half of the 1980s, when various factors— including rising wage rates, a depreciating NT dollar, and large foreign exchange reserves—encouraged the outflow of capital directed mostly toward China and Southeast Asia.

2.2 Reform of its Financial Sector and State Enterprises

In the course of giving enterprises autonomy and reforming the property-right system, the essential question is how to ensure that enterprises can effectively raise and use funds. The foundation for developing a market economy is a developed market system, and the financial market is the core. First of all, resources must flow freely in competitive use, and this will inevitably promote investment by the people, thus necessitating the formation of an effective shift from savings to investment. In this way, people's savings resulting from their increased income can be effectively accumulated to increase savings deposits.

At the end of the Cultural Revaluation there were no financial markets, bonds or securities in China. By 1995 there were active bond and securities markets, gradually being brought within a legal and regulatory structure. Commodities markets are now well developed, with fourteen commodities futures exchanges. An October 1995 Insurance Law sets out the framework for a further opening up of the insurance market, already growing very rapidly with a number of foreign participants. Stock trading has emerged since the 1980s; and the first officially approved were opened in Shanghai and Shenzhen in the 1990s.

The banking sector is also under reform. Until 1979 there were, in conventional terms, no banks. Now the four large state banks have been asked to become fully commercial with their policy lending obligations relieved. However, they did suffer from a large chunk of bad loans to state owned enterprises. The central government is now taking the legacy of socialism—1.2 tillion yuan of bad loans—off the state banks' books. In return, the banks are under intense moral and financial pressure to behave more commercially. New commercial banks have been started, fostering a more competitive environment. Some 250 foreign banks are operating in China but they are restricted only to non-Renminbi transactions.

From the government's point of view, the cost of state-owned enterprises is unsustainable. That lesson was leant after the economic boom of the early 1990s--- an indiscriminate lunge for economic growth urged on China by its ancient Deng Xiaopng. There are four types of enterprises in China: state-owned enterprises, collectively owned enterprises, privately owned enterprises, and other enterprises. In 1991 there were about 105,000 state-owned enterprises, while the total number of enterprises came to 8.1 million. The output value of the state-owned enterprises in 1991 was as much as 52.9 per cent of total industrial output. The success of the Chinese economy depends to a great extent on the efficiency of these enterprises. The government has been trying hard to improve efficiency, but the industrial sector seems much lower than the agricultural sector to respond to the government call for reform (Soon, 1999).

There appear to be several major obstacles to improving the performance of state-owned enterprises. First is the lack of enterprise independence from administrative entities. Second is the burden of out-of-business responsibilities borne by these enterprises; and thirdly distorted price structures. Stated owned enterprises are used to guarantee lifetime employment to their employees. Enterprises have tried to institute changes by creating a contract system of employment, restructuring enterprise organization, establishment of an efficient index for wage rates. Despite all those efforts, little progress has been made. The enterprises remain to count on government, with some even more than before.

The distorted price structure exacerbated the problem of reliance of the state-owned enterprises. Such distortion lies in: (1) the relatively lower prices of energy, agricultural products, and transportation as compared to industrial products; (2) one same commodity carrying more than one prices; and (3) many prices used by enterprises are administrated prices, and not market-determined ones.

The state has launched, amongst other things, some measures to address this and cut off the reliance of the enterprises. As early as 1984, the government stipulated that (1) enterprises are authorized to produce and sell in excess of planned amounts; (2) enterprises can negotiate with their buyers on goods within 20 per cent of the stipulated prices, and (3) enterprises are allowed to freely dispose of retained profits as production funds, new output development funds, and welfare funds. In April 1988 the government enacted the Law on State-owned Enterprises, which further broadened their autonomy. In 1992 the Regulations of Conversion of Management Mechanism of State-Owned Enterprises was promulgated. The regulations stipulated the rights of enterprises to hold possession of and use government properties and to dispose of the products thereof. They further set out ways in which production plans were to be settled, price determined, employment of personnel managed, and the social cost assigned. This shows that China has made effort to clear the way for greater efficiency in state-owned enterprises. At the same time, however, one cannot be sure that these policies, ingenious and innovative as they are, are adequate to unleash the kind of entrepreneurial ability inherent in the Chinese people. This is because prices, profits, sales and markets are still heavily determined by the state administratively.

2.3 Balance between Rural and Urban Regions

China is physically very big. Mao Zedong once said that China was like "another United Nations". At present it has 31 provinces, including four municipalities with province-level status and the five "autonomous regions", which (especially in case of Xinjiang and Tibet) are anything but autonomous. In addition, there are two "special administrative regions": i.e. Hong Kong and Macau, which really are special and autonomous. However, regional equalities, particularly in terms of rural and urban sectors, have become very serious, and Beijing's leadership is beginning to wake up to them. Equally worrying is the wealth gap between city and countryside.

Two thirds of China's 1.3 billion people still live in the countryside—has almost reached its natural limits, given China's severe shortage of water. In cities, 90% of households have washing machines and colour televisions. On farms, the most widely owned consumer durable, found in 70% of all households, is the sewing machine. For example, Shanghai's GNP per head in 1998 was at more than US$1,000, compared with Tibet at only US$250-500 (China Statistical Yearbook). Meanwhile, there are huge differences in wealth within the same locality, along with dire cases of poverty, even in the "prosperous" coastal cites. The central government has by and large kept control of the reform process and the country as a whole. Interestingly, while devolving responsibility for economic growth to local level, it still centralizes the collection of tax revenues and, more importantly, the rationing of credit to the state sector. It is this way that the State addresses the imbalances between rural and urban sectors in different regions on the Mainland. More recently, the Chinese authorities have planned to develop China's western provinces, on the ground of economics and rural/urban imbalances. Their campaign is to develop the vast but poor western regions of China promises to catch up with the eastern provinces in the country over the coming years.

By the government's definition, the "west" consists of the provinces of Sichuan, Gansu, Guizhou, Yunnan, Qinghai and Shaanxi, the municipality of Chongqing, the tiny, "autonomous" province of Ningxia and the two vast ones of Tibet and Xinjiang. Together, they account for just one-quarter of China's population of 1.3 billion, but more than half its land. Prosperity has passed by great swathes of this region. Well over half of China's poorest 80m live in the west. A farmer there earns about a third of a coastal farmer's average of 3,600 yuan ($435) a year. This half of the country has attracted less than 5% of the foreign investment committed to China in the past two decades.

The case for bringing more prosperity to the west is a strong one, but this campaign was cranked up officially only after 2001. That is testimony to the huge political and economic influence that China's coastal provinces have long brought to bear. With little sign that eastern prosperity has trickled west, it is hard these days for China's leaders to ignore western backwardness.

However, the government's "go west" campaign is not without problems. First, it is not clear how much money the central government is able to spend. Some $13 billion is said to have been made available during 2000. And it is suggested that equal, or larger, sums will be available for the years to come. Yet, that seems to be difficult, if not impossible. The central government collects revenues equivalent to a mere 14% of GDP, which greatly constrains its policy options for the campaign. Therefore, a large part of the central government's efforts lies in better-off provinces, and state banks, to help with its western plans. Foreign investors and even banks are now being courted. Second, there is curiously little emphasis on one key issue, i.e. the backwardness of the western region. More particularly, the region is dominated by the state in the economy. Nowhere is this clearer than, for example, in Xinjiang, where four-fifths of the province's industrial assets remain in state hands. If the state enterprises lose money, the central government makes up. Third, the "go west" campaign has little on offer in alleviation of poverty and imbalances between rural and urban sectors. It is been argued that the government's endeavours currently lie in gigantic, and correspondingly expensive, infrastructure projects. To address the imbalances, however, it needs to spend more money on schools and health; and local roads that tie isolated communities to the broader market.

2.4 Conclusion

The Chinese Communist Party has taken an economic path with great success. The economic reform, which took precedence over political liberalization, was hailed by some, if not all, as a more rewarding way to transform state socialism. The reform without doubt was essentially associated with urban land reform in many cities in China. This urban land reform has much to do with the Mainland's land use and property rights; land administration and land leasing system. All these have repercussion effects on the way the real estate market was transformed. That made the market so much different from what it was. The next part will look at the urban land reform in China, with particular reference to Shanghai.

3. Urban Land Reform in China: Shanghai

The aim of this part is to examine urban land reform and the real estate market in China, with particular reference to Shanghai, the most dynamic leading commercial city in China. We first introduce the development of the city, which grasps the essence of the reform as a dramatic change of economic structure brought about by a highly autonomous government. At the core of the study, because of its intrinsic importance, is Chinese land use rights reform, in which land administration and land leasing system will be brought into picture. It deals with China's property market in three levels: the State, real estate development companies, the medium for land use right transactions, i.e. the secondary market. Second, the part examines the transformation of real estate market in Shanghai as a case study. As a result of the land use rights reform, there have been tremendous changes since 1985, when the first land use rights reforms started were introduced, in the distribution of land use rights and real estate as a tradable commodity. Finally, we will discuss Shanghai's plan for a comprehensive housing reform. That comprises a distinctive feature with housing provident funds that made the city notably different from other housing reform models in China.

3.1 Background

Shanghai is a Chinese coastal city directly administered by the central government in Beijing. Located at the mouth of the Yangtze River Delta and situated on the eastern coast of Asia facing the Pacific Ocean, Shanghai is China's principal gateway to the world. To the north of the city is the mouth of the Yangtze River, to the east the East China Sea, to the south Hangzhou Bay and to the west Jiangsu and Zhejiang provinces.

The total area of Shanghai province is 6340.5 sq km, with the urban land area covering 792.53 sq km (12.5%) and the rural land area comprising 5547.97 sq km (87.5%). The population of Shanghai at the end of 1994 reached 12.95 million with 9.48 million population living in the urban area and 3.47 million of the population residing in the rural area. The population density of Shanghai is currently 2042 per sq km, the highest amongst all provinces in China. Shanghai, today, arguably is the country's most modern city. The urban area is founded on the west bank of the Huangpu River and is called Puxi (west of the river). On the other side of the river the Pudong New Development Zone, an area of 522 sq km, was established in April 1990 by the authority to speed up the rate of urbanization of Shanghai.

In the mid-19th century, Shanghai was opened as one of the treaty ports under the Treaty of Nanjing (1842) and subsequently an influx of foreign nationalities established the international settlement on the banks of the Huangpu River. The city's orientation to the sea and its excellent accessibility to the Yangtze River resulted in an expansion of trading and shipping activities. After the city opened as a treaty port, Shanghai emerged as China's largest economic centre and its urban functions became increasingly diversified to include banking and finance, commerce and manufacturing. By 1947 there were 14 foreign banks, 128 government-owned and privately owned banks, 13 trust companies and 70 money exchangers in the city. The west bank of the Huangpu River developed as a financial and commercial centre with a strong representation of foreign banks and trading companies. The present European-style buildings in the Bund area provide reminders of the western influences and the past prosperity of Shanghai.

In 1949, the establishment of People's Republic of China led to the withdrawal of foreign capital, foreign companies closed their businesses in Shanghai and economic development began to slow down. Light and heavy industries became the dominant industries as the centrally planned economy placed greater stress on production rather than on services.

Between 1949 and 1982, investment in urban infrastructure and housing in Shanghai accounted for only 12.2% of total new fixed capital formation. However in 1984, together with thirteen other coastal cities, Shanghai was designated by the central government as an open port city to serve as a recipient point for capital investment and technology transfer from developed nations. As an economic locomotive, Shanghai needs more infrastructure. It was anticipated that if the economic development of Shanghai succeeded, the economic reforms would trickle down through the entire Yangzi Delta and eventually spread to the lower and middle Yangzi Basin. At that time, the Shanghai government established Hongqiao, Caohejing and Minhang development zones to attract foreign investment into the financial and industrial sectors and invest in the city again (Byrd, 1991; Ishihara, 1993; Seldon, 1993; Solinger, 1993).

Until the late 1980s foreign investment and economic development focused on Puxi but in April 1990 the Shanghai government announced Pudong as a new development zone in order to accelerate its infrastructure development and economic growth. The newly developed area is similar to the size of the urban area in Puxi and has become the focus of China's reform and open policy in the 1990s. Shanghai has been involved in a building frenzy aimed at transforming the farmland into a bustling manufacturing, finance and trade metropolis to help link the mainland with the world. The cost between 1990 and 1995 – for infrastructure construction alone – amounted to US$3.0 billion. The objective is to transform Pudong into a 522-sq km district of office towers, high-technology factories and port facilities. As part of second-phase development, US$12 billion is slated to be funnelled into infrastructure in the five-year period ending in 2000.

On the other hand, the government helped guarantee success of the project's start-up by channeling foreign investment to the new district through the use of preferential income tax and other investment policies. With the support of the Shanghai government, Pudong has considerable growth potential and by the beginning of the twenty-first century is expected to be the largest commercial centre in China, an open and multi-purpose free trade zone, the most advanced export processing zone in China, and a modern agricultural production base. Furthermore GNP is expected to reach RMB 50 billion constituting 22.5% of Shanghai's total GNP. At the end of May 1998, Podong had 5,150 foreign-funded projects, involving investment of US$16 billion. The district has attracted some of the world's leading manufacturers, such as Intel, which has invested heavily in a facility to manufacture test flash chips, and NEC, which has formed a US$700 million joint venture with Shanghai Huahong Microelectronics to establish the mainland's largest manufacturer of integrated circuits.

During the first half of 1994 Shanghai exported US$3.7 billion worth of products, an increase of 28.5% and its total foreign trade volume reached 4.1 billion US dollars, an increase of 24.5%. Six years of double-digit growth has expanded its GNP to 336 billion yuan, 4.6 times the size 20 years ago. This rapid growth has enabled the incomes as well as savings of both urban and rural residents to increase quickly with living standards having improved significantly. The GNP per capita in Shanghai was 3.4 time above the Chinese average in 1993 with growth rates of 15%, 24% and 42% in real term in 1991, 1992 and 1993 respectively. The city handles nearly 19% of the mainland's sea cargo, 18% of foreign trade, while accounting for 12% of national revenue collected and 8% of fixed-asset investment. It has been planned for the city area to be enlarged by 100% to 2000 sq km by year 2000.

3.2 The Land Use Rights Reforms

Land Administration

China's property market comprises three levels. At a primary level the market operates between the State or the Municipal Land Administration and real estate development companies with the former granting virgin land to the latter for a definite period subject to payment of a premium (land use conveyance fee). The ownership and the land use rights of the same piece of land then become separated: the state holds the land ownership but the right to use can be transferred. The land administration bureau of the local government negotiates the sale of the land use lease, with the contract stating the land use rights and terms of the lease. Typically, these leases are of 70 years duration for residential land uses and 50 years for non-residential uses. The transfer of land use right can be adopted by three methods: private negotiation, tender and auction. Upon expiration of the term, the land use rights and the superstructure thereon reverts to the State without compensation unless there is a renewal of the grant contract (which is normally assumed to be the case).

The secondary level concerns real estate development companies and property/land users. The development companies, after acquiring the land use rights from the State, have to develop the basic infrastructure and facilities, in accordance with the contract terms. Usually, this is referred to by the government as "the seven utility connections and one formation". In the other words, development companies normally have to be responsible for the connection of public utilities such as gas, water and telephone lines. After satisfying all the obligations, these companies can, if they so wish transfer the remaining period of the land use rights to property/land users. The State has the right to withdraw the grant if the companies fail to comply with those regulations stated in the contract of assignment.

The tertiary level is the medium provided for the transactions of land use right amongst the property/land users, that is the secondary market. The types of transfer may be assignment, subletting, mortgage, inheritance or grant as gift. The first two types are the most common modes. However, this market still remains in the primitive stage in China. The details of the system are illustrated in Table 3

Table 3: The Basic Structure of the Property Market

	First level	Second level	Third level
Market player	State or Municipal Land Administration Authorities	Local real estate development companies	Foreign investors and other local land users
Type of market	Monopoly	Competitive	Open with limits
Scope of business	Master planning, land use design, resumption of land, relocation and demolition	Comprehensive development of large tracts of land (virgin land).	Laterally transferring the interest of land with period
Mode of business	Disposal of land by auctions, tenders or negotiation with compensation (progressively adopting the policy of transfer of land use right for Value	Assigning or letting the developed land (with or without buildings on ground)	Further assignment or sublet the developed land(with or without building on ground)
Land price	Monopolistic price (land rent)	Fair price	Remaining value of the fair price

Source: Shanghai Land, 1993, vol.3

Land Leasing System

Interest in the real estate market in China from both a local and an international investor perspective occurred after the launch of the urban land use rights reforms in 1988 (Walker, 1991; Walker and Li, 1994; Linge, 1997). In April 1987, the State Council proposed a new policy for the transferability of land use rights in the free market, and the Special Economic Zones Office, under the State Council, was delegated to test the idea in the four open cities of Tianjin, Shanghai, Guangzhou and Shenzhen.

On 12th April 1988, Clause 4 of Article 10 of the Constitution of the People's Republic of China was amended as:"... *No organization or individual may appropriate, buy, sell, or unlawfully transfer land in other ways. The right of land use can be transferred in accordance with the law*...This makes possible the operation of a real estate market mechanism similar to that of Hong Kong. Ownership in land still belongs to the State (on behalf of the people), and is not contrary to the basis of the socialist doctrines. Moreover, in December 1988, the Land Management Law of the People's Republic of China was also amended so that in Chapter Two of the Ordinance the original statement of "No enterprises or individuals can possess, sale or rent or by any illegal means transfer land" now reads "No enterprises or individuals can possess, sell or by any illegal means transfer land".

As such, the basis for the conveyance of land (or land use rights to be exact) in China's legal as well as the ideological framework is the concept of "land lease". It should therefore be emphasized that the reform programme of the real estate market in China is basically to release the leasehold value of real estate, not the real freehold ownership (Li, 1996a; 1996b).

Under the Provisional Law on the Conveyance, Grant and Transfer of the Land Use Rights over the State-Owned Land in Cities and Towns 1990" which was enacted by the State Council's Order 55 decreed on 19th May, 1990, land use rights (LURs) are separated from the ownership right and become tradable in the market by private treaty; negotiation and auction. LURs are rights with time limits for different kinds of land use (normally residential use for 70 years and commercial use for 50 years etc., but it varies according to local government policies). Moreover, LURs are capable of being mortgaged and transferred.

The land-leasing system started in the city of Shenzhen and was subsequently extended to other coastal cities. The number of property companies increased from 12,400 at the end of 1992 to 33,482 in 1995. While the percentage of real estate companies suffering from losses increased from 33% in 1994 to 52% in 1995, the real-estate enterprises in Shanghai still gained profits. On average, the profits of the real-estate companies in Shanghai reached RMB 4.1 billion in 1995. However, it appears that most of the real-estate companies lack an appreciation of risk. The state-owned company is unaware of risks, simply because the managers are not accountable for losses. On the other hand, the property right of land is still unclear. While the ownership of land belongs to the state, practically it is the local government (i.e. government of cities, districts, towns, villages) that are responsible for the transfer of the right of land use.

3.3 Transformation of Real Estate Market in Shanghai

Distribution of Land Use Rights

The role of Shanghai in the process of land use rights reforms started much earlier than the rest of China in December 1985 when a pilot study on land valuation was carried out by the Shanghai Urban Economics Society (1987) sponsored by the Shanghai City Planned Economy Research Institute (Li, 1995 and Tse 2000). The research examined 1,161 samples from the major commercial land use zones (including general retailing, hardware, cigarette and candies, clothing, trading etc.) from which the average 3-yearly profit between 1982-1984 was obtained. Assuming a 12% average profit, the differential profit was regressed as:

$Rn = 254.68 * (1+0.435)n - 254.68$; where n = the grade of the land zone.

The study area was then divided into seven zones with grade R7 zone being the most profitable location. From the above, the differential land profit of each zone was derived:

R7=2936.6 RMB per sq m
R6=1969.2 RMB per sq m
R5=1295.0 RMB per sq m
R4= 825.3 RMB per sq m
R3= 497.7 RMB per sq m

R2=269.8 RMB per sq m
R1=110.8 RMB per sq m

This study became the milestone for subsequent research on valuation of land in China. Despite early interest in land use rights reform it was not until 1992 when the late leader Deng Xiaoping re-emphasized the need for reform that Shanghai became a focus for land development. Prior to this urban land use was a mis-match (Figure 1). Furthermore, after 1992 land sale was to become a popular economic activity by local government.

Figure 1: Distribution of Major Land Use Types and Population Density in the Urban Districts in Shanghai in 1992

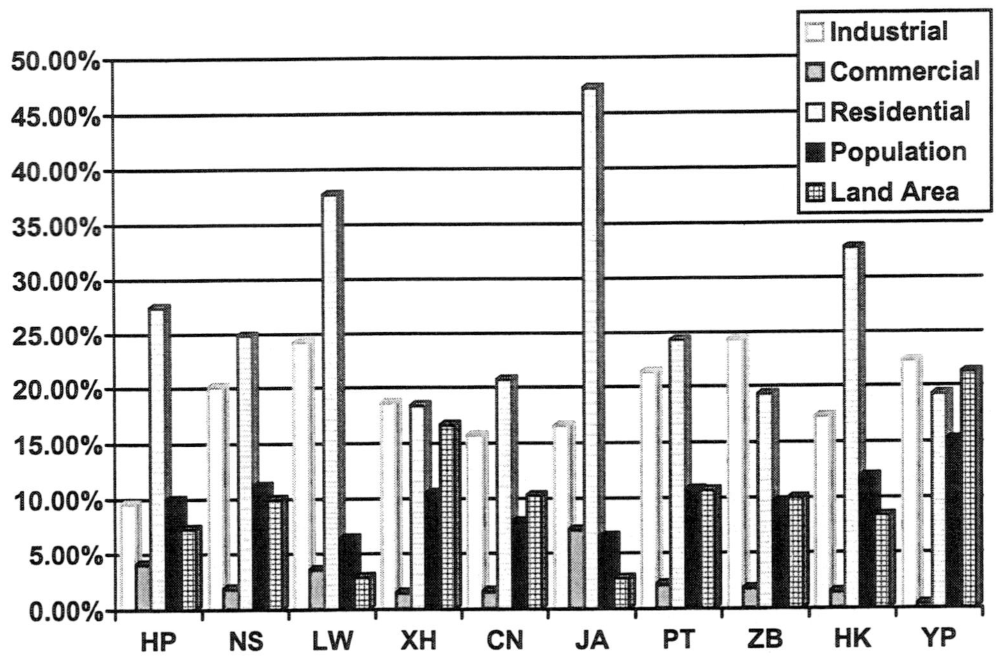

Source: Shanghai State Land Administration Bureau and Statistical Yearbook of Shangai
Where these Districts are:

HP= Huangpu	NS= Nanshi	LW= Luwan	XH= Xuhui	CN= Changning
JA= Jingan	PT= Putuo	ZB= Zhabei	HK= Hongkou	YP= Yangpu

With the exception of the Yangpu, Jingan and Luwan Districts, most of the urban districts have more or less the same percentage of total population. However, the size of the land area of each urban district varies with some of the urban districts densely occupied by both industrial and residential users, a situation which is rather uncommon in developed market economies. Furthermore, the commercial content in the land use pattern is very low and varies substantially between different districts. The highest increase in both industrial output as well as the number of industrial employees occurred in the Huangpu district or the CBD of Shanghai, although only 11.15% of land in that district is currently used for industrial and warehouse use (Table 4) In contrast some of the districts with the largest industrial content in their land use distribution show only minimal increase in the industrial production and even decrease in the number of industrial employees. These districts include Luwan; Xuhui; Jingan; Zhabei and Hongkou.

Table 4: Industrial output in the Urban Districts in Shanghai in 1992

District	Total employees at the end of 1992 (10,00 persons)	% increase of employees over 1991	Total worth of industrial output at the end of 1992 (0.1 billion Yuan)	Industrial Content : % of industrial & warehouse land in the total land areas in each district by the end of 1992	% increase of industrial output over 1991
Huangpu	20.44	25%	142.53	11.15%	107.02%
Nanshi	19.53	7.25%	117.74	20.97%	80%
Luwan	11.27	-7.62%	56.77	24.91%	12.24%
Xuhui	22.78	-5.00%	129.47	21.31%	2.86%
Changning	16.02	-3.14%	81.91	16.59%	11.11%
Jingan	13.58	-4.03%	59.34	16.74%	8.86%
Putuo	20.67	-8.30%	95.13	26.49%	6.05%
Zhabei	18.47	-7.65%	81.44	26.465	11.45%
Hongkou	17.31	-11.14%	98.69	18.39%	13.33%
Yangpu	43.29	22.08%	300.59	26.43%	48.81%

Source: Statistical Yearbook of Shanghai, 1992 and 1993

Such mis-matches were reflected in the local governments preference in the sale of land use rights in the urban and sub-urban areas (Li, 1997). From 1988 to the first quarter of 1996, there were over 600 pieces of land (or land leases) sold to various land users. Table 4 shows the land areas sold for various uses in Shanghai from 1992 to mid-1996. It is apparent that while most land sold in the earlier years was designated for residential and mixed use (which consists of high class residential and office), land granted to industrial use especially in the rural area increased substantially when oversupply of offices occurred (Shanghai Statistical Bureau, 1996). This reflects a gradual learning curve on the part of the local government to try to be pro-active in the overall land policy.

Although the land area sold for mixed use development accounts for a smaller percentage than that for residential use, the more favourable plot ratio policy towards mixed use development (which normally carries a very high portion of office space) means the actual supply of developed properties in this category is much higher (Figure 2). Following guidelines from municipal planning departments, the negotiating land administration bureau also designates the maximum permitted plot ratio for the intended development. In 1995, a new Planning Commission (this refers to land use rather than economic planning as traditionally interpreted in China) was formed to take care of all planning issues. This new Planning Commission works in parallel with the Construction Commission which is the traditional supreme body at local government level in charge of all land, housing and construction issues.

Table 5: Land Market Activities in Shanghai

1992						
Land Area:						
	Comprehensive	Residential	Mixed	Industrial	Others	
Urban	67.890%	22.400%	4.620%	0.001%	5.050%	
Pudong	91.285%	0.900%	1.030%	0.000%	6.784%	
other districts	0.000%	82.200%	14.540%	3.270%	0.000%	
GFA allowed:	(excluding comprehensive)					
Urban		35.937%	60.225%	3.630%	0.208%	
Pudong		21.801%	76.363%	0.000%	1.836%	
Other districts		37.740%	58.167%	4.092%	0.000%	
1993						
Land Area:						
	Comprehensive	Residential	Mixed	Industrial	Commercial	
All districts	89.670%	6.300%	1.310%	2.680%	0.030%	
GFA allowed:	(excluding comprehensive)					
All districts		34.359%	42.510%	23.053%	0.078%	
1994						
Land Area:						
	Comprehensive	Residential	Mixed	Industrial	Commercial	Others
All districts	35.279%	14.937%	7.874%	37.394%	0.030%	4.486%
GFA allowed:	(excluding comprehensive)					
All districts		12.421%	35.177%	48.916%	0.148%	2.898%
1995						
Land Area:						
	Comprehensive	Residential	Mixed	Industrial	Commercial	Others
All districts	25.580%	7.140%	4.750%	62.440%	0.010%	0.080%
GFA allowed:	(excluding comprehensive)					
All districts		7.186%	17.920%	74.267%	0.012%	0.615%
1996	up to April only					
Land Area:						
	Comprehensive	Residential	Mixed	Industrial	Commercial	Others
All districts	0.000%	14.510%	8.840%	75.970%	0.000%	0.680%
GFA allowed:	(excluding comprehensive)					
All districts		14.420%	28.590%	54.320%	0.000%	2.660%

Notes:

All districts basically refer to the Metropolitan Shanghai, sub-urban and rural Shanghai, and Pudong Area.

GFA is the gross floor area allowed to be built on site.

Comprehensive use means comprehensive development of a massive land area (sometimes equivalent to a new town) which was a common way of attracting foreign developer to input investment into the relatively remote area of a region.

Figure 2: Comparative Analysis of Expected Floor Areas Sold in Shanghai for Different Uses between 1993 to 1996 (up to April)

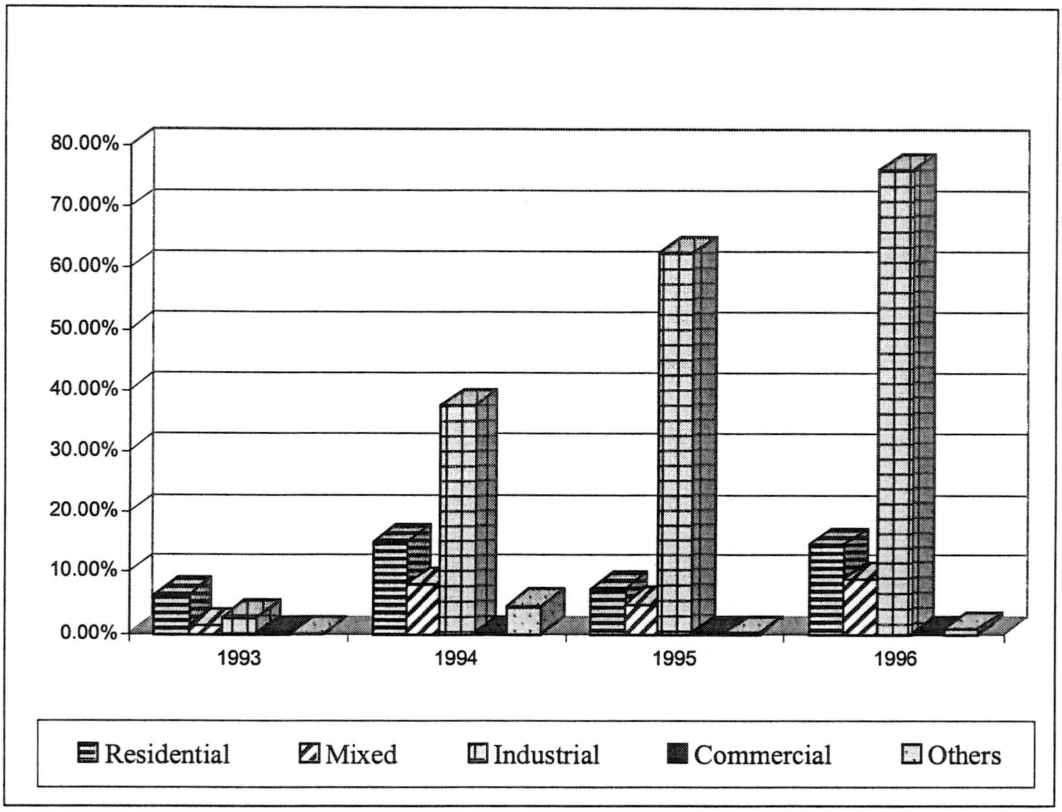

Source: *Shanghai Land* 1993-1996

Real Estate as a Tradable Commodity

Shanghai has been the major recipient of foreign investment amongst all the open cities (Table 6).Out of the total foreign investment in the city in 1995 about 38% was for property related projects. This is a very high figure given the rudimentary nature of the real estate market in the city though it provides a reflection of the attractiveness of the market to foreign, especially Hong Kong, real estate developers (Table 7).

Table 6: Foreign Investments in Shanghai by 1995

	Agreed amount on contracts		Actual utilization of investment funds	
	In 1995 (in US bn)	Cumulated sum by 1995 (in US bn)	In 1995 (in US bn)	Cumulated sum by 1995 (in US bn)
Grand Total:	12.588	43.92	5.298	19.944
1) Direct invest (total)	10.54	34.271	3.25	11.519
joint ventures	4.636	18.673	1.754	6.007
Co-operation	2.072	7.073	1.088	3.342
Solely-owned	3.726	7.858	0.363	1.197
2) Indirect invest (total)	2.048	9.649	2.048	8.425
Loans	2.033	8.129	2.033	7.983
Other Investment	0.015	1.52	0.015	0.442

Source: Shanghai Real Estate Market, 1996

Table 7: Foreign Investments in the Real Estate Market in Shanghai by 1995

	Agreed amount on contracts	
	In 1995 (in US Mn.)	Cumulated sum by 1995 (in US Mn.)
Grand Total:	4870.5	13293.79
Hong Kong	2183.2	8832.9
Britain	774.48	993.49
Singapore	664.39	892.33
Japan	338.25	568.49
S. Korea	270.27	270.27

Source: Shanghai Real Estate Market, 1996

In terms of the Shanghai property market, tradable private properties are called commodity properties (Figure 3). These can be classified into commodity housing (for residential use) and commodity buildings (for non-residential use). Commodity housing can be further sub-divided into internal commodity housing sold to local enterprises and citizens with all transactions in the Yuan. Foreign Chinese exchange commodity housing developed by companies with special certificates and better building standards and sold mainly to foreign Chinese who work in Shanghai, and any individuals stipulated by the relevant policies including local Chinese enterprises and individuals. This type of housing is sold inside China and is conducted in foreign exchange though it can be sold to both local and foreign individuals and enterprises.

Prices of internal commodity residences are controlled by the Chinese government. A maximum limit is set periodically by the government, under which the property companies can freely adjust the price according to the supply and demand situation. The Shanghai Housing Administration Bureau conducts a pricing survey periodically to set the guideline for the maximum price ceiling. Over the years, as construction costs have increased, the price of flats has also increased steadily.

Figure 3: Structure of the Private Property Market in Shanghai

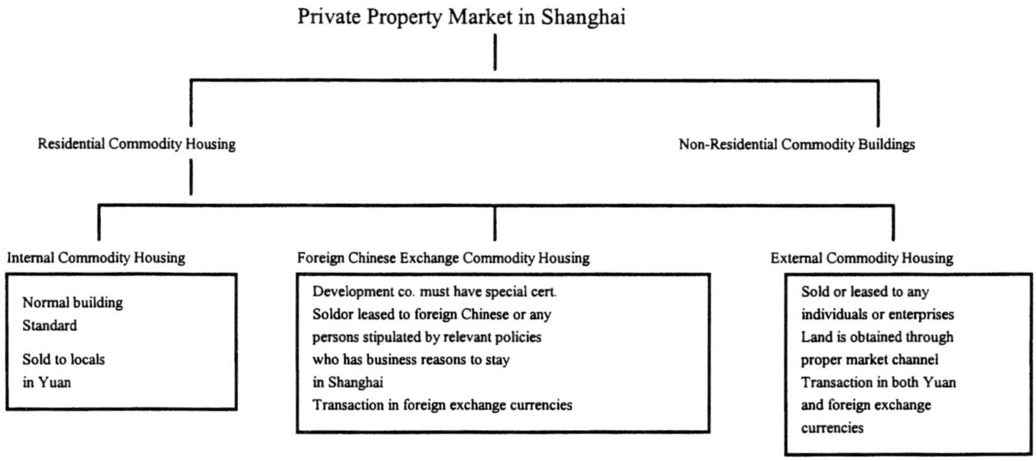

For the residential commodity housing sector, there is no time limit on the property rights of internal commodity housing because land is not obtained through the sale of land use rights. The situation is very different from properties developed with land use rights sold through the market channel. However if internal commodity housing is developed by a foreign investor, who provides housing for the foreign employees of his joint venture, property rights of such housing stand so long as the joint venture is good. In this case, the development of internal housing is not a market itself but a provision mechanism of welfare benefits.

In fact, one of the effective ways to absorb the surplus funds of the public sector is to develop a commodity housing market, allowing private ownership of dwelling units. Privatizing urban land use rights could also attract private capital to assist in redeveloping dilapidated urban areas and in improving housing conditions which have been severely under supplied due to the low-rent policy. In urban areas of China, most state enterprises own housing which are allocated to their employees as a welfare commodity and rents are only symbolic, even lower than the maintenance costs. The problem is that urban housing tends to deteriorate prematurely when housing rent is lower than the maintenance costs. China's urban housing reform which began in 1978 introduced market mechanisms such as raising rents and commercializing some newly built flats. While the state enterprises are cash poor, they are land rich. Thus, selling a part of the land use rights would improve their financial situation and provide the enterprises with investment capital with land flowing to the higher-valued users. On the other hand, the local government uses the revenue from the land sales for improving urban infrastructure and resettling displaced residents, and without government participation there would be substantial costs in the redevelopment of urban cities.

3.4 Housing Reform

At present the houses completed in the cities and villages of China is as many as one billion square meters per year. It amounts to 30% of the society-wide performed investment in fixed assets. According to a report by the China Mainland Marketing Research Co. and the economic news department of China Central Television, Chinese Urban Residents' hiring conditions have improved in the past two decades. Between 1979 and 1997, 14.8 billion sq.m of houses have been completed in the cities and villages of the country, including 30.15 billion sq.m for urban residents and 11.65 billion sq.m for rural residents. Nearly half a number of inhabitants moved into new houses. Their per capita living space was raised from 3.6 sq.m in 1978 to 8.8 sq.m in 1997. The scale of housing construction in the villages was kept as large as six hundred million sq.m in more than ten years on end and reached seven hundred and ninety five million sq.m in 1996.

The per capita living space in the rural areas has been raised from 15.9 sq.m in 1984 to 22.6 sq.m today. In general, everyone has already had one room. One hundred million sets of village houses has been built, and half of the peasant households have moved into their new houses. But the housing level is low in both per capita floor area and quality of living environment by comparison with developed countries in spite of the fact that housing construction is going on rapidly in China. At present, about 45% of urban and village houses have not been provided with public utilities, and per capita floor area for 3.25 million households in the cities is as low as 4 sq.m. Three hundred and thirty four billion sq.m of houses needs to be rebuilt. Village houses are generally low in quality and function. Consequently, there is an enormous potential demand for housing. The market prospect is broad. It is urgent to increase an effective supply.

Statistics indicate that the current house sales price in the country averages 1500 yuan per square meter. In fact, the house sales price in many big cities is far greater than the average price given above. For instance, in Beijing the house price within the Second Ring is as high as 10,000 yuan/M2, and the house between the Second and Third Ring sees at the price of 5,000-7,000 yuan/M2. On the one hand, there exist about 60 million households with no permanent house to live in; on the other hand, seventy million square meters of new buildings (including fifty million square meters of residential houses) stand idle by the end of 1997. The situation is caused by the reason that the housing system reform lag behind the times. In many places and organizations the practice of providing free houses only 1.2 yuan/M2. In addition, the current house sales price is extremely irregular because only 40% of the price is the immediate cost of construction and installation. The remainder of the price is the expense for land and public utilities. So it is necessary to speed up China's housing system reform.

Shanghai's plan for a comprehensive reform in the housing system was formally introduced on May 1st 1991 with the approval of the State Council in the central government. Strategies of rent increase, housing subsidy, and private investment in housing were incorporated in the plan. The most significant difference between the Shanghai model and other housing reform models in China was the introduction of the provident fund system.

In Shanghai the establishment of an experimental scheme to provident funds is expected to be followed by other cities in China. Under the provident fund system, modeled on the Singaporean approach, every citizen (with a legally registered household account in the population and household registry) must deposit 5% of their wages into the fund, though this is adjusted according to economic growth and changes in workers' income in the future. The work units and the government also supply about the same amount. Local banks act as agencies for funding and tenants can apply for the use of the provident fund for the down payment of the flat purchased in the open market. If the tenant resells a flat purchased by using the provident fund, the same amount of money must be repaid to the fund's account. Restrictions in the use of the provident funds limit usage to house purchase, house building, or major repair/ renovation. Routine decoration, maintenance and rental payment cannot be paid from provident funds.

Apart from paying for provident funds, citizens in Shanghai also have to buy housing bonds to contribute to housing development funds. The amount of housing bonds to be bought by each household is based on the area of living space and other characteristics of the flat. Work units can use their workers' housing bonds to construct new residential buildings to provide housing for their workers.

Furthermore in Shanghai it is stipulated that citizens who buy their homes at lower-than-market prices are only allowed to resell their units after five years of residence. In addition, the difference between resale price and the original selling price must be returned to their work units. Hence trading profit of public housing is not allowed.

4. Conclusions

This chapter has looked at the most recent economic reforms towards marketization in China and the policy shifts necessary for its further integrating into the Asia Pacific economy from the viewpoint of economics and politics. It specifically discussed the salient aspects associated with these reforms and policy shifts: such as economic co-operation, reform of its financial sector and state enterprises and the regional imbalances. The first part of this chapter addressed a number of key questions: such as the way China should improve its financial structure and state-owned enterprises that depress competition, cause corruption and increasingly burden the government financially. The second part looked at urban land reform in China, with particular reference to Shanghai, the most vibrant and cosmopolitan city in the Mainland.

What has been the most stunning economic event of the past century? Many people might cite the case of China in the two decades since it opened up. Over the period, the Chinese economy has grown more than fivefold. Incomes have quadrupled, and 270m Chinese have been lifted out of absolute poverty. Much of China's growth up to now has been largely of a catch-up kind, after agricultural communes were disbanded and restrictions on travel and informal enterprise were lifted.

The coming two decades may offer the possibility of an even more extraordinary pace of economic change. These could be the decades when China truly joins the world, and when the crushing legacy of a socialist economy is swept away. China certainly has the potential, over this period, to become the second largest economy in the world. WTO membership is the first of its future reform initiatives. The central government is developing financial markets that bypass a decrepit state banking system and award capital to the deserving. It is building a national infrastructure of roads, railways and fibre-optic lines that promise for the first time in history to tie up the disparate parts of the Chinese empire, creating a unified economy. Also, there have been clear signs of China's economic power within the Asian Pacific region, through economic co-operations and trade. During the Asian Financial Crisis of 1997-98, Asian economies counted upon strong American demand for their exports to pull them back from trouble. China, on the other hand, was marginally affected. Jun Ma, an economist at Deutsche Bank in Hong Kong, estimates even if China's net exports declined by a quarter, a mere half-percentage point would be knocked off the country's growth. This reinforces the point China's is a continental economy, driven by domestic demand.

Over the past century, China has witnessed the collapse of state socialism throughout Eastern and the former Soviet Union. One after another Communist party lost power, and the nascent democratic regimes that replaced the old party states struggled to make transformative economic reforms. Like many other Communist countries, China underwent tremendous strain as they adjusted to the unprecedented changes brought about by the reform. Urban reform is town planning concepts and controls are not very strong in the Chinese cities. There is always an element of negotiation throughout the real estate development process from the conveyance of land to the negotiation of plot ratio. In this type of market it is sometimes assumed that chaos and uncertainty will exist which will drag the pace of development into a sluggish state. However, the gradual approach to reform in the real estate sector has led to a very active market without causing the price fluctuation which occurred in eastern European countries after their so-called "shock-therapy" (Berry and McGreal, 1995; Li, 1997). In the case of Shanghai, the city government's attempt to improve general living standards in the urban area over the last ten years has been accompanied by an increase in the per capita living area from 6.0 sq m in 1986 to about 8.0 sq m in 1995 (Table 8), expecting to rise even further to 14 sq.m. by 2005.

Table 8: Changes in Stock of Commercial Floor Space in Urban Shanghai (Unit: 10,000 sq.m.)

Use	1980	1990	1994	1995	1996	Annual %*
Offices	336	599	813	955	1127	7.38%
Retail shops	243	403	515	562	656	6%
Hotels	54	237	271	280	288	10.3%
Factories	2646	4822	5511	5573	5513	4.4%

* represents average percentage change since 1980
Source: Statistical Yearbook of Shanghai 1995-1996

The role of the government remains instrumental in the establishment of a proper real estate market. Given that China is creating a market-socialist economy, instead of a capitalist economy, the gradual approach being adopted seemingly works better than the complete reform package. Although Shanghai's economy is not as free as Hong Kong's, nor is its information flow, it has a strong manufacturing base and the cost of doing business, though rising, is lower than Hong Kong's. Shanghai was the most vibrant and cosmopolitan of Asian cities-a magnet for capital and talent. It was where influential foreign and domestic banks based headquarters, and the country's cleverest people gathered. However, the successful reform of the real estate market depends fundamentally upon the overall reform packages being applied to the socio-economic system in China. It is believed that a more liberalized market regime would be conducive to the pace of economic growth in China. And such a regime is an effective way to integrate the Chinese mainland into the global economy.

REFERENCES

Beijing Review, March 20-26, 1989, pp. 15-17. Cited in Lardy, op. cit., 1990, p. 104.

Berry, J.N. and McGreal, W.S European Cities, Planning Systems and Property Markets, E&FN Spon, London pp. 289-393.

Bertaud, A. and Renaud, B. (1992) *Cities Without Land Markets*; World Bank Discussion Paper No. 227, Washington D.C.: World Bank.

Byrd, W. A. (1991) *The Market Mechanism and Economic Reforms in China*, New York: Sharpe.

Gao S. Liu G. & Ma J. (ed) (1999) *The Market Economy and China*, Beijing: Foreign Languages Press.

Ishihara, K. (1993) *China's Conversion to a Market Economy*, Tokyo: Institute of Developing Economies.

Lardy, N. (1990) "China and Asia-Pacific Economic Cooperation," in John P. Hardt and Young C. Kim, eds., *Economic Cooperation in the Asia-Pacific Region*, Boulder: Westview Press, p. 105.

Li, L.H. (1996a) *Privatization of Urban Land in Shanghai*, Hong Kong: Hong Kong University Press.

Li, L.H. (1996b) The Advent of Valuers in China, *Australian Land Economics Review*, Vol. 2, No. 1, pp.33-39.

Li, L.H. (1997) Privatization of Urban Land Market in Shanghai, *Journal of Real Estate Literature*, Vol. 5, pp.161-168.

Linge, G.J.R. (ed.) (1997) *China's New Spatial Economy: Heading Towards 2020*, Oxford : Oxford University Press

Seldon, M. (1993) *The Political Economy of Chinese Development*, New York: Sharpe

Shanghai Statistical Bureau (1996) *Office Sector Analysis in Shanghai Real Estate Market 1993-1996.*

Shanghai Urban Economics Society (1987) *Research Report on the Model, Methods and Standards of the Charging of Land Use Fees for the use of Urban Land in Shanghai*, 1987 second edition; Shanghai Urban Economics Society.

Shen G. (1990) "Trends and Proposals with Regard to China's Policy Toward Pacific Economic Cooperation," *Social Science*, Shanghai, 1987, No. 10, pp. 12-15, reprinted in *Shijie Jingji* (World Economy), 1987, No. 12, pp. 57-60. Cited in Lardy, op. cit., . 103-104.

Solinger, D. J. (1993) *China's Transition from Socialism*, New York: Sharpe.

Tse R. (2000) China's Real Estate Market and the Asian Financial Crisis, *Emerging Markets Quarterly*, **4**(4), pp.51-59.

Walker, A. (1991), *Land Property and Construction in the People's Republic of China*, Hong Kong: Hong Kong University Press.

Walker, A. and Li, L.H. (1994) Land Use Rights Reform and the Real Estate Market in China, *Journal of Real Estate Literature* , Vol. 2, pp.199-211.

World Bank (1993) *China. Urban Land Management in an Emerging Market Economy*, World Bank Country Study, Washington D.C.: World Bank.

Chapter 9

DIMENSIONS OF DOING BUSINESS IN CHINA

Heidi Dahles and Harry Wels

1.1 INTRODUCTION

Doing business in China is a popular topic in current management books and expat manuals boasting of tips and tricks in order to ensure successful business deals for Western businessmen who enter China with great hopes and expectations. Listing the do's and don'ts of Chinese business etiquette, the task seems easy: never lose your temper, keep your face in place, cultivate friendships with the Chinese business partners, inquire after their family members and eating habits, show stamina at opulent banquets, and master the art of using chopsticks (cf. Schneiter 1992). However, as those who have failed in China can tell, operating successfully in the Chinese market is not as easy as the business manuals suggest (cf. Stross 1991). There is more to business in China than toasting at banquets and singing along with new business partners in karaoke bars.

The large number of management manuals to guide Western businessmen in their China adventure implicitly or explicitly start from the presupposition that Chinese business culture strongly contrasts with Western business culture. Inspired by Hofstede's analysis of cultural differences (1991), it is claimed that Western capitalist market cultures characterized by individualism, rationality and secularism meet with collectivism, familism and Confucianism in China. The West and the East: will there ever be cultural convergence toward a universal market culture? And will this convergence signify the dominance of capitalist thinking? Or will 'the East' move away from capitalism turning to Confucianism as the "Asian values' debate seem to suggest? For the time being, there is evidence that "capitalist markets exert comparable pressures everywhere in the world but that local systems react differently to those pressures" (Weller 1998:79). This suggests that tensions between value and market, community and individual are inherent to every society entering the world market.

When in 1978 Deng Xiaoping announced his Open Door Policy and invited foreign organizations to invest in China in the form of joint ventures or otherwise, he set the pace for China's formidable economic growth in the years to follow (White 1993). With around 1.3 billion people, China is the world's most populous country. In the 1990s, the Chinese economy has achieved annual average growth rates of over 13 per cent per year (with China's most dynamic coastal provinces such as Guangdong, Fujian, Jiangsu and the Shanghai region producing growth rates of over 20 per cent per year, whereas some of the interior and western provinces lagging far behind the national average; Henderson 1998:377). As the World Bank Atlas of 1995 predicted based on the extrapolation of financial indicators, China would be the biggest economy of the world by 2010. Considering Greater China (including mainland China and Taiwan), as many economists do, the status of largest economy would be gained as early as 2002 with a Gross National Product of 9.8 trillion dollar, against 9.7 trillion dollar in the United States of America (cf. Van Kemenade 1996). As the last giant 'untapped market', China infused many firms around the world with a straightforward euphoria regarding the economic possibilities. The euphoria is based on a simple idea: 'if every second, or even third or fourth Chinese buys one piece of for example chewing gum or toothpaste of my brand, the economic performance of my company will sky-rocket'. As a result many firms rushed towards China as in a new gold rush. Expecting world economy to further globalize and integrate (of which the entry of China was regarded as a clear signal), the practicalities of doing business and running joint ventures in China were not seen as a problem. However, the economic opening of China did not run parallel with a cultural opening of China as many Western firms learned the hard way (cf. Mann 1989).

The upsurge of foreign direct investment in China during the 1990s and the emergence of more and more Sino-foreign joint ventures have raised concerns about management, organizational culture and corporate identity. After all, long-standing cultural stereotypes are part and parcel of the intensified cultural exchange between China and the West. Traditionally, Westerners have been considered 'barbarians' and, as all people living beyond the realm of Chinese civilization, they were dehumanized (DiKötter 1992: 6). Within the Chinese cultural tradition, covering some 5000 years of uninterrupted cultural process, the respective nature of the Chinese and the barbarian were considered incompatible (ibid.: 18). But stereotyping is not a one-way process. Vice versa, from a Western perspective, many publications testify to the different-ness of China and the Chinese in general and of doing business in China in particular (Wilpert & Scharpf 1990; Jia 1993; Hofstede 1991; Bogstra et al 1993; Van Buuren et al 1995; Harmsen & Nelissen 1995).

In China, as in many other societies, business strategies rely heavily on personal social networks. For the Chinese it is claimed that the effective mobilization of family and other personal ties are a distinctive feature serving the purpose of avoiding Western individualism (Weller 1998:79). In particular in urban areas with its dynamism and uncertainty of opportunities, personal ties are extremely important to get things done. Writing about Beijing, Buckley (1999:209) contends: "Entrepreneurs and their backers strive to survive in an environment where, as well as individual skills and resources, they often depend on the skills, resources and influence on others – especially access to bureaucratic influence and reliable information." Being a successful businessman or woman requires a combination of skills: individual entrepreneurial zeal and access to bureaucratic power through family relations and friendship. In order to understand how business works in China, one needs to understand how personal networks are operated, what cultural norms and values are at their basis and how these networks are related to bureaucratic power. These matters become extremely important against the background of increasing co-operation between Chinese and Western businesses. The relationship between China's unique social and historical heritage and the global context of doing business raises the question of how tensions and conflicts, uncertainties and frustrations are dealt with in the face of negotiating and managing different national cultures, corporate identities and business pressures and objectives.

Questions raised in this book therefore center around the ways in which personal relations are handled in China in general and in particular between Chinese and Western business partners. As will be elaborated in the subsequent sections of this introduction and supported with empirical material in the following chapters, the instrumental dimension of personal social relations seem to be unusually (though not uniquely) important in China for a variety of reasons, among which two may be identified as outstanding. First, the role of social connections in Chinese life is very visible and surrounded by many explicit and implicit rules of conduct. Second, the importance of the instrumental uses of these social connections has been accentuated by the tremendous social, economic and (to a lesser degree) political changes China has undergone in the recent decades.

This chapter is arranged as follows. First, the often quoted concept of *guanxi* and related terms will be discussed against the background of theories on European versus Asian capitalism. Secondly, the 'art of maintaining ongoing social relations' will be positioned in the context of political power relations in post-Mao China and the requirements of the global market. Finally, the structure of this book and the contribution of the different chapters to the central question will be briefly presented.

1.2 Social Connections in Chinese Culture

Ever since Max Weber's pessimistic diagnosis of Chinese culture as generator of capitalism, many scholars have followed in his footsteps arguing that Confucianism and related familism has been at the root of China's failure to modernize its economy. After having dominated the writings on China for decades (known as the Weber Trap), the image of the Protestant West versus the Confucian East generated Redding's (1990) analysis of China in terms of an indigenous capitalism. This analysis identified Confucian values and family networks as assets offering the key to the East Asian economic success (Holbig 2000:16; Weller 1998:81). Redding's contribution marked the emancipation of China from the Weberian predicament. After all, capitalism seemed not to be limited to Western societies based on rationalist principles, but could also emerge under different social and cultural conditions. This altered perception of China has to be understood against the background of the booming Western investments.

It has become a trope in the literature to describe Chinese capitalism in terms of a 'network capitalism' characterized by both hierarchical relationships within the family (based on Confucian responsibility toward the elders) and a system of reciprocal relationships between individuals known as *guanxi* (cf. Redding 1990), while the concept of *guanxiwang* refers to a network of exchanges between two parties and beyond (Wu Wei-ping 2000:38). The frequency of this discourse may arouse suspicion and one may question the soundness of the argument - pointing out particularistic competitiveness and conflicts within families undermine collectivism and Confucian harmony, loyalty and respect (cf. Weller 1998:83). However, it is also true that "real, non-metaphorical family business has been at the heart of the economic boom in Taiwan, Hong Kong, and the people's Republic" (Weller 1998:84). The basic building block for Chinese business is the extended family, which is patrilineal, patrilocal and patriarchal. Chinese families pool incomes and contribute unpaid labor to the family enterprise as this is regarded as a corporate undertaking (Hefner, 1998:13). However, success is defined not in terms of growth and a vertically integrated corporation, but by the establishment of independent firms loosely structured in a multi-firm business group (Hefner, 1998:23). This business group is generated as a spin-off from a successful family business, the owner of which assigns to each of his sons different spheres of influence in the business or an entirely separate business. While family networks among the Chinese are hierarchical and close-knit, *guanxi* tend to be relatively egalitarian, reciprocal, and broad in their reach. Those active in a *guanxi* network may include distant kin, neighbors, former schoolmates, people with the same surname (Hefner, 1998). Some scholars have traced these family-operated and *guanxi*-based Chinese business networks to a Confucian value system that presumably emphasizes harmony and consensus, trust and responsibilities towards the lineage (cf. Kotkin, 1993; Thompson, 1998).

Closely related to *guanxi* are the concepts of *mianzi* (face) and *jen-ching* (human obligations). To start with the latter, human obligations are intrinsically linked to the reciprocal relations within a *guanxi* network. The principle of reciprocity implies that the exchange of services, favors, money or other valuables establishes and reinforces longstanding ties between people, as no immediate compensation is required. 'Face', or rather 'loss of face' comes to play in the *guanxi* context when a person cannot fulfil the duties or obligations based on his or her social position or the requirements of his or her network ties. This is the debtor's perspective. Vice versa, people can create debt for other people by 'giving face', such as bestowing honor upon other or doing unasked favors, which others have to return in due course.

Another concept related to the *guanxi* network is *xinyong*, personal trust, a concept of pivotal significance for doing business in China. Instead of focusing on closing a deal – as Westerners use to do, Chinese entrepreneurs attempt to develop *xinyong* first. From a Western perspective, this is a time consuming approach as it implies investing into the relationship with a business partner. In contrast with their Western corollaries, Chinese business communities operate on a 'basis of limited and bounded trust" (Holbig 2000:17). Chinese society lacks the level of legal codification and law enforcement characteristic of Western society. Therefore, business deals are based on specific trust bonds which involve personal obligations, reputation and face and include members of their family and lineage (absolutely) and friends and business partners (to a degree), but exclude people outside these networks (ibid.). Instead of Chinese society being a trust-based society, the opposite is true: in a context of general mistrust, personal trust bonds establish the only reliable foundation of economic co-operation. It must be clear then that *xinyong* is of crucial importance for *guanxi* ties, while loss of face affects negatively *guanxi* as well as *xinyong* (Menkhoff 1992).

1.3 The Role of the State

The rise of China as an economic power since the 1980s has puzzled those neoclassical thinkers who deny that economies under strong state control can grow as spectacularly as China has done. The Chinese government still engages in central planning and domestic market protection. The version of capitalism that has emerged in China is coined as Market Stalinism. This term refers to a 'set of institutional arrangements that are (presumably) transitional between state socialism and capitalism in the East Asian context, the defining characteristic is the continuing decisive economic role of an authoritarian, repressive, 'Stalinist' state in a context where resource allocation has been partially marketized, and the economy partially connected to the world economy, primarily as a result of insertion into overseas Chinese business networks' (Henderson 1998:367).

Under Mao, the Chinese economy was subjected to a rigid system of central planning, which created a multi-layered bureaucratic system. The coping strategies of individuals and organizations who attempted to survive in this system implied and required "cultivating and maintaining personal relations with people who had access to those goods and resources" (Buckley, 1999:220). The economic reforms that characterized the post-Mao era since 1978 mitigated centralism and bureaucratic control. But instead of undermining the importance of personal connections, the market reforms even enhanced the necessity to activate one's personal network to get things done. After all, liberalization introduced many new uncertainties that were absent under rigid state control. The unpredictability of the 'free market' has been added to the ongoing impediments of red tape in the surviving bureaucratic structures. Nowadays, commercial interests have to reckon with political and bureaucratic agendas. Economic life in reformed China is rather complex, in particular for business people and entrepreneurs. "In these circumstances, the trust and certainty that comes through close personal relationships is in itself an important asset, especially where the people concerned occupy influential positions. In this unstable context, where becoming wealthy is often based on reading the unpredictable currents of market forces and official policy, friends and kin play an important role in 'making it'" (Buckley 1999:221).

Connections between Chinese firms are highly personalized, fluid, and changeable. Sources of finance tend to be informal (family savings, loans from trusted friends, revolving credit associations, other forms of informal lending). In such a structure, management is highly centralized and authoritarian. On the other hand, the flexibility of such a system allows for fast adjustments to new products, to new processes, and to new markets. Through alliances between families, and their corresponding networks, capital turnover is accelerated, and allocation of resources is optimized (Castells, 1993). The weak point in these small-scale Chinese business networks is their inability to undertake major strategic transformations, requiring for instance R&D investment, knowledge of world markets, large-scale technological modernization, or offshoring of production (Castells, 1993). This weakness has been compensated in some parts of Asia by the developmental state. In Taiwan, Hong Kong, Singapore, and more recently China, the state has come to support Chinese entrepreneurialism. As Castells (1993:189) points out, "the form of Chinese business networks is also a function of the indirect, subtle, yet real and effective form of state intervention in the process of economic development in various contexts."

In the rich variety of norms, affinities and obligations expressed in terms such as face (*mianzi*), connection (*guanxi*) and sentiment (*renqing*) that are found in modern Chinese culture, the struggle to overcome uncertainty and risk in an unpredictable social and economic/political environment is expressed. Success and wealth are often dependent on combining individual resources and talents with the opportunities and information that comes through relations with others. Hence, developing trust and social reciprocity among close friends, partners and colleagues is an important element in social life.

Aspiring successful business operators must win and maintain the trust and respect of their peers, a requirement reflected in the forms of sociality and consumption that characterize their lifestyle – helps to mitigate the problems of running a private business in China, such as reducing and avoiding tax, choosing, ordering and pricing goods.

The recent re-entrance of China into world economy may contribute to the wealth of Chinese business networks within China and across the Chinese borders into East and Southeast Asia, transforming the power balance in the region. Since the opening of China to foreign investors, the number of joint-venture companies in which foreign and domestic interests collaborate has boomed, often involving major multinationals and the one hand and state or private Chinese companies on the other. Overseas Chinese businesses from East and Southeast Asia and beyond have come to play an increasing role in foreign investments in mainland China (cf. Douw et al 1999; Chan Kwok Bun 2000). These joint ventures can be observed in particular in the manufacturing industries. In China, manufacturing largely consist of consumer electronics, microcomputers, semiconductors, automobiles, auto components and garments and toys. This export profile brings Chinese firms into competition especially with their Japanese counterparts, and it may loom as the major economic problem to the USA (Henderson 1999:372).

1.4 About this Chapter

Methodology

This book brings together a number of case studies that focus on Chinese business practices from an anthropological perspective discussing either legal or organizational-cultural matters. The authors in this book are organizational anthropologists. They study and write about people in organizations, managers and employees and their interrelatedness, rather than statistics and aggregate figures, management strategies and models. The hallmark of an anthropological approach is to see complexity where others see uniformity and look from within and below where others look from above and without. Two of the four chapters in this volume are based on ethnography, i.e., dense description of the daily practices and interactions in à Chinese company. It is widely agreed that ethnography conveys some insight or understanding into 'the native's point of view' and reflects the multiple voices in a local setting (Hirsch & Gellner 2001). Rooted in the anthropological tradition of long-term fieldwork, 'doing ethnography' within organizations pose specific problems of access (formal barriers impeding researchers from wandering freely about offices, executives rooms and workfloors), disclosure (protecting the privacy of the researched organization) and academic detachment (problems of company secrets, censure and embargoes on publication) (cf. Chapman 2001).

Three of the contributors to this volume were graduate students at the department of Culture, Organization and Management (COM) at Vrije Universiteit Amsterdam (the Netherlands) at the time they were conducting their research on cultural aspects of Chinese organizations and organizational co-operation between Western and Chinese firms. This research resulted in graduate theses that received an excellent rating. Usually these theses go unnoticed to a broader audience. Upon graduation they end up on a half forgotten bookshelf in the university library. But as the developments in China continue to attract our interest, it would be a waste to leave them there and not to build on the knowledge accumulated by them. For the purpose of this volume three graduates produced a condensed and revised version of their thesis to be published under the editorship of their former supervisors. Their thinking reflects the theoretical and empirical orientation of the research program of the department of COM, which addresses the issue, which cultural and social repertories organizations establish in negotiating new alliances and in constructing new identities. The research addresses new forms of identification in organizations. Integration and fragmentation, homogenization and individualization, increasing conformity and distinction raise the question as to how individuals in organizations (both managers and employees) respond to these partly converging and partly conflicting processes. Which types of organization, linkages and identification are conceived and practiced, and which survival strategies are applied? How are identities being constructed, individually and collectively, in late modern organizations, which explanations can be given, and what are the implications for the management of organizations?

The Chapters

Upon entering the Chinese market, Westerners attempt to formalize their relationships with their Chinese counterparts in a contract, which they expect to offer them juridical protection. How widely accepted and obeyed is contract law? How do the respective parties perceive formal contracts? What influence does culture have on the formulations and perception of business contracts? In chapter one, these and related questions are answered by Axel Hagedorn, a lawyer by training, who compares Western and Chinese contract law. Based on a comparative literature review, Hagedorn investigates the complexities of the Chinese legal system, and in particular contractual law in China, which is contrasted with the Western legal system. The central argument of his chapter is that in order to gain some understanding of the Chinese legal system the restricted approach to law characteristic of Western thinking has to be abandoned in favor of a multiple perspective that includes cultural values and practices. Such a perspective throws different light on Sino-Western business contacts and enables persons involved in intercultural legal transactions to operate more effectively.

What happens if a co-operative organizational structure becomes operational in China? Do cultural differences subside, or do they remain as confronting as in the first phases of forming a joint venture? Two case studies of Sino-Western joint ventures tackle these questions. In chapter two the case of an international joint venture is presented consisting of a number of European partners, one private Chinese company and a Chinese state enterprise. This joint venture (in the storage sector) is between the second largest storage company in the world, Van Ommeren, and its two Chinese counterparts, Zhejiang Chemicals & Light Industry and the Ningbo Port Authorities, in Ningbo, south of Shanghai. Ever since the research, Van Ommeren merged with Pakhoed. Nowadays this merger, operating under the name of Vopak, is the largest storage-company in the world. The author, Bas Rozemuller, questions the general assumption held in the West that Chinese culture is characterized by the concept of collectivism, in contrast to the individualism of the Western world. The very diversity of this joint venture raises questions about intercultural communication, commitment, decision-making and power processes at management and work floor levels. An in-depth analysis of social relations within this joint venture leads Rozemuller to conclude that simplistic concepts about Chinese collectivity versus Western individualism miss the point when held against the daily practice and routines in the company.

Another view from inside an organization in China is offered by Marc David Brand in Chapter three, which presents the case of a state-owned hennep cotton factory in Dong Ping in Shandong province in China's Northeast. This factory entered into a joint venture with an American private firm in 1993. The discussion focuses on the process of adapting to a market-economy and the related coping strategies employed by the Chinese firm. Central to Brand's argument is that instead of adjusting to American ways of doing business, the Chinese reflected on their cultural traditions as a frame of reference in their co-operative efforts with the Americans.

In the fourth and final chapter, the editors reflect on the case studies at a more theoretical level and reconsider the cultural concepts that have turned out to be of pivotal significance in Chinese business practices. The chapter concludes with an outlook on possible lessons learned from highlighting the cultural dimension of organizational processes in China. In the end, a few considerations may be of interest for Western managers who already are or intend to get involved with Chinese business partners. These considerations highlight cultural aspects of initiating business co-operations and maintaining ongoing relations of reciprocity and trust with Chinese business partners. Needless to say that these considerations reach beyond the art of handling chopsticks.

REFERENCES

Bogstra, A.J., B. Liu, J.Tang, & H.Wateler (1993) *The road to China. Marketing opportunities for industrial and consumer goods in southern China.* Amsterdam: Chain

Buckley, Ch. (1999) 'How a revolution becomes a dinner party. Stratification, mobility and the new rich in urban China'. In Michael Pinches (ed.), *Culture and Privilege in Capitalist Asia*. London/New York: Routledge, pp. 208-229

Castells, M. (1993) *The Information Age I: The Rise of the Network Society*. Oxford: Blackwell Publishers.

Chan Kwok Bun (ed.) (2000) *Chinese Business Networks. State, Economy and Culture.* Singapore: Prentice Hall.

Chapman, M. (2000) 'Social Anthropology and Business Studies: Some Considerations of Method'. In David N. Gellner & Eric Hirsch (eds.), *Inside Organizations. Anthropologists at Work.* Oxford: Berg, pp. 19-34.

DiKötter, F. (1992) *The discourse of race in modern China.* Hong Kong: Hong Kong University Press.

Douw, L., Cen Huang & M.R. Godley (eds.) (1999) *Qiaoxiang Ties. Interdisciplinary approaches to 'cultural capitalism' in South China.* London/New York: Kegan Paul.

Harmsen, P.J. & Nelissen, S.H.F. (1995) *China, a business survival guide*, Maastricht: Foundation Study Projects EFM.

Hefner, R.W. (1992) 'Morality in the New Asian Capitalisms', in: R. Hefner (ed.), *Market Cultures; Society and Morality in the New Asian Capitalisms*. Boulder (Colorado): Westview Press, pp. 1-40.

Henderson, J. (1998) 'Danger and opportunity in the Asia-Pacific'. In Grahame Thompson. *Economic Dynamism in the Asia-Pacific. The Growth of Integration and Competitiveness*. London and New York: Routledge in association with The Open University, pp. 356-384.

Hirsch E.& D.N. Gellner (2001) 'Introduction: Ethnography of Organizations and Organizations of Ethnography'. In David N. Gellner & Eric Hirsch (eds.), *Inside Organizations. Anthropologists at Work.* Oxford: Berg, pp. 1-18.

Hofstede, G. (1991) *Cultures and organisations. Software of the mind.* London: McGraw-Hill Book Company.

Holbig, H. (1999) 'Trust and Its Limitations: A Changing Discourse on Money during the people's Republic of China's Reform Period'. In Chan Kwok Bun (ed.), *Chinese Business Networks. State, Economy and Culture*. Singapore: Prentice Hall, pp. 14-34.

Jia, X. (1993) *Creating Sino-Foreign equity joint ventures. Technology transfer: negotiation, product selection and localization*. Enschede: Print 2000.

Kotkin, J. (1993) *Tribes: How Race, Religion, and Identity Determine Success in the New Global Economy*. New York: Random House.

Mann, J. (1989) *Beijing Jeep: unhappy romance of American business in China*. Simon & Schuster.

Menkhoff, T. (1992) 'Xinyong or How to Trust Trust'. In: *Internationales Asienforum*, vol. 23, no. 1-2, pp. 261-288.

Redding, S.G. (1990) *The Spirit of Chinese Capitalism*. Berlin, New York: Walter de Gruyter.

Schneiter, F. (1991) *Getting Along With The Chinese For Fun And Profit*. Hong Kong: Asia 2000 Limited.

Stross, R. (1991) *Bulls in the China shop and other Sino-American business encounters*. New York: Pantheon Books, Random House.

Thompson, G. (ed.) (1998) *Economic Dynamism in the Asia-Pacific*. London and New York: Routledge.

Van Buuren, S. & E. Van Doorne (1995) *Visible from the moon: the Chinese market investigated*. Amsterdam: Chain

Van Kemenade, W. (1996) *China, Hong Kong, Taiwan BV. Superstaat op zoek naar een nieuw systeem*. Amsterdam: Uitgeverij Balans

Wilpert, B. & S.Y. Scharpf (1990) 'Intercultural management – Joint ventures in the People's Republic of China'. *International Journal of Psychology*, vol. 25, no. 5/6, pp. 643-665.

Weller, R.P. (1998) 'Divided Market Cultures in China. Gender, Enterprise, and Religion'. In Robert W. Hefner (ed.), *Market Cultures. Society and Morality in the New Asian Capitalisms*. Boulder (Colorado): Westview, pp. 78-103.

White, D.G. (1993) *Riding the tiger: the politics of economic reform in post-Mao China*. London: Macmillan Press.

Wu Wei-ping (2000) 'Transaction Costs, Cultural Values and Chinese Business Networks: An Integrated Approach'. In Chan Kwok Bun (ed.), *Chinese Business Networks. State, Economy and Culture*. Singapore: Prentice Hall, pp. 35-56.

INDEX

A

accountability, 119
achievement, 130
Aerospace Industries Association of America (AIA), 82
agriculture, 29, 80, 82, 90, 96, 130
all-Asia Boao Economic Forum, 26
Amphibious Assault Vehicles, 47
ASEAN Regional Forum (ARF), 26, 32, 37
Asia, 15-18, 20-22, 25, 32, 34, 36, 37, 43, 46, 47, 51, 53, 58-60, 63, 65, 66, 69, 70, 76, 78, 81, 85, 95, 100, 110-115, 121, 126, 127, 129, 133, 134, 137, 149, 157, 158, 160, 161
Asian Development Bank, 95
Asian economies, 110, 112, 114, 115, 132, 149
Asian Financial Crisis, 60, 110, 111, 114, 115, 149, 151
Asia-Pacific Economic Cooperation (APEC), 132-134, 151
Association of Southeast Asian Nations (ASEAN), 16, 25, 32, 36, 37, 51, 53, 63, 65, 110, 111, 113-115, 133
Australia, 26, 37, 53, 54, 59, 95, 133

B

ballistic missile defense, 47
banking system, 78, 79, 149
Beijing, 3, 4, 5, 14, 18-26, 29, 32, 35, 40-42, 44, 46-48, 52, 67, 73, 75, 77-79, 88, 90, 94, 103, 107, 119, 124, 131-133, 136, 137, 148, 150, 151, 154, 161
bilateral trade agreements, 86, 87
Britain, 28, 146
Bush Administration, 70, 71, 90, 97
Bush, President, 71, 72, 94, 97
business relations, 104

C

capacity, 26, 28, 56, 85, 95, 100
capitalism, 24, 153, 155, 156, 160
capitalist markets, 153
Central Intelligence Agency (CIA), 17, 33
Central Military Commission (CMC), 41, 120
chemicals, 35, 52, 102, 159
China's accession, 15, 53, 71, 72, 86, 91, 92, 96, 97, 100
Chinese Communist Party (CCP), 15, 19, 24, 25, 29, 70, 73, 137
Chinese economy, 52, 69-71, 75, 77-79, 88, 95, 96, 122, 126, 132, 133, 135, 149, 153, 157
Chinese enterprises, 51-66, 146
Chinese Institute of Contemporary International Relations (CICIR), 20, 21
Chinese market, 84, 96, 114, 153, 159, 161
Chinese military, 16, 27, 44, 45, 46, 122, 124
Chinese Petroleum Corp, 104
civil liberties, 48
Clinton Administration, 31
Clinton, President, 70, 71, 72
Closer Economic Partnership Agreement (CEPA), 110
Cold War, 17, 18, 25
commercial banks, 135
Commercial Law Development Program (CLDP), 96
Communication, 19
communication, 26, 45, 83, 159
competition, 23, 27, 53, 55, 59, 61, 64-66, 72, 73, 74, 77, 79, 80, 84, 88, 90, 96, 129, 149, 158
competitiveness, 52, 53, 64, 66, 113, 155, 160
comprehensive national power (CNP), 21
computers, 83, 101, 102, 107
confidence-building measures (CBMs), 16, 25, 26, 30-32, 34-37

Constitution, 140
conventional weapons, 46
corruption, 79, 87, 120, 123, 129, 132, 149
countervailing duty (CVD), 96
crime, 23
cultural exchange, 40, 154
Cultural Revolution, 130
Culture, Organization and Management (COM), 158

D

Defense Authorization Act, 47, 125
defense relations, 49
democratization, 18
Department of Defense (DoD), 27, 34, 40, 43, 44, 46, 47, 49, 118, 121, 126, 127
developing countries, 95, 131
direct investment, 17, 23, 24, 51, 52, 59, 63, 65, 74, 100, 126, 131, 132, 154
Dispute Settlement Understanding (DSU), 92
drugs, 23
dynamic Asian economies (DAEs), 132

E

Early Warning (EW), 46
Economic cooperation, 129
Economic Development Advisory Conference (EDAC), 103, 104
economic development, 24, 25, 48, 52, 54, 56, 58, 59, 61, 64, 65, 72, 110, 115, 117, 138, 157
economic growth, 15, 21, 24, 27, 52, 63, 65, 69, 70, 74, 75, 77-79, 95, 101, 102, 106, 110, 114, 115, 125, 126, 127, 129, 132, 135, 136, 138, 148, 150, 153
economic integration, 19, 48, 72, 96, 103, 104, 106, 107, 109, 114, 115, 134
economic interests, 132
economic reform, 1, 23, 63, 65, 69, 70, 72, 75, 77, 80, 81, 88, 113, 114, 125, 129, 130, 133, 137, 138, 149, 150, 157, 161
economic reforms, 1, 63, 65, 77, 80, 88, 114, 125, 129, 133, 138, 149, 150, 157
education, 24, 85, 94, 130
emerging power, 15
employment, 9, 78, 80, 81, 86, 107, 125, 135
environment, 17, 24, 25, 33, 46, 52, 53, 61-63, 74, 133, 135, 148, 154, 157
equality, 25, 133
Europe, 17, 18, 22, 26, 34, 53, 85, 94, 130, 133
European Union (EU), 21, 25, 37, 93, 95, 97, 131, 133
exchange rate, 130
expansion, 57, 74, 76, 104, 106, 108, 109, 117, 125, 126, 138

F

farmers, 132
flexibility, 104, 157
Foreign Broadcast Information Service (FBIS), 18, 19, 24, 33, 34, 41, 44, 73
foreign direct investment (FDI), 17, 23, 24, 51, 52, 53, 55, 56, 59, 60, 66, 67, 74, 100, 109, 110, 111, 114, 125, 126, 131, 154
foreign exchange reserves, 125, 134
foreign exchange, 56-58, 64, 65, 91, 125, 126, 134, 146
foreign investment, 23, 56, 58, 60, 62, 63, 65, 69, 74, 76, 102, 109, 110, 113, 125, 132, 136, 138, 145, 158
foreign investors, 26, 158
foreign military aid, 121
Foreign Operations Appropriations Act, 49
foreign policy, 16, 19, 21, 28, 32, 48, 51, 56, 65
France, 26, 28, 76, 120
free trade, 51, 53, 63, 65, 86, 139

G

General Agreement on Tariffs and Trade (GATT), 81, 86, 93, 97, 108, 132
General Agreement on Trade in Services (GATS), 81
General Armaments Department (GAD), 121, 124
General Logistics Department (GLD), 120, 124
Genetically Modified Organisms (GMOs), 89
Germany, 18, 26, 28, 76, 120
global economy, 100, 113, 129, 150
government officials, 77, 94
government policies, 141
government policy, 53
Government Procurement Agreement(GPA), 85, 108
government support, 51
Great Leap Forward, 130
Gross Domestic Product (GDP), 2, 8, 76-79, 114, 118-122, 130, 136
Gross National Product (GNP), 136, 139
gross value of industrial and agricultural outputs (GVIAO), 2-12
Guangdong Province, 9
Guangzhou, 91, 140

H

Hong Kong University, 151, 160
Hong Kong, 20, 41, 53, 56, 64-67, 76, 78, 87, 91, 100, 101, 103, 109-112, 131, 133, 134, 136, 140, 145, 146, 149-151, 155, 157, 160, 161
housing, 137, 138, 143, 146-149
human rights, 18, 28, 36, 71

I

independence, 40, 43, 48, 49, 135
India, 16, 25, 32, 34, 35, 120
Indigenous Defense Fighter (IDF), 45
Information Technology Agreement (ITA), 83, 89
information technology, 82, 102, 104, 107
Information Warfare (IW), 27, 46
infrastructure, 29, 41, 45, 53, 78, 79, 94, 103, 124, 137-139, 147, 149
intellectual property rights (IPR), 74, 83-87, 91
interference, 64, 133
international competitiveness, 54
International Monetary Fund (IMF), 121
international relations, 93, 133
investment, 19, 23, 24, 25, 26, 27, 28, 51-66, 72-74, 76, 78, 79, 82, 85, 86, 99-101, 103-107, 109-111, 113, 114, 125, 126, 131, 132, 134, 136, 138, 139, 144-148, 157
investments, 26, 102-104, 132, 134, 155
Iran, 54, 93
Iraq, 22

J

Japan, 17, 21, 22, 25, 26, 37, 43, 52, 55, 76, 95, 97, 100, 102, 110-113, 115, 120, 122, 125, 133, 146
Japanese, 66, 113, 115, 133, 158
Jiang Zemin, 20, 24, 27, 30, 35, 52, 94, 105, 123
Joint Commission on Commerce and Trade (JCCT), 94
Joint Commission on Science and Technology (JCS&T), 94
Joint Declaration, 35
Joint Economic Committee (JEC), 13, 94

K

Korea, 1, 26, 36, 37, 111, 112, 113, 132, 133, 146

L

land use rights (LURs), 137, 139-143, 147, 151
Land Use Rights, 139, 141
Leadership, 70, 71, 72
leadership, vii, 16, 19, 27, 28, 41, 43, 48, 70, 72, 74, 80, 87, 88, 95, 109, 118, 136
learning, 64, 143
legal system, 61, 64, 84, 87, 88, 94, 159
legitimacy, 30, 31, 43, 70, 75
liberalization, 37, 69, 70, 72, 76, 96, 104, 132, 137, 157
Libya, 93
Line of Actual Control (LAC), 35
living standards, 139, 150
loans, 55, 78, 79, 90, 134, 157
local government, 80, 124, 139, 141-143, 147
low tax, 118

M

Macau, 87, 136
mainland, 43, 105, 107, 109, 129-138, 139, 150, 154, 158
manufacturing facilities, 105, 106, 113
manufacturing sector, 132
manufacturing, 57, 58, 61, 64, 88, 99-101, 102, 105-107, 113, 114, 123, 129, 130, 132, 138, 150, 158
Maoism, 132
market access, 69-72, 74, 81-91, 96, 97, 114
market economy, 72, 73, 96, 113, 129, 130, 134
market mechanism, 140, 147
media, 16, 18, 19, 28
Memorandum of Understanding (MOU), 86, 87
Mexico, 25, 131
military budget, 119-123, 125-127
military relations, 16, 35
Ministry of Finance (MOF), 120
Ministry of Foreign Trade and Economic Co-operation (MFTEC), 131, 133
Ministry of Foreign Trade and Economic Cooperation (MOFTEC), 60, 62, 67, 89, 94
Ministry of National Defense (MND), 45
money, 46, 109, 118, 121, 122, 136, 138, 148, 156
most-favored nation (MFN), 18
Muslims, 21

N

National Defense University (NDU), 23, 31
National People's Congress (NPC), 41, 119, 121

negotiation, 16, 139, 140, 141, 150, 161
non-market economy (NME), 92, 96, 97
nuclear proliferation, 31

O

olitical liberalization, 69, 70, 72, 137
Open Door Policy, 153
output, 1, 2, 6, 8, 9, 11, 12, 54, 127, 130, 131, 135, 142, 143

P

Pacific, 21, 25, 31, 43, 46, 54, 111, 129, 130, 133, 137, 149, 151
People's Armed Police (PAP), 121, 123
People's Liberation Army (PLA), 27, 28, 30, 33, 41-43, 45, 46, 48, 117-119, 121-126
People's Republic of China
per capita income, 10, 131
performance, 61, 62, 75, 135, 154
Permanent Normal Trade Relations (PNTR), 70, 97
population, vii, 6, 44, 80, 130, 136, 138, 142, 148
poverty, vii, 23, 136, 137, 149
PRC, 151
private sector, 74, 131
production, 2, 23, 24, 43, 44, 54, 55, 57-59, 76, 80, 82, 84, 86, 89, 92, 99, 100, 102, 104, 106, 107, 113, 114, 121, 123, 124, 130, 135, 138, 139, 143, 157
profits, 56, 57, 121, 123, 132, 135, 141
public sector, 147

R

Reagan, President, 47
reference, 108, 129, 137, 149, 160
reform of financial sector, 129
reforms, 15, 59, 65, 71-76, 95, 103, 119, 129, 130, 133, 137, 138, 140, 141, 149, 150, 157
regional cooperation, 133, 134
regional imbalances, 129, 149
religious freedom, 21
Research Development Test and Evaluation (RDT&E), 121
Revolution in Military Affairs (RMA), 27
rural areas, vii, 80, 148
Russia, 16, 17, 20, 21, 25, 26, 28, 32, 35, 37, 46, 48, 125, 126, 133

S

Senate, 80, 132
Shanghai Cooperation Organization (SCO), 16, 26, 32, 35, 36, 37
Shanghai, 3, 4, 5, 16, 26, 30, 32, 35, 36, 79, 91, 95, 102, 109, 113, 129, 134, 136-151, 154, 159
Shenzhen, 102, 134, 140, 141
Singapore, 37, 53, 60, 61, 62, 66, 76, 100, 111-113, 115, 146, 157, 160, 161
small or medium-sized enterprise (SME), 57
socialism, 24, 77, 134, 137, 149, 156
South Korea, 113, 120, 132
Southeast Asia, 32, 36, 37, 51, 53, 58-63, 65, 84, 113, 115, 134, 157
sovereignty, 28, 48, 133
Soviet Union, 17, 18, 21, 30, 31, 34, 35, 84, 130, 149
Special Economic Zones (SEZs), 140
state enterprises, 78, 129, 132, 137, 147, 149
state-invested enterprises (SIEs), 85
state-owned enterprises (SOEs), 51-53, 56, 64-66, 74, 76-81, 85, 88, 124, 129, 131, 135, 149
State-Owned Enterprises, 135
statistics, 3, 60, 61, 77, 78, 109, 134, 158
stress, 104, 138
submarines, 42, 44, 45, 47

T

Taiwan Government, 99, 101, 103-106
Taiwan Relations Act (TRA), 39, 46-48
Taiwan Semiconductor Manufacturing Company (TSMC), 105
Taiwan, 15, 17, 22, 26, 28, 31, 32, 39-49, 51, 71, 72, 76, 99-109, 111-113, 118, 121, 122, 126, 127, 132-134, 154, 155, 157, 161
Tariff-Rate Quotas (TRQs), 89
tariffs, 55, 71, 72, 76, 77, 81-83, 87, 89, 132
taxes, 132
Technical Barriers to Trade (TBT), 81
technology transfer, 24, 29, 82, 84, 99, 138
telecommunications, 81, 83, 102, 123, 132
threat, 25, 30, 42, 43, 46, 49, 73, 80, 87, 133
Tianjin, 3, 4, 5, 140
Tibet, 2, 3, 136
township and village enterprises (TVE), 10
Trade Policy Staff Committee (TPSC), 90
Trade Promotion Coordination Committee (TPCC), 96
trade union, 133
Trade-related Aspects of Intellectual Property Rights (TRIPs), 81, 83-85, 97

Trade-related Investment Measures (TRIMs), 81, 84, 85
transition, vii, 39, 40, 56, 113, 132
Transitional Review Mechanism (TRM), 91, 92

U

U.S. Agency for International Development (USAID), 95, 96
U.S. Department of Agriculture (USDA), 82
U.S. exporters, 71, 89
U.S. trade law, 92, 96, 97
unemployment, 80, 131
United Nations, 26, 52, 136
United States, 131-133
urban land reform, 129, 137, 149
urban residents, 10, 148

W

wealth, 70, 74, 95, 136, 157
weapons of mass destruction (WMD), 18, 21, 31, 33
workers, 10, 25, 76, 77, 80, 131, 148, 149
World Bank, 95, 118, 129, 130, 150, 151, 154
world economy, 154, 157
World Trade Organization (WTO), 15, 18, 19, 23, 26, 37, 51, 53, 66, 67, 69-97, 99-101, 103, 108, 110-112, 114, 115, 131, 132, 149
World War I, 132
World War II, 132
Xiaoping, Deng, 23, 24, 25, 27, 29, 130, 132, 142, 153

Y

Yunnan, 4, 5, 7, 11, 136

Z

Zero Base Budgeting (ZBB), 119